Careers
and Creativity

Social Inequality Series
Marta Tienda and David B. Grusky, Series Editors

Careers and Creativity

Social Forces in the Arts

Harrison C. White

Westview Press

BOULDER • SAN FRANCISCO • OXFORD

ᵛ *Social Inequality Series*

Published in 1993 in the United States of America by Westview Press, Inc., 5500 Central Avenue, Boulder, Colorado 80301-2877, and in the United Kingdom by Westview Press, 36 Lonsdale Road, Summertown, Oxford OX2 7EW

A CIP catalog record for this book is available from the Library of Congress.
ISBN 0-8133-1543-3

Printed and bound in the United States of America

The paper used in this publication meets the requirements
of the American National Standard for Permanence of Paper
for Printed Library Materials Z39.48-1984.

10   9   8   7   6   5   4   3   2   1

Contents

Illustrations

Preface

I develop two basic themes in this book:

1. *The shaping of identities—which includes celebrating and arguing for competing identities—generates and energizes the arts.* These identities are for groups—be they families or clans or corporations or categories such as gender—more than they are personal, even in our day. These identities find expression both in private and to various publics.

2. *Particular artworks emerge from a dialogue between artist and art world.* Artistic production is stimulated and sustained by an art world—a working community of artists and others—not isolation in some garret. Such stimulation and support are emotional and communicative as much as they are material. Shared ways of arguing and seeing, and of using technology, are essential, as are distinctive personal themes and specific triggering events.

These two themes weave together into narrative of art. Sometimes this narrative is self-conscious; artists observe and analyze it for us in case studies. Artists typically struggle within, and also depend upon, several overlapping art worlds in order to create or perform on a continuing basis. Informal networks of acquaintance link artists to each other and to various patrons and organizations across these worlds. But so do alliances and divisions over recognition and content—alliances and divisions that become concrete in various and changing audiences and that bind all into broader social formations. Artworks thus are shaped under competing commitments of both artists and audiences into identities of both selves and larger social groups, whether of ethnicity or locale or class or nation or gender.

Particular styles in distinct arts condense out of such narrative process. *I will show why and how styles in arts change.*

Spelling out and backing up these assertions will take up a book. Reading this book will be eased by referring repeatedly to these assertions. They remind you of the central themes while you are following complex arguments and detailed cases in alternating chapters. Field observation reported in case studies is the primary authority, but general argumentation also is needed about both the arts and the practicalities of social organization. So the readings drawn upon are diverse.

*   *   *

This socially grounded perspective on the arts can serve interests in traditional art history, musicology, literary criticism, and so on as well as interests in the social sciences. Such perspectives also, I think, can ease and aid the practice of art. The subtitle of this book could be "how to survive as an artist"—especially in college settings that relate art practice to more general liberal education. Yet inversely, art worlds can provide very helpful windows on how social life works in general—on how businesses are administered as well as how priests influence flocks and scientists accomplish research. To look for familiar social logics in apparently different situations is indeed the hallmark of the sociological vision.

You may be interested mainly in current art scenes, which you can examine through fieldwork. Field observation by you is important, in any case, because there are too many arts (and art worlds are endlessly different) to be covered in any one book. Some of your best insights can come from contrasting various arts, various periods, and locales secondhand through reading. Videotapes, reproductions, photographs, and interviews in journals can lessen the gap between book learning and field observation.

You may have little experience of any art worlds and may not know how to observe and keep the observation unobtrusive. Circulating quietly on the fringes of a party or watching others watch, or not watch, facades on buildings or sitting around a painter's studio—are all examples of unobtrusive observation. The text should help you spot and introduce apt topics. One that is current in artists' shared talk is the twin motif of careers and rebellion, which is central in the discussion that follows.

The arts have many social faces. Each not only can tell us something about artistic content (and so contribute to appreciation of styles across many arts) but also can offer a fascinating window on social organization, in general, and on the multiplicity of competing claims for identity, in particular. From reading this book you can expect as outcome a heightened appreciation not only of artists and arts but also of the social forces through which art, along with everything else, comes into being.

*   *   *

My focus is the social surroundings for production in, as well as perception of, particular arts. This means concentration on a middle range in scope and scale. I emphasize how a set of locales interacts to constitute an art world: For example, in the dramatic arts how do dinner theatre and high school plays fit together with Broadway and how is Broadway foreshadowed by avante-garde experimentalism?

To help readers orient themselves, let me say a bit about what this book is *not*. Art experts' evidence comes from diary and archive as well as from trained perception of the work of art, stroke by stroke, be it painting or other composition. *I shall not do much of such microscopic examination*, either of visual or of other arts. I seek more general patterns and relate each world of art production to social process surrounding it and to other such worlds.

Arnold Hauser, in a multivolume work, draws direct connections between, on the one hand, contents and style of artworks and, on the other hand, social and political processes throughout the environing society. Hauser assumes, in a Marxist vein, a mirroring by art of society and its class structure. *This is an opposite extreme that I also avoid.* And Pitirim Sorokin speculates on an even broader scale about evolution of art, from "ideal" to "sensate," over whole centuries and for sets of societies that he calls civilizations. I shall instead try to be explicit about mechanisms of influence through specific art worlds in particular periods.

What I do aim for is understanding systems of production of art. Much sifting and matching occur among art works and also among artists with differing specializations. These siftings and matchings are made both by (and of) brokers and agents of various sorts. During such processes, several quite different arts may influence each other through overlaps among producers, among audiences, and among patrons. I trace out these claims of overlap and influence and thus uncover the ways and extent to which they become aspects of a system.

*   *   *

I have kept this book short. Although it can be read by itself, readers will benefit from having the text fleshed out by discussion with some expert who can supply exhibits, add illustrations, and suggest further readings. Or readers can develop supplements for themselves with the aid of the chapter appendixes on readings and fieldwork.

This book started with questions that grew out of discussions, in both my teaching and research, of social facets of several arts: How do arts change? How does an art world get built and maintained? Does art provision flight from everyday life, or instead does art aid control over ordinary life? Can one interpret society, or persons, by their reflections in arts? Today in America, how can artists both survive and be able to grow in stature? I build toward answers to these questions.

Harrison C. White

Acknowledgments

Several students from versions of a course that I have taught at Harvard and then Columbia over a number of years are acknowledged in chapters where field reports or papers of theirs are used. I am grateful to them and other students for their listening and discussions, for their memos and exams, all of which helped in evolving this picture of social forces in the arts. In the earlier Harvard versions of this course, David Brain was thoughtful and helpful as teaching assistant, and Cristina Bodinger-deUriarte provided insights and perspective on Bauhaus times, as did Marge Theeman on modern dance. Dean Kathryn Yatrakis gave wonderful support with the new version of the course for Columbia, and I thank Professor Robert Hymer and the other members of the Committee on Instruction for their comments on my draft syllabus. Seth Rachlin was creative and helpful as he guided Barnard and Columbia students in fieldwork and in discussion sections of the course, which I taught largely from a draft of the present book.

The writings of many colleagues in sociology of arts are cited in the chapters that follow, but I also learned much by listening to them, especially to my earlier coauthor, Cynthia White. Professors Vera Zolberg of the New School and Robert Alford of CUNY–Graduate Center and I started a monthly New York circle (artists as well as professors) on social faces of the arts, and I am grateful to them and to all the members for broadening my horizons. I benefited particularly from the session where my draft of Chapter 4 was critiqued. Dialogues with Debra Friedman, John Padgett, and Alessandro Pizzorno shaped my ideas about layers of identity, as did Andrew Abbott concerning layers of contingency. Charles Tilly and Eric Leifer and Robert Eccles were endlessly patient and helpful with my attempts to formulate how identity related to control in social institution. Discussions with Ken Dauber, Carlos Forment, Doug McAdam, Walter Powell, and Jonathan Rieder on rhetorics were helpful, as were discussions with Roberto Fernandez and Cal Morrill on fieldwork.

I am indebted to several colleagues at Columbia for opening up quite different windows on art worlds, especially to Professor Lynn Cooper on perception and style both in theory and practice, to Professor Herbert

Gans on the media, and to Andras Szanto on galleries. Professor Priscilla Ferguson was helpful not only through her own writings on literature in its French setting but also through an incisive critique of my manuscript.

I am grateful to Professor Daniel Schacter of Harvard University and to Richard Bowman of Redwood City for supplying detailed biographical material. I am indebted to Harold Prince, chairman of the advisory group of the Theatre Research Project, and to its sixteen other members, and to Harold Horowitz of the Research Division of National Endowment for the Arts, which sponsored the research leading to the 1981 report. Our discussions were coordinated with the research and fieldwork of the Mathematica, Inc., staff by the report's author, Dr. Robert J. Anderson, who was assisted by other social scientists: Drs. Hilda Baumol, Sonya Maltezou, and Robert Wuthnow.

I thank Paul DiMaggio for the subtlety, verve, and precision in his detailed critique of an early draft. Comments from Steve Berkowitz and Kenneth Dauber and Stuart Plattner helped me improve a later draft. Dean Birkenkamp of Westview Press contributed to the book through incisive and patient editorial suggestions on several drafts. David Grusky and Marta Tienda as series editors made suggestions both of substance and of style, and I am indebted to Vera Zolberg for her comments as reader for Westview. In the last phase, Sarah Tomasek helped me improve accuracy and clarity, and Libby Barstow brought it all together.

H. W.

1

Introduction

Artworks shape and are shaped by our very identities, from before a hit song first captures us in adolescence to our being awed by the headquarters architecture of a possible employer. Artworks and performances—be they painting or music or dance or story—help orient us also to who others are. We are brought together and kept apart by social formulas and identities that the arts help to represent and even to shape, whether as flower and dress ceremonials or as oil portraits of founders of some shared corporate identity.

Works of art furthermore help us find who we want to be and how to control, or seem to control, both nature and the social groups that are always being reconstructed around us. Punk rock fans can testify to this and so can tuxedo-clad first-nighters at the Metropolitan Opera. Thus artworks are also coin of manipulation that can serve to embed people and groups into hierarchies, be these of domination or of admiration. Beauty and entertainment are two possible outcomes from the arts, but first the arts serve to overawe and mystify us by imputing new levels of reality.

Long ago, artists emerged as the agents who led the rest of us to artworks, and they developed thereafter as specialist members of distinctive art worlds. In the past few centuries, artists in some fields gained the status of professionals, with claims for cognitive training and expertise greater than that of their clients. Just in the past century, in some arts certain artists also were proffered as geniuses, and certain groups of artists were proffered as making up an avant-garde whose visions and processes of creation should seize our attention as a public. Regardless, the production of artworks continues through all such fireworks to be bound up in networks of brokerage and reception in and across various art worlds.

Both in arts for the populace and in arts for elites, star systems have emerged to offer enormous disparities in reward and recognition across artists and artworks. Such systems compete with alternative systems centered around education or around careers sponsored by governments and other bureaucracies. But even stars, together with their masterworks, result as much from social machinery as from cultural sensitivities and may be only of the passing moment.

So I aim beyond particular reputations and artworks, and even particular arts, as I build toward a heightened appreciation of how social forces and cultural production in an art shape one another—and especially how they change only together (Chapter 4). In the final two chapters I examine how arts are becoming new vehicles of exploration in identities for selves and for other social formations as new publics develop for new professions. Creativity and career shape but also are shaped by broader sociocultural constraints and opportunities.

Excitement and entertainment are part of art, which is a matter of the surface as well as the depths of life. Let us begin with a frothy example in which current social life is captured, and dissected, within an art. We will also note backstage arrangements for production and then proceed to introduce in this chapter a sociological perspective for the exploration of social forces in the arts.

The Small World of Social Networks

As I began this manuscript, I happened to see *Six Degrees of Separation*, a Broadway hit starring Stockard Channing. John Guare's title for the play takes off from some social science results of the 1960s, from Stanley Milgram's probes of what he called the "Small World." Stockard Channing, playing the lead character, Ouisa, muses that you can reach almost anyone else in our country in about six links. Social networks are implicit as the skeleton for this Small World of Milgram and Guare. They also are central to this book.

Like many other plays, this one offers sociology in three layers. First, it portrays, with crackling wit, some very New York types (including a nude male hustler) in interactions that build upon one another in ways that seem universal. Second, the troupe seizes us on behalf of another level, or realm, of reality through its magic, its labor of art—just as sociology and anthropology attempt (in much more ponderous fashion) to convince one of both unseen impacts from a larger context and the fragility and effort going into construction of everyday reality among persons. Third, the play's own scene, its backstage, drips with social stigmata begging for sociological interpretation.

The theater is the Vivian Beaumont within Lincoln Center—on Broadway but not quite "Broadway." Lincoln Center is a quango (quasi-autonomous nongovernmental organization)—neither government nor business but yet not the artists' own either. The only names in lights are those of patrons, affixed permanently on the plazas and buildings their donations created. Tax dollars did contribute too, but only New York, not the United States, gets name recognition—and even then not in lights.

Arts as wholes come to be, and stay, separate through responses across audiences. Whole separate real arts appear in issue 12 of the ninety-first volume of *Playbill: The National Theatre Magazine.* This magazine licenses issues also in Boston, Dallas, Florida, and Washington/Baltimore. (Note that the word "theater," as opposed to "theatre," refers to movies and such.) We learn that the Vivian Beaumont Theater company itself has had a succession of lives, separated in turn by "several dark seasons" before a new director (or, lately, a new producer) steps forward.

Ouisa, in the play, is of two minds. She finds comfort in this six-step closeness to any other person yet is bemused at how to know about one's own networks. Ouisa and her husband are art dealers, posh art dealers, and they gamble on their skills at making such contacts in the processes of acquiring and then speculating in Sotheby-quality paintings. She orients to ties, just as the male hustler orients to and gambles upon mores of acquaintanceship.

The abstraction of relations as ties in a network has always been true in reckoning kinship, as in "meet my cousin's wife." Like the rest of us in current social life, artists are woven together in networks through ties of acquaintance of various sorts—and we all have come to recognize this. Today, sociometry of acquaintanceship has penetrated general consciousness.

A special sort of tie has become equated with particular behaviors and attitudes as reported in stories of relations so that the elements of networks are stereotyped stories—such as acquaintance, enmity, dependence. Network becomes a verb, and we tell stories in network terms; so, for example, Ouisa could speak in terms of one network of social acquaintance and another network of business dealings and yet another of personal antagonism. But "networking" is just more dull sociologese until it is brought to life as actual process before one's eyes in the magic land of theatre.

Sociologists have found that Ouisa's particular region of the Small World is quite compartmentalized as well as specialized. For one thing, to guard against an expanding supply, a dealer may prefer that the painter be dead; such dealers need never see live artists. These dealers rely on critique of art developed about the swirls of acrylic on the canvas rather than on the social swirls among artists and their students and collaborators in studios.

The pecking order of actors stepping forward in turn for applause at the end of the evening was meticulously kept. This was despite the alphabetical listing in the program of all but the three stars, and these three are spread out together just below the director and the producer at the top. Yet Stockard Channing, no mistake, is *the* star: She is prime mover, even down to signaling scene changes, and of course she steps up last, to the loudest applause, because this New York audience is knowing.

Succession in roles is meticulously noted. Several slips were inserted into the program identifying the understudies appearing that night for four (of a total of seventeen) roles in place of their usual players. Three of the understudies were proclaimed by career—each had from eight to twenty lines of credits in previous plays, with Broadway productions listed first, then Off Broadway, then Off-Off Broadway, then regional (largely League of Resident Theatres like the Guthrie in Minneapolis), only then film, and last of all television. But at least TV did appear, unlike dinner theatre, summer stock, and other peripheral stage billings. The fourth understudy had actually just moved (up, naturally) to a vacancy, from the role of Hustler to the role of MIT wonk being hustled, so his proclamation of thirteen lines (mostly Off-Off Broadway) was already in the *Playbill*.

The various notes included in the *Playbill* for *Six Degrees of Separation* discuss a variety of arts. There is a piece on college education for future careers of dancers (whose vocation, though consuming, is all too brief in years), followed by reviews of high fashion and, on one of the last pages of the *Playbill*, reviews of the London theatre scene. These latter reviews were written in an in-the-know tone and presupposed audiences widely interested in several arts, both vulgar and refined, pure and applied. If only that were true!

Ostentation and Exclusion

Celebrations of identities, and accountings of relations, in works of arts come to be mediated by agents of increasing variety and independence, artists and others. These agents do, however, continue to give viewers some focus on and rooting in particularly significant social groupings. This is a continuing process down to our day—a day in which we are likely to think in terms of social strata and classes as the sites of appreciation of particular art.

This process is also a devolution into segregated enclaves, which can be ethnicities—and can also be worlds of science and learning, or of art for that matter. Part of this devolution is defusing and deconstructing sacredness. As objects of personal and home decoration descend from ritual ones, vestiges of sacredness remain. For example, today's split between professional and amateur is a cultural displacement of sacredness that is often explored in art.

Wealth and social prestige are other vestiges of sacredness. Return to the *Playbill* for *Six Degrees of Separation*. In its last pages, the *Playbill* became quite literally a social treasure trove. It listed patrons of the theatre by strata, from $100,000 and more down through six further levels to $1,000 and more. Then came a more elegant statement, of patrons for the overall Lincoln Center for the Performing Arts, but listed now in *chronological* order, by when they gave. There was a separate listing of corporations that donated, in circles of leadership from Outstanding, at $150,000 and more, down four levels to Pacesetters, at $25,000 and more, and three steps later at Donors, which cut off at $3,000 and more.

Do the arts and their works sustain invidious hierarchy in general? An evolutionary perspective can suggest answers. The central thread of any animal society, among wolves as among chickens, is comparability. Comparability is achieved within these most primitive societies as strict pecking orders. One hen defers to another without explicit fighting or challenging; it defers in eating and walking, not to mention sex. Each such pecking order yields strict interlockings among announcements and celebrations by the contending identities. Pecking order becomes strict hierarchy and as such remains the simplest way to achieve the comparability that is the meaning of the social.

Actions interact with ceremonial formulas for action in and as any social institution such as a pecking order, which may be reflected in artworks. This remains as true today in any of the dozens of art worlds in New York City as it proves to be among aborigines on Groote Eylandt (an obscure island of aborigines off the Australian coast), who have been studied exhaustively by anthropologists. A social institution is some pattern that persists among endless challenges for control. Such a pattern is robust and tends to absorb the continuing fresh actions. In part the pattern does so by celebrating and announcing them by the use of arts.

Tribes don't stay separate. Superdisciplines put tribes together in all sorts of ways, but always tending toward a simplest order—a linear order echoing pecking orders. It might be a caste system or a slave system or later an empire. Art helps to certify being higher and to regulate being lower. Achieving comparability is the key, for without it there are no relations but only physical encounter and destruction. Paradoxically, the simplest way to comparability is strict hierarchy. In more complex societies it becomes a stratification if not a rigid class system. There always are humans, as there are chickens, swarming to be at the top of the heap.

Beyond simple tribes, ostentation seems commonly to be at the root of art. Ostentation is the format of social ordering. Sculpture continues to be a good example. While holding a guide to outdoor sculpture, I can wander all over New York seeing persons (almost entirely men) made great, literally and figuratively. Many were long dead when the work was commissioned, and there the ostentation was by the patron (civic or private) as well as the sculptor, perhaps for the celebration of the city (or some particular institution) as such.

For long eras, nobody thought of art in our current sense: There was no term for art and no term for beauty. Instead there was the sense of size and glitter and rarity and wondrous feats of shaping and realism—all as celebrations and announcements. In the early era of commercial empire, for example, along with Pericles' acropolis and its statues were the festivals of Greek plays paid for—as "liturgies"—by the wealthy of the day in lieu of taxes and in honor of honor.

Elites are like the downtrodden in attempting to announce identity, but they go further and act so as to impose the superiority of their identity vis-à-vis preexisting elites as well as everyone else. For example, the Boston Brahmins reasserted hegemony last century in a city awash in immigrants and "new men," that is, those who have become recognized as significant persons; so did the New York City elite. Each used a combination of methods: building (both literally and figuratively) new institutions of art, and doing so for several arts, notably orchestral music, opera, and the fine arts. In this process, canons for style and genre were reshaped along with the meaning and social uses of the museum and the concert hall.

Identities and Artists

Proclaiming particular identities and announcing particular relations are two main impetuses to the production of artworks. Identity arises from a primordial and continuing urge to control, which can be seen always and in all contexts. For example, a new child on a playground has an overriding need to find some sort of stable social footing so that the child can know how to act in an otherwise chaotic social world. Only occasionally does this lead to bullying. Identity in this first sense is the expression in social context of the same urge for secure footing that in physical settings induces behavioral patterns of posture. A group's identity in this first sense is its solidarity, and in seeking celebration it helps build art.

A second and more elaborate and quite distinct sense of identity is akin to "face." It is identity achieved and expressed or operationalized as part of some distinct social discipline or group in which each member has a face just because it is a social face, one of the set of faces that together make up that discipline. The group or discipline may range from loose to strict. A simple example is a group at a table in a dormitory dining room. Chances are that these students know each other and are accustomed to eating together often, and so have come to tend to take certain stances—one as topic selector, another as clown, and so on—and may celebrate themselves by story or other work. The naming of each such identity—the process of establishing "face"—is perhaps the first particular art to emerge.

Naming goes with levels. The earliest name was "us" and presumably the earliest art proclaimed "us" as an aspect of our endless attempts to control nature and other "us"s. Today something like this can be seen in the culture of remaining aboriginal peoples, who are hunters and gatherers. Identity always is a matter of levels; it induces distinct levels. One's own identity is achieved only as part of a larger identity into which it is inducted and of which it is a reflection. Identity in this second sense appears in our usual idea of the individual: as an actor in a role that supplies preferences to guide the actor toward goals. Ordinary life induces levels not visible but not unlike distinct levels of reality in theatre. Culture provides aids:

> In their metaphoric interaction with society, cultural objects organize and illuminate social concerns by presenting the structure of the particular concerns in an arena removed from everyday life ... a cultural work enables human beings to examine the dilemmas represented and assess the solution offered, in terms of attitude or behavior, without being distracted by the complexities and randomness of the real world. (Griswold 1986, p. 202)

Artworks are tangible realizations of culture, in support of identity.

Art starts as performance, and the power of art is in the now and present. But we can speculate about the emergence and evolution of art and performance. At first, art is performance by all and announcement to all. A later, difficult step is when distinct audiences separate out. Once audiences emerge, everything is possible.

Once a fixed "us" can come apart into different audiences, many new kinds of namings can emerge. One art can then differentiate from another. Some audiences become clans, and some become age grades or secret societies. Naming grows into chants and into dances and into stories. Much later some of the individual humans get names.

Once there are many namings, deaths and endings become more problematic. Pictures of totemic animals are an art that shields against the animals' disappearances for whatever reason and thus against the clan's own disappearance. Sculpture of figurines for burials of some humans is one of the early arts.

Once some namings become stories, further levels develop. Levels interlock with and pile upon one another and thus build into social institutions. Announcements and accountings, all sorts of them, are essential constituents in institutions. A picture—or an ornament or a dance or a song—is worth a thousand words, and even in aborigine tribes many thousands are needed.

Specialized artistic expressions develop while the larger social context is evolving. Art is distinguished long before individual works of art are given much notice. The evolution of arts reflects something of general social evolution, during early tribal phases as well as now. Art already develops within a tribe in many facets, from story-dance on to sculpture for graves. In multitribal settings, arts become differentiated and alienated into specialized activities.

Once pottery comes along, distinctions between arts seem to be recognized. And at the same time, distinctiveness between different individual works of art seems to come in. This is a big step—a step that never is complete because so much of art always is ceremonial and announcement, which means that much of its power consists in being recognizably the same.

Later these activities become embedded into still larger socioeconomic-political settings, in which artisans' work spins off as an activity separate from but concomitant to that of priests. Ceremonies then can replace tribal consensus. Still later, fashion in entertainment supervenes and joins with grieving and ceremony into variable forms of celebration and accounting. Commerce may come to broker artworks as commodities. In these earlier eras when artists were workmen or artisans, the focus was the work of art. Its conception was attributed to the principal or patron and so represented the patron's identity and ties, not the artist's.

The further step to recognition of artists is a long one. It requires enough cycles of recurrence among specialized activities and groupings. It requires a distinct art world, which can exist only as a spin-off of more general social formations. So artists, like art as beauty, come late indeed, and they come interwoven into social institutions. Actual live production of art today involves practical and immediate pressures and options, which may not tie explicitly to either class struggles or individual career perspectives and which exhibit few signs of art's evolutionary paths.

Art World as Agency

Artists' production is supported not by individual inspiration in some lonely garret, but rather by some community, call it an art world, that brokers art to us. The support and stimulation are emotional and communicative as much as they are material because shared ways of arguing and perceiving are required to embed the raw material of idiosyncratic themes and events into and through identities. Artworks emerge today from a dialogue between the artist and some art world that stands as agent for most of us.

Art is special in many ways, which is why we are so interested and involved in the arts. But, at the same time, the social mechanics of art worlds are not so different from those in all the other worlds in which we build our social lives. These similarities can help us—through recognizing varying degrees of kinship with art worlds—to relate to and deal with art more effectively and comfortably. And sometimes we can turn this around and learn a great deal from art worlds about other sides of our life, both secular and religious. As Shakespeare said, all the world's a stage.

An art world combines artists and their works with others into a pattern that can reproduce itself, may become aware of itself, and does impose itself as reality upon those in it before its products reach out as a reality for others outside it. Endless questions are raised. Which art worlds focus more on works and which more on artists? Or how, for example, are authors tied with patrons? To start answering such questions we can look back at the beginnings of art.

Artisan work comes early. By the third millennium before our era, there appear to have been in Sumeria (now Iraq) separate full-time occupations for artisans, along with specialized farming and trade. These artisans were part of a central city-temple-palace complex that could be recognized as a world of its own embedded in a system with outlying simpler communities of farming and herding. But an art world—a self-recognizing and -reproducing social world—comes along late indeed.

Such an art world has identity; it is recognized as an entity. There is also the second sense of this identity, identity as "face." The larger identity of an art world depends on and exists only as realization of a dovetailing of many individual "faces" that make it up. Artworks can be so charged with importance because in expressing various identities, artworks may also be announcing ways in which identities are subject to reshaping and manipulation.

Art worlds today are the principal social institutions for art production. They interpenetrate with each other as well as with other institutions within broader social systems. Expressed in the economic idiom of today, these institutional systems around arts embrace the production, pricing, distribution, and consumption of art. Many of the principles and forms of organization and recognition that appear in art worlds can be found also in other worlds such as, say, today's sport worlds or business worlds or professional worlds.

Just as priests in their religious creed pay heed to social networks and attend to social intimacies and closeness, so also do critics trace and help to build networks of cultural cues in ways that resonate among patrons and other audiences. The critic is going on to become a new and flexible kind of priest, bringing together artistic liturgies of celebration and accounting in new and flexible rhetorics.

There is also an inside perspective on an art world. The interior of an art world builds up an intensity and involution of perceptions and attitudes that often are sufficient to encapsulate most of the emotions and strivings of its constituent artists and hangers-on. Yet the artworks produced by the world must also achieve resonance with outsiders.

Consider the challenge faced by the solo performer, say a violinist. The performer is assessed in reviews by critics both in terms of known standards and in terms of originality and freshness of interpretation. It is exactly in this contradictory situation that there is room for coding to develop and persist: as style concerning both social enactment and artistic substance.

Performance is not restricted to drama or to that together with music and poetry. Performance can have very different impacts according to sensory modality, for example, dance versus spoken language. And even within the latter, the effects of words accompanied by music are greater, that is, the sense of reality is more intense, than from words without music even when accompanied, as in drama, by gesture, placement, and the like. This is the distinction critics make between the mimetic and the rhetorical in art.

Performance is a feature of ordinary social life, as we recognize in speaking of roles and the like. More abstractly, performance can be seen as one side of the pair of enactment and plan. The whole point of performance is to achieve spontaneity and what we today call sincerity, even though the audience knows, at some level, that performers are carrying out a preset plan. This is a paradox. For acting on the stage, much the same conclusions about paradox can be derived from a more psychological point of view. Scripted speech is literary language, and thus it is a memory; it is past. Performing as a character is basic, and it is not primarily language.

An art world resembles a cruise ship. It spends time at sea, lost in self-absorption as a separate universe in which everyone is more concerned with who sits where at the captain's table than with the rise and fall of empires back on shore. Yet a cruise ship may be on a mission, for example, to view the art of Crete or other ancient place. An art world also is on a mission—a mission to continue weaving strands of styles and techniques into a rope of artworks that limn identities in cultural terms for the passengers as well as for the crew.

The ship metaphor can help in clarifying the difficult matter of boundaries for an art world. Viewed from outside, the relation of audience to producing artists in an art world is an image of the relation between the passengers and the crew of a cruise ship. Part of the audience is afforded by fellow producers in this or a neighboring art world, but much of the audience cannot be entirely inside the art world. Most patrons are not idle heirs able, and willing, to spend all their time figuratively inside the fence with "their" artists. Only a few audience members are hangers-on who somehow manage to camp out permanently on picnic food in an art world. An art world must capture, in external and internal perspectives, the same symbiosis found between cruise ship and shore support.

Illusion—illusion of some sort of reality—is the business of and production from any art world. This leads to confusions and conundrums. For example, both the hustler role and the author of the play *Six Degrees* become jointly entangled in curious mixes of "real life" and "play acting":

> David Hampton, the man whose confidence scheme gained him access to the homes of several prominent New Yorkers and inspired John Guare's award-winning play "Six Degrees of Separation," was acquitted yesterday on one count of harassing the playwright in an effort to obtain money from him. A jury deadlocked on a second count of harassment. ...
>
> The play was based on a widely-reported hoax in which Mr. Hampton posed as the son of actor Sidney Poitier to gain entrance to the Manhattan homes of Osborn Elliot, the former dean of the Columbia University School of Journalism, and John J. Iselin, the former president of Channel 13, among others. Mr. Hampton, who claimed to have been mugged and to need a place to stay, accepted spending money from his hosts and took property from their homes.
>
> Mr. Hampton served 21 months in state prison after being found guilty of attempted burglary in the 1983 incidents. ...
>
> A State Supreme Court justice in Manhattan ruled last April that Mr. Hampton, 28 years old, was not entitled to civil damages for the fictional use of his story. (*New York Times,* October 2, 1992, p. B1)

No doubt Osborn Elliot and John Iselin were in the audience of some performance of *Six Degrees.* Where does this "art world" end? Where does illusion begin? Who, after all, is agent and who is player and who is artist? Identities abound and interlock in dizzying profusion in and around art.

Overview

Social forces impinge on each aspect of the arts. Each social face of art can tell us something about artistic content besides offering a fascinating window on social organization in general. The arts also impinge back upon the social, shaping our perceptions and announcements of selves and situations. This book will help you to understand how production and appreciation of art relate both to art's own social worlds and to broader social organization. I will also highlight how identities emerge and become recognized through artworks.

Several different perspectives on the arts within social context are valid simultaneously and are combined in this book. An internal perspective is art worlds as seen by those who constitute them. One external perspective is evolutionary and anthropological, in contrast to another, which is cross-sectional in time and is systemic. And furthermore, specific accounts may be either sociological (talk of class or ethnicity or gender) or historical (ancient or recent grudges).

Similarities between arts and other social process will come into focus in this book more than will differences among the arts, which depend upon both historical specifics and differences in human physical senses about which I have little to say. Some readers will want to think only about certain arts, and the chapters are set up with that in mind. But I do hope that both social science and culture buffs will be fascinated by the widest variety of comparisons.

This book is short, through being brief on any one topic or case, because I would wish it to be as handy as, and to orient you as efficiently as, a nature field guide does. I provide pointers and guidance so that you can follow up your particular art or chosen interest more fully. One important way to do that is through fieldwork of your own. The result can become a case study that you author to go with the reading.

Specific suggestions, useful as triggers for your own ideas, are best offered in connection with specific topics. At the end of each chapter is a section "Fieldwork Ideas." As one encouragement, I occasionally quote from fieldwork memos done for me by students in previous years.

Broad coverage is important to support arguments about how arts interlace with practicalities of social organization, so I have drawn upon diverse readings. There are no footnotes, but at the end of each chapter, before the fieldwork guide, appears a "Guide to Further Reading." This points to sources where assertions in the text, roughly in the order given, can be checked and further explored. It also includes general sources that themselves list many further readings for your edification and delight.

And there is a further section, "Measures and Models," both qualitative and quantitative, which, however, is kept on an elementary level. All of these sections, as well as quotes within the main text, key, by author's last name and date of publication, to the "References" at the end of the book. In the hope of providing at least a lead toward the special interest of each reader, far more items are included in the "References" than any one reader will require.

Creativity and career involve and use both social mechanism and cultural content in weaving narrative about identities in art, about the labor and effort of making art. Many identities and careers besides those of artists are represented and influenced by artworks and their production. In this book I develop how artistic content is shaped as narrative reflections of identities within social process. The juncture of content and process establishes style in the production of art (Chapter 3). In this first chapter and Chapters 5, 6, and 7 I use ideas of social networks and agency to portray the social mechanism of art production and some of its impact on the resulting artworks.

The complicated situations surrounding art can be sorted out only with the help of explicit theory. I hope to make this theory more digestible for you by building it up in layers and interleaving it with examples. Fully understanding these situations requires, after all, contexts sufficient to permit deciphering how rhetorics and strategies evolve over time around some particular art form. This means case studies, and alternate chapters (2, 4, and 6 plus 7) will focus on such studies.

The book builds in these terms toward answers to two main empirical questions: How have major changes in style come about? (Chapter 4) and How do struggles for careers and support in American arts center around identity problems, both narrow and broad? (Chapters 6 and 7). In Chapter 2, I examine the broad impact of a secret brotherhood of very young English painters in Victorian times and how their art mirrored their dramatic era. In Chapter 6, I trace in some detail how modern American theatre works as a system of inputs and outputs among social networks of professionals. The Conclusion returns to difficult questions about boundaries between arts, about levels of reality, and about competing identities.

GUIDE TO FURTHER READING

Citations, by author's name and the date of publication, are to the References at the end of the book.

The perspective developed in this book, primarily the high arts viewed as whole systems, is different from but complements a perspective that Howard Becker beautifully develops in his *Art Worlds* of 1980. He offers views from the inside and from the fringes, especially of popular art worlds. Becker is a jazz musician and photographer as well as a sociologist of note. Becker's is a populist avenue to parsing art in the modern world. He develops views of the social construction of reality that have long been inculcated at the University of Chicago, where Everett Hughes taught Becker along with Erving Goffman, whose books you are more likely to have read. They continued a tradition that explored odd and vulgar roles—such as the jackroller who preceded the mugger—for clues to universal processes concealed by conventions of daily life. Zolberg (1989) is a recent and Tomars (1960) is an early comprehensive scholarly survey of sociologies of art.

For reading related to the ideas presented in this first chapter, Poggi (1968) gives a fine survey of how theatre has developed in America. Kochen (1989) recently edited a survey of research using Small World techniques and formulations.

Chase (1980) compares humans with animals on hierarchy and ostentation. Paul DiMaggio (1982) examines with great perspicuity how Boston and New York fine arts institutions came to be constructed in their own honor by local elites in the nineteenth century. Cannadine and Price (1988) examine hierarchical aesthetics of royal events. Bourdieu (1984) develops the importance of arts in establishing gradations of social class in an important but difficult book; for a review, see Gartman (1991).

Naming interacts with technologies, as Boster (1986) shows for useful species of plants, as much as with other arts. Archaeologists help one orient to the arts of bygone tribes; see, for example, the wonderful survey by Nissen (1988). Rostovtzeff (1930) remains a great read for the art of early Mesopotamia and ancient Greece.

The Australian government has subsidized production of a book providing an overview of Australia's aborigines and their hundreds of tribes, which date back thousands of years in that continent. In this book (Isaacs 1980), which is superbly illustrated in color, Chapter 9 is devoted to aboriginal arts, notably designs on bark and dances with ceremonial masks. Norbert Lynton (1980), in surveying modern painting, points out how much it borrows from visual arts of such remote cultures.

Most great anthropological field reports deal with what the arts are and do among the social institutions of a particular people, be it tribe or city or whatever. Spencer and Gillen (1903) provide wonderful accounts of dances and ceremonies that they witnessed across a swathe of aborigine tribes in the central Australian desert. Meyer Fortes (1945, 1949) introduces you to cults, of sacred trees as well as less impersonal myths, and to how cults are proclaimed in complex ceremonies among lineages and clans of the Tallensi spread across West African plains. Adrian Mayer (1960) ferrets out, across a region of villages in central India, values and aesthetics that complement the official Hindu hierarchy of caste.

Berger and Luckmann (1967) are insightful on the construction of social reality as a tangible setting for identities. *Art world*, as I mentioned earlier, is the term coined by Howard Becker (1982) to evoke the interdependencies established in field studies of the production of art—studies made by himself and allies such as Richard Peterson (1976) and Paul Hirsch (1972). Whiteside (1981), Hirsch (1972), and Faulkner (1983) expound the systems yielding big hits (for book publishing, record publishing, and movies respectively), which undergird the inequalities of stardom.

Recent discussions of art worlds in terms of networks can be found in Baker and Faulkner (1991) and Faulkner and Anderson (1987). Early and readable discussion of thinking in terms of social networks are Barnes (1972) and Granovetter (1974).

FIELDWORK IDEAS

Keep fieldwork simple. You are to examine how the social relations within which current artists work can affect the forms, styles, and contents of their work. Videotapes, photographs, and printed interviews in journals of many sorts can be used to lessen the gap between the approach via book learning and that via your own field observation or direct participation. But published case studies are not enough—even those based directly on field observation.

Go backstage, or poke around artists' studios, or poke into some writer's agenda of activities. Do any of these and you will find interesting commonalities between the art world and mundane organizing, whether that be in business or government realms or in still other realms such as colleges and hospitals. Ties between persons, and how they chain together and spread out in social networks, always prove the key, in art worlds as in other social formations. Getting out of your chair to do some field exploration is the best way to size up this claim and to improve your general understanding. Get out and ask and watch. For guidance on theatre in particular, turn to the end of Chapter 6.

Your own fieldwork, observation, and questioning are hard to bring to bear on areas so historically involuted as, say, the prehistory of art. But you can try, for example, to find some museum with a wide range of American Indian art or other tribal art from Africa, India, Latin America, or Neolithic Europe of interest to you. Then ask, Why is this museum here? Who selected these works? and How did these, and not other, works come to be selected?

The guide to outdoor sculpture mentioned earlier is Gayle and Cohen (1988). For Washington, D.C., an even larger guide is available from the Government Printing Office. If you are in Los Angeles, go to the UCLA Sculpture Garden—and poke around campus for pokier statues. In New England, there is a superb tour of sculpture at MIT that leads you all across its campus on the Charles River (where I went to school). When in the Midwest, you do better with architecture than statues. In the South, you'll do better with ceremonial gardens.

Inspection of New York's outdoor sculpture with the help of a guide was informative about reputations. I learned which statues are unkempt and where still other statues had been pulled down. I saw that the whole style of presentation changes, that one fashion succeeds another in statuary. Sculpture shifts away from definite persons to mythical beings. Then it shifts away from statues altogether to abstract sculptures, such as Henry Moore's, which dot my own university's campuses here in New York.

MEASURES AND MODELS

I take networks as both commonsense constructs and avenues for eventual measurement and theorizing. Stanley Milgram introduced the Small World problem in 1967. He developed a trace procedure that relied upon each successive person in the probe chain (which was being tracked by Milgram through a deck of postcards sent along with the probe) and that used ordinary social skills and sense to pick, as the next link to the target, some acquaintance closer to that target. Milgram used various sorts of people as targets, and each probe included the person's name, city, and occupation. To obtain reliable estimates of the distribution of chain lengths and its mean for each target, hundreds of chains were launched with the use of a random sample of persons as initiators (Travers and Milgram 1969; Korte and Milgram 1970). I calculated (1970b) the distribution of chain lengths assuming that none of the intermediaries had abandoned the task.

Explicit tools such as networks are needed to analyze and predict complex intertwinings of art with the social. A totally different context can set off the best ideas for measures and models:

Question 1.1. Can we predict changes in artworks, aesthetic effects, from the surge toward ethnic identities in Europe or Russia or the United States? Can we predict changes in the operation of markets and other systems of social transactions in artworks?

2

The Pre-Raphaelites

Before that day in Irvine, California, the Pre-Raphaelites had slipped from my mind. After all, they were but a minor wave in the art seas of the nineteenth century. Then one gorgeous afternoon I saw a tournament in a wooded and hilly glade, an artificial dell plunked down in the middle of the university campus. It was a reproduction of a medieval tournament, enacted amid the eucalypti by the Society for Creative Anachronism, which was a band of demoiselles and youths complete with swords and armor. Their displaced medievalism had overtones that seemed to me eerily like the vibrations set up by a band of very young artists who formed the Pre-Raphaelite Brotherhood in the heart of London a century earlier.

The London group—call it the PRB hereafter—did not put on tournaments, but some of their obsessions in both painting and poetry assumed the looks and aura of medievalism. Painterly and broader social influences fitted together in making medievalism and romanticism favored vehicles. Both the Orange County and the London examples vividly illustrate that performances and artworks can reflect compulsions to assert identity even against what seems common sense, against "reality." Elsewheres and elsewhens become important venues for claiming identities.

The PRB, unlike the Irvine crowd, also sought full material support from an audience. The art worlds of English painting were, however, raw and primitive compared to those across the Channel, and this rawness gave freer rein to influences via audiences external to the artists. In subsequent chapters I will deal with better-established and institutionalized art worlds, which are worlds more opaque to outside influences, worlds of self-elaborated circles of production that bare their professional hackles at outsiders. In contrast, the Pre-Raphaelites were gloriously though erratically open to much of the greater world in which they were trying to reshape some sorts of new being, some new identities.

Painting and Industry

Raphael, painter of an exquisite realism, was of the Renaissance of Italy, so in art history terms those who preceded Raphael included Giotto and late medieval Italians, all of whose modes of composing and painting pictures appear stereotyped and hieratic. Their prints and paintings were what the dozen or so youths who were to constitute the PRB enthused about to each other and their peers, over tea and in London cafes. But this enthusiasm accounts only partly for the *Ivanhoe* paintings of crisply idealized knights that came from the brushes of PRB members.

Amidst the coal smoke of Victorian London, they urgently sought identities utterly different from those implied by the works—and the ways of working—of then-conventional artists. One of the PRB obsessions was for clear, bright, new paintings that were evenly detailed rather that focused on some elite figure. Dark paintings of ancient tales were admired then, as were pompous portraits of current elites, to whom deference was shown. Look now at some of the pictures from PRB brushes. In mood they are dreamy and of the Good: The Pre-Raphaelites favored fluid and melodramatic phrasings. Yet in execution their work is precise, hard edged, and brilliantly colored. The composition was typically frontal. Instead of depicting women, they painted large-eyed and long-haired maidens staring right out at you.

English industrial cities were the Chicago and Los Angeles of that midcentury time of the PRB. Manchester and Leeds and Liverpool seemed weird to the world, ugly yet fabulous. Medieval themes of a fixed, hieratic society made an odd juxtaposition to such Manchester scenes, yet these PRB themes were fabulous, and England bulged with scrambled metaphors as well as vitality. Through medievalism the young PRB members could celebrate brash new identities with strikingly novel thematics suitable to brash new men and forces.

Dreams and words, more than a consistent rhetoric, characterized the PRB mentality. It would be as if a club calling itself the pre-Beatles emerged in the late 1980s among a swath of young instrumentalists and students and hangers-on in Japan. By their own initial account, the PRB was a secret society. Gabriel Dante Rossetti sparked the Brotherhood, along with two other youths, John Everett Millais and Holman Hunt. There were seven youths in the beginning if one includes some ephemeral hangers-on.

The PRB members not only thought well of painting but also were already—or were to become—painters. Millais had amazing painterly skills by anyone's standards. Most of the PRB acquired some art school training. They tutored each other with gusto and set up art training for many others. They did need mentors in painterly technique. Some guidance came from older, yet sympathetic, painters like Ford Madox Brown, and from a critic of towering influence, John Ruskin, came much advice, mixed in with his philosophical effusions.

One joint project of the PRB exemplifies their combination of energy with ignorance. Rossetti, then approaching thirty and already a guru for the new young adherents William Morris and Edward Coley Burne-Jones, went to Oxford and persuaded the architect of the new Oxford Union debating hall to let his crew paint ten scenes of Arthurian legends on the walls. Their correspondence reports having a wonderful summer, but six months later hardly a stroke's worth of paint was left: Neither Rossetti nor the others knew anything of fresco technique for freshly plastered walls.

Their works show originality and force sufficient to reward looking for its own sake. The PRB were passionate about their tastes. These changed sometimes, and individuals differed about them, but some formation of collective identity was signaled in their common rejection, along with elders like Brown and Ruskin, of tastes then current among established painters. Their art world became transparent to outsiders because it was simple. There was little veiling by intricate secrecies of guild, or profession, or of aristocratic patronage.

Pre-Raphaelitism did require material sustenance, which doing portraits could supply only in part. They came from diverse social backgrounds, from which some drew part or all of independent incomes. But many over time built up substantial incomes from their paintings. The industrial powerhouse of Manchester and the commercial entrepôt of Liverpool were both important as sources of recognition and support for Pre-Raphaelitism.

Between 1851 and 1857, Hunt, Millais, and Brown each won two annual prizes at the Liverpool Academy. Several local painters, such as William Windus, began to pick up themes from the PRB, whose paintings were being acquired by a tobacco merchant, a shipping magnate, a banker, and later by soap baron William Lever, first Lorde Leverhulme. Liverpool was important also because it later remained committed to Pre-Raphaelites in its galleries through intervening decades of disdain before they once again rose in London esteem.

Poetry and London

The Pre-Raphaelites were preprofessionals who mixed with literati and, in addition to painting, wrote. London was a writing capital of the world and had been for centuries. When building other art worlds, young English always were awash in literary metaphor. William Hogarth's caricatures are the most famous early example among visual artists. The few older English artists to whom the PRB keyed, notably Ruskin and Brown, were very literary, and young Rossetti grew up within a literary ambience. Rossetti's father was a liberal expatriate from Italy who had become a professor of literature in London. Dante Rossetti often slipped back into the writing of poetry. Holman Hunt had fixations in Old Testament narratives that led to hideous though strong paintings.

No one art survives long in isolation from production of other arts, which are needed to help sustain both ambience and audience. One sees this again and again in the United States as one bold regional experiment after another, now in this art and now in that, folds after a brief solo flowering. In England, having a turf within London was vital for being able to mix with other high arts, because no other location could sustain an array of arts. Artists came to claim particular areas in the metropolis, and the PRB pioneered in a scruffy neighborhood near a literary area of London. Their evolution shows "style" spreading in variations accounted for better by networks of ties and influences rather than by abstract categories of independent cognition.

London was no Paris, but it did offer dutiful training in visual art, especially bread-and-butter painting of portraits, landscapes, and still lifes. Several members of the PRB were trained in the Royal Academy of Arts in London and studio schools loosely tied to it, in a system that aped the royal mantle long draped over French painting. This training was off and on and not very good. There were relatively few incidents and relations about which to gossip and to angle for advantage. Would-be painters of England thus were free to think deep thoughts and have striking opinions about many matters—in short to be young amateurs more than professionals. It was a time in which identities as artists were closely embedded within broader social formation.

London was able to beckon provincials toward a whole nexus of arts, but information and connections in any art did have to be spun out to the provinces. An art requires a broad base for recruitment as well as material support, just as it requires cultural stimulation. The PRB members oriented to the dominant universities of Oxford and Cambridge in their provincial cities, as well as to their avid supporters in industrial cities of the Midlands.

The "Central" Class

Some external influences reach artists directly along personal networks from social kindred not tied into arts at all. Others are more public. In Victorian England these latter influences included newly rampant prejudices and goals among a new and broad array of people who had new and enlarged sources of income and thus were able to support new art in new ways according to tastes that could be changed. Members of a buoyant new socioeconomic stratum came to see Pre-Raphaelite artworks as celebrating their importance.

In hindsight, the Pre-Raphaelites appear an odd lot: a warehouseman's son, the offspring of a transplanted Italian literature professor, a boy wonder from the Channel islands, and so on. Hindsight, however, is exactly the wrong perspective. A feel for the times leads us to sense that what was being shared was a necessarily inarticulate and partial sense of new identity emerging, emerging before their eyes in larger social as well as immediate personal scope.

The "middle class" was attempting to be born in Victorian England. There was no such term then; there were neither linguistic nor accepted symbolic markers for it. Earlier, in the Wesleyan Methodist movement, what we would now call a lower middle class had pushed itself into existence. It was recognized though disdained by gentry and nobility, who meanwhile continued their mutual, centuries-long gavotte in pretensions to ancestry and honor and in accrual of cash. Industrialists were bursting forth from textiles and from steam and elsewhere on over to Wedgwood in pottery. Workmen opponents to industrialists were roiling England with huge Chartist demonstrations, to which PRBs were sympathetic spectators.

But there was as yet no center. There was no middle class. This middle class has since been made real for all of us, both here and there, in terms of Rotarians and respectability. In dynamism as well as Philistinism, this central class is not the bourgeoisie of continental Europe, who looked backward as much as forward. Seemingly the new class would lie between others above and below it, but the urge was too strong to settle down as a mere stratum. The urge, shared by an array of odd sets of persons such as the PRB, was for a class bursting forth to claim moral preeminince (with success eventually more complete in the United States in its Calvin Coolidges than in the UK even with its Margaret Thatchers). "Central" seems a more apt description than "middle."

The Pre-Raphaelites, as a group with hangers-on, mirrored the problematics of the new middle class, but on a much smaller scale. Like other young men, they passionately sought identities both jointly and severally. Nascent identities always seek some sort of control, often through explicit organization such as the Brotherhood and its later spin-offs. Such explicit organization thereupon attracts outside attention that can erode and overwhelm, as it almost did the PRB.

In this Victorian context a new class was stirring; it was moved to seek identities in and through new interpretations of art, as much as in specific new artworks or styles:

> The collection and contemplation of art were among the chief preoccupations of the upwardly mobile Victorian middle class. … Art managed to extract itself from its moral harness and become the source of more complex aspira-

tions for a diverse group of patrons. ... The Reform Bill of 1832 granted more recognition to the middle classes, gave them greater confidence in asserting their aesthetic preferences. ... English parvenus may have wished to emulate the aristocracy by buying or building country houses and furnishing them with precious possessions, but they did not imitate the upper classes in bidding for pictures by the Old Masters. Like the merchant "princes" of Renaissance Italy and the burghers of seventeenth-century Holland, they hung their walls with freshly-painted canvases by living artists. ... Although a few of the nobility supported the trend, most considered modern art inferior to the art of the past. ... Contemporary art was given a major boost in 1843 by the appearance of the first volume of John Ruskin's *Modern Painters*. (Macleod 1987, pp. 328–329)

The Pre-Raphaelites thus are an example of the awkward process by which the "middle class" was trying to come into existence, by constructive self-discovery, in Victorian England. This was to be a new class not of mere lackeys of the higher classes, whether nobility or its shadow gentry. This was to be a new class with a morality and spirit distinctively its own, a class in itself and not merely a stratum better off than lower strata. It was to be, in its own view, not so much the "middle" class as the *central* class, whose values were best and most significant and therefore at the core or center of society.

Like most other social passages, this one in England was uneven and irregular. Within the complex dynamisms of the first industrial nation, this passage was bound to, and did, fractionate into a set of middle strata only partially nested into *the* central class. Many cultural themes and styles could and did contribute. People did care, also, about the art for its own sake. But the need was all the more urgent for classwide myths. Individualism became the central new myth.

Individualism and Ruskin

Ruskin was the preeminent critic and aesthete of the whole century in Britain. Why? He was particularly the aesthete for the PRB, being personally close to many of them, but his closeness had a unique flavor. It was with equanimity that Ruskin let his wife be wafted away by Millais, first as model and then as wife. There was an extraordinary absence of tangible, flesh-and-blood humans in the visions that Ruskin promulgated in his four volumes of commentary.

This is just the paradox of creating a wider individualism: It must shun concrete individuals! Particular individuals as prototypes are hard to divorce from preexisting classes and strata that must be overridden by an emerging new class identity. Every identity, whether class or person, is at once seeking control.

Notes to Plates

John Ruskin, *Fragment of the Alps*
Watercolor and gouache over graphite, on cream wove paper.

Three facets of Ruskin's identity connect to this watercolor drawing. It is the very model of the practice Ruskin, the critic, valued in Pre-Raphaelite paintings: exquisite attention to rendering detail of form and texture in nature. It also represents Ruskin's methods and identity as a teacher of drawing, at the Working Men's College (founded 1854) in London, and in his best-selling manual, *Elements of Drawing* (1857). He bade students to see naively and freshly and to record that vision. "If you can draw that stone, you can draw anything ... that is drawable," he wrote. Finally, Ruskin the religio-scientific exegetist saw truth to nature as figuring forth transcendant meaning, a glimpse of the mind of the creator. The drawing was made in 1854, when Ruskin traveled to Switzerland to get away from the painful scandal of his wife's flight with Millais. It was later a gift from Ruskin to Charles Eliot Norton, a key American connection.

Courtesy of Fogg Art Museum, The Harvard University Art Museums. Gift of Samuel Sachs.

Edward Burne-Jones, *Sir Galahad*
Pen and ink on vellum.

"Remember, I have set my heart on founding a Brotherhood. Learn 'Sir Galahad' (by Tennyson, 1842) by heart. He is to be the patron of our order." So wrote Burne-Jones to a friend in 1853. William Morris and Burne-Jones, outsiders who gravitated to each other at Oxford, shared an enthusiasm for Arthurian legend. In 1855, they were houseguests in the home of the painter Val Prinsep, as was Tennyson. There, Burne-Jones made a number of Arthurian drawings. This drawing, from 1858, has reference to Ruskin as well. The careful buildup of crosshatching, especially in the horse's body, is a technique recommended by Ruskin in *Elements of Drawing*. Basically, it is pen and ink imitating engraving. Ruskin, an avid collector of the prints of Albrecht Dürer, was especially fond of the famous *Knight, Death and the Devil*. *Sir Galahad* has echoes of that print. Ruskin, who had "taken up" Burne-Jones, gave him an original of the Dürer print in 1863.

Courtesy of Fogg Art Museum, The Harvard University Art Museums. Bequest of Grenville L. Winthrop.

Edward Burne-Jones, *The Days of Creation* (The Third Day)
Watercolor, gouache, shell gold, and platinum paint on linen-covered panel. 1875–1876.

With the founding of the Firm by William Morris (1861), Burne-Jones began to come into his own as a master designer with an unmistakable trademark style. Stained-glass designs were his specialty in the Firm. *The Days of Creation* were originally designed in 1870 for church windows. The panel paintings, in which he conveyed a sumptuous quality by a surprisingly limited palette, were first exhibited in 1877 at the new, no-less-sumptuous Grosvenor Gallery (enterprise of an enormously wealthy couple, Sir Coutts and Lady Lindsay). By this time, Burne-Jones had his own large studio, with several assistants. Usually, he made detailed pencil drawings that an assistant transferred to an underpainting on canvas. Burne-Jones then did all the final overpainting. But in the Six Days, the entire work was his.

Courtesy of Fogg Art Museum, The Harvard University Art Museums. Bequest of Grenville L. Winthrop.

Gabriel Charles Dante Rossetti, *The Salutation of Beatrice*
Graphite, pen, black ink, black wash, white gouache on cream paper.

Made in 1849–1850, the first year of the Brotherhood, these drawings show artistic, imaginative, and personal sources for Rossetti's art. The treatment of space and the figures, especially on the left, are from the work of Rossetti's chosen mentor, Ford Madox Brown. The insistently thin, rather dry line and the flattened-out planes it creates appear in other Pre-Raphaelite drawings of this era: Nineteenth-century engravings illustrating early Italian paintings from Pisa were a widely used source. The drawings also signal Rossetti's lifelong identification with the Italian poet Dante. Several years earlier, Rossetti had taken Dante as his first name. During his lifetime, he made over one hundred drawings and paintings of Dantesque subjects. In 1859 Rossetti repeated this subject as the decorative panel on a cabinet by William Morris.

Courtesy of Fogg Art Museum, The Harvard University Art Museums. Bequest of Grenville L. Winthrop.

John Everett Millais, *The Good Samaritan* and *The Lost Piece of Silver*
Watercolor and gouache on white paper. c. 1876.

These are part of a series of six Parables from the New Testament, painted as bases for a set of stained-glass windows in the church near Millais's home in Perthshire, a memorial to one of his sons, who had died. They are a selection from the original *Parables of Our Lord and Saviour Jesus Christ,* twenty book illustrations drawn on the block by Millais, turned into wood engravings, and printed in 1863 by the firm of the Brothers Dalziel. Millais, with Rossetti, Holman Hunt, and Arthur Hughes, was a star of the "golden age of English book illustration" (c. 1855–1870). He worked slowly, with great care, meticulously drawing everything in reverse; he was paid twenty pounds each for his designs. The Dalziels photographed some of them onto other blocks, so that the originals could be preserved and sold. They owned the copyright for the Parables, later selling it to the magazine *Good Words* for a thousand pounds. Effie Millais, the model for the exquisitely painted *Lost Coin,* often corresponded with the Dalziels on her husband's behalf, especially when the publisher was pressuring him to finish a commission.

Courtesy of Fogg Art Museum, The Harvard University Art Museums. Bequest of Grenville L. Winthrop.

Ford Madox Brown, *Death of King Lear: Lear and Cordelia*
Pencil on light green paper. 1856.

This drawing, part of a series of scenes from *King Lear,* was a study for an oil painting later exhibited in the United States. Madox Brown, conservatively trained by a Belgian muralist, nevertheless provided pictorial ideas far more influential than has been generally recognized. The shallow stagelike foreground space opening out into a glimpse of a far background is almost a Pre-Raphaelite cliché. The exaggerated, somewhat awkward, often freshly observed gestures and the odd bunching and twisting of figural groups are also an F. M. Brown trademark absorbed by his younger colleagues. Rossetti's debt to him is very obvious here.

Courtesy of Fogg Art Museum, The Harvard University Art Museums. Bequest of Grenville L. Winthrop.

Gabriel Charles Dante Rossetti, Study for *The Blessed Damozel*
Black crayon on gray-green paper with touches of red crayon and white chalk. 1876.

This pattern of sinuously entwined lovers became the background of one painted version of The Blessed Damozel, an image from Rossetti's poem about Dante's Beatrice in Heaven. The combination of abstract pattern, exaggerated, softened, rounded forms, and a sticky sensuality is an unfortunate example of Rossetti's late style. Jane Morris, with whom Rossetti developed an intense relationship, is the model for the two women in the foreground. Like most of Rossetti's later work, the final painting is dominated by a large, extravagantly sensuous female figure; the lovers become a more abstract backdrop. Collectors of these paintings of the 1870s, like Liverpool shipping magnate Frederick Leyland, found in Rossetti's women the key into the new aesthetic of beauty for beauty's sake. In Leyland's London mansion, rooms were specially designed as settings, almost shrines, for these paintings.

Courtesy of Fogg Art Museum, The Harvard University Art Museums. Bequest of Grenville L. Winthrop.

Notes prepared by Cynthia A. White

John Ruskin, *Fragment of the Alps*

Edward Burne-Jones, *Sir Galahad*

Edward Burne-Jones, *The Days of Creation*
(The Third Day)

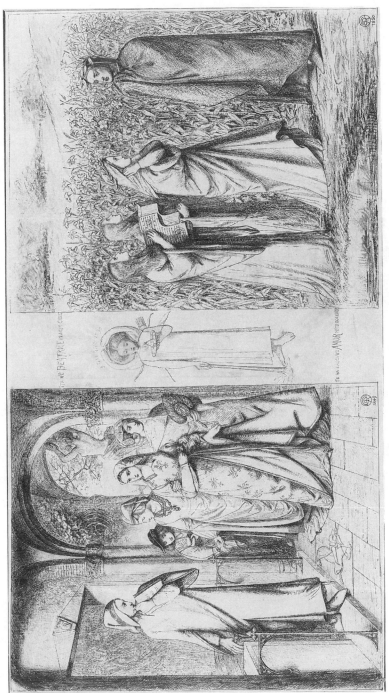

Gabriel Charles Dante Rossetti, *The Salutation of Beatrice*

John Everett Millais, *The Good Samaritan*

John Everett Millais, *The Lost Piece of Silver*

Ford Madox Brown, *Death of King Lear: Lear and Cordelia*

Gabriel Charles Dante Rossetti, Study for *The Blessed Damozel*

Individualism is the vehicle suitable for creating a class out of what starts as some set of odd lots that are scattered across different regions and very diverse niches in both businesses and industries and encompassing new professions as they displace guilds. No wonder Ruskin was the paramount pundit of the century. He wrote unending volumes in which one never saw concrete human artists but rather roles of artists. And in them one never encountered tangible rights and duties, say Chartist rights as unions or gentry duties in parliament, but rather Beauty and Truth and so on. Identity always must seek control, and a newly minting identity is best off avoiding the familiar turfs on which existing classes and strata assert their control.

Works on medieval themes by naive young PRB artists provided very suitable visual dress for Ruskin's themes. These themes required resonance to and among and for a class-in-the-making, which necessarily seeks new sociocultural space for itself. Just claiming location in some existing social tapestry will not suffice. Individualism, being formed across all these class fractions, could not settle well into such existing tapestry; individualism therefore fled sometimes to medieval fantasy, in which all bits and pieces of the would-be central class could share.

Pre-Raphaelite painting attracted renewed interest and attention, it seems to me, just around the late 1970s and early 1980s in the United Kingdom and then also in the United States. Was not this a time in both countries of a resurgent but conflicted would-be central class? Many fractions of the would-be class were nostalgic for 1960s myths about classless utopia, but others were ferociously antiunion. And many fractions resented divergences away from would-be central values that had become all too manifest. Again in this later era individualism becomes an apt resolution. Among many possible symbolizations, resurgence of a medieval never-never land is made more likely by the memory of Pre-Raphaelitism.

Pre-Raphaelite Women, Medievalism, and Spirituality

Forming perceptions of a new class may go with a dynamic in which some other, and apparently unrelated, dichotomy is brought into focus. In this section I show that spirituality led to one such dichotomy (with religion) in the formation of the Victorian middle class. Another dichotomy in the nineteenth century was gender, gender reconstrued and made central in a new way. Women as disjunct from men, via a new construct of femininity, gave leverage to the production of a new social class. This was in part substantive, with women cast in a special new relation to the strong new modes of commerce. But it was an ideological struggle as well. Bringing to light new conflicts that are unresolvable can generate the energy requisite to creating a new class culture. Eventually the conflict becomes the "common sense" of a new culture: "Class and gender come together and sustain themselves within the family. As the middle class prospered and cohered, it increasingly treasured a sexual division of labor. Although men worked for and with their families, women became more detached from the processes of production, a separation that moving the home to the suburbs both symbolized and insured" (in the Foreword, by Catharine Stimpson, to Davidoff and Hall 1987, p. 9).

Relations of Pre-Raphaelites with women fell into a stereotype. Morris and Rossetti both became deeply attached to shop girls of great beauty and little education. Each built an inward-looking cocoon around that relationship, segregating it from broader social context. Medieval or other unreal contexts were especially suitable for PRB paintings of women. Jan Marsh (1988) speaks of

> The opposed but complementary aspects of womanhood, as defined in the Victorian age, whose variants and influences on life and art form the subject of this book [*Pre-Raphaelite Women: Images of Femininity*]. Woman as desirable, woman as chaste, woman as dutiful, woman as witch: these are among the images that both reflected and shaped the ideas of the age regarding the relations of the sexes and the ideals of masculinity and femininity. Such ideas were powerfully expressed in both painting and poetry ... [and] images of women dominate Pre-Raphaelite art—the term is indeed now synonymous with a specific feminine appearance, with loose hair, large eyes, elongated neck and soulful expression. (p. 9)
>
> It is not easy to account for this preoccupation. (p. 10)

Such a puzzle invites more indirect solutions.

Speculation 2.1. If the various feminist movements of today succeed in eroding the dichotomy about femininity, does this imply that the middle class as construct will unwind too?

Perhaps this process is already under way and can be seen in a number of other social developments, visible in our arts as well as our general social life—developments that on the surface have nothing to do with feminist debates. There may be dissolution of our middle class back into either a stack of strata or perhaps just a messy congeries of all sorts of class fractions, with only elite and underclass hanging on as effective constructs from previous reality. Social formations are complex, however, and the causal nexus may not be the dissolution of gender. Instead one might focus speculation upon the dissolution of a working class, taking as given that the underclass does not provide sufficient cultural contraposition to sustain a middle class. One can examine our current art productions for clues as to which if either speculation is worth pursuing.

It seems likely that PRB usages of the feminine are related to the PRB usages of medievalism. Did medieval troubadours also exemplify a correlation between the formation of a new class and a new apotheosis of female gender? If so, the PRB members were replaying the troubadours. Perhaps the PRB use of medievalism in art is not just an arbitrary borrowing of style and symbol.

Turn to analysis by an expert on medievalism:

> Courtliness is, in many ways, synonymous with the psychologizing of social reality—the conversion of a set of reciprocal social relations, sensed as external and objective, into moral values. The courtly lexicon represents a virtual inventory of feudal terminology whose meaning has shifted toward the designation of an internal quality or state ... the objective obligation of the feudal lord to provide his vassal with material support as well as protection becomes ... the virtue of generosity. ... The decision-making process most characteristic of the epic is the public *concilium* which serves as a forum for the resolution of matters of both personal and collective concern. In romance, however ... the individual, and not the assembled community, bears the sole responsibility of choice. (Bloch 1977, p. 231)

What Bloch emphasizes in his analysis is how individualism ties together courtliness to women with the emergence of a new class, a class in the middle. This is not so far from what we found about Pre-Raphaelite women. Neither the troubadours nor the PRB who emulated them were much concerned with daily reality and concrete individuals. The great cleanliness and tidiness of PRB medieval scenes surely are an anachronism. What both troubadours and PRB members were sensing and representing was the new aspects of invidious social relations that were painfully beginning to emerge. The new character given to women in both eras may have served in part to deflect and subsume some of the pain of asserting change in invidious relations—just as did the new ideology of the individual. In both eras, reflections can be found in poetry as well as in music in the earlier era and painting in the later era.

Let the analyst continue to expound these subtle interconnections:

> There is no problem more confusing than the relation between the concept of individualism and the forms of social organization that have tended historically to accompany its repeated disappearance and revival. Nonetheless, the twelfth century is generally considered to be one of the great eras of liberation of the individual, the first in a series of steps leading to Renaissance humanism and to the democratic revolutions of the eighteenth century. The literary legacy of that liberation is, however, unclear. On the one hand, the free-

dom of a knight to leave the community in search of adventure ... seems to establish the autonomy not only of the individual, but of the entire chivalric class. The power of the lyric lover ... the privilege of noble souls, reinforces a similar claim to moral superiority and to dominance. ... And yet, the individualism of both adventurer and lover is, at the same time, perfectly consonant with the political strategy of monarchy and bourgeoisie ... the lyric pattern of constant conflict ... represents an important step in the direction of the individualist and materialist vision of human nature characteristic of Old French satire ... in more recognizably popular forms ... the courtly text can be situated somewhere between the collectivism of the epic and the ardent individualism of the satire. It does not conflict, but rather coincides, with the ideological interests of a nascent bourgeoisie. (Bloch 1977, p. 225)

With the advent of inquest and appeal, along with the emergence of the office of public prosecutor, the dynamics of the judicial encounter shifted from a conflict between opposing families to a contest between the individual and the broader body politic. Intention as the foundation of ethical theory served to individualize the notion of sin itself. ... The twelfth century was, in fact, a period of transition from the fixed penances of an earlier era—the tariffs of punishment which, like the *wergeld*, consisted of codified sanctions strictly applied in order to produce automatic absolution—to more individual sanctions prescribed according to the age, sex, and social status of the sinner and according to the circumstances of the sin. Absolution ... depended upon signs of inner contrition ... part of a global transformation by which the individual became a self-governing legal entity. (Bloch 1977, p. 228)

Ruskin was not so learned as Bloch, but his aesthetics, like the artwork he praised, fits the same mold. And this supplies some insight into possible sources of energy and motivation for Pre-Raphaelitism as well as PRB members' choice of medieval models.

Perhaps medievalism was related to new tendencies in spirituality as well. Medievalism was a choice, but religion was an inescapable part of the social and cultural landscape for the PRB. It is hard to appreciate how deeply religion permeated life in Victorian England, in part because many of its most prominent figures had ostentatiously forsworn religion.

There were social constraints on choice of religious terrain for a new identity. The Anglican church, which was the state church, was taken up by squabbles over precedence among nobility and gentry. Lower reaches of society escaped variously from such tutelage into Wesleyan and more fundamentalist sects or into freethinking or atheism. Ruskin had a solution for this, as for all else. Ruskin, and many PRB members partly under his influence, turned to spiritualism. Spirituality was left as unclaimed cultural terrain for some dimly apprehended class-to-be, a middle class seeking superiority intellectually and culturally. This was not spiritualism in any explicit form like theosophy or the Swedenborgian church; rather it was admirably vague and was suitable for bracketing religion without denying it.

Perhaps the great vogue for classical Greece and Rome in the Europe of that century came from somewhat the same source, namely, joint striving for high respectability by a nonnoble, nongentry class-to-be. And spirituality had the virtue, for the PRB and others, of sidestepping the "Catholic question" that bedeviled nineteenth-century England: Protestantism is an anachronism in medieval times. In that context, the Catholicism of Hunt, Rossetti, and others, born or acquired, could lie in peace with Chapel and High Church.

Any real world of cultural and social formations is, however, always irregular and messy. Independent of the rationalizing aesthete Ruskin, there also was a fiery spiritualist artist, William Blake, who had some kinship with PRB vision and ideas. Blake was a working man, a printer, who, unlike those in the rising labor movement, turned away from explicit concern with social class. But Blake turned to the Old Testament, whereas the PRB medievalists turned to the New Testament. Blake turned to Milton, and the medievalists to Chaucer. It is hard to draw stylistic lessons, however, for Blake was original in more fundamental ways than any of the other PRB members and was technically inept in drawing, much like Rossetti.

Design for Industry

Each of the two recent surveys of the Pre-Raphaelites offers Ford Madox Brown's *The Last of England* as the plate for its front cover. Yet this painting is not spiritual, not medieval, not romantic. It is instead a picture of class choice, of rejecting England for a try at life in the colonies.

The collective identity of Pre-Raphaelites also required creative choice, choice that could help engender some sort of tangible art world with regular support and attention from the outside. Industry was a site for such choice. Industry as art was taken up by William Morris. Stained glass was a product for which middling sorts as well as elites paid eagerly, as they also did for the new strains of furniture and of design in wallpaper and textile. All of these soon came from Morris's business, called The Firm, to which other Pre-Raphaelites contributed and which spread their fame.

The Morris products followed designs that were rigidly controlled and regimented by Morris (and Burne-Jones). Yet PRB art celebrated a new individualism, via medievalism and a new femininity. This was an individualism without concrete individuals. It seems fitting that this array of Morris products distinctive of Pre-Raphaelitism should bypass individualized designing and also bypass femininity yet continue to cast a medieval tone.

Read a Marxist critic on William Morris to gain a new angle of vision on Pre-Raphaelitism:

> The fundamental distinction between the Arnold and Ruskin view of society and that of William Morris lies in the attitude towards class and the interconnections between history and class struggle. Of course, Morris had to first overcome the assumptions and prejudices of his own class and the powerful influence of such men as Ruskin, Rossetti and Burne-Jones, the great mid-century aesthetic-cultural movement, its aversion to and its pessimism about the explosive energies of the capitalist market ... the path that led from Pre-Raphaelite admiration for the anonymous artisans and craftsmen of the Middle Ages and the culture of an idealized past ... Morris almost alone [led the way]. (Hampton 1990, p. 107)

Across the Atlantic

The analysis so far, if valid, should hold good in other settings too. Across the Atlantic many of the themes and fervors of the PRB circles—especially those enunciated by Ruskin and Morris—were activated a generation later in the United States. I argue that it is worth seeing whether in this other setting the same wrestling to realize a new central class was again the prime source of artistic themes and tone that on the surface had no direct relation to a new class.

In the United States these themes were especially associated with the increasing role of women in art. Kathleen D. McCarthy writes:

> The Philadelphia Centennial Exposition of 1876 triggered a national stock-taking of the place of women in American society, as well as the place of art ... the Ladies Centennial Committee solicited samples to highlight all forms of feminine achievement, literature, legal briefs ... photography, "and the fine arts; but not the lighter fancy work (such) as wax flowers, embroidery, etc., unless a very high order of artistic skill is manifested in the work." ... The decorative arts movement that developed in the aftermath of the Fair changed the artistic ideals of the entire country, elevating domestic handiwork to a new level of dignity and respect, and moving feminine artistry to the center of the creative process. ... *The movement received additional stature from the endorsement of revered art critic and philosopher, John Ruskin, and his disciple William Morris ... Ruskinites had fashioned the cause of art into a social and moral crusade. ... Crafts that had traditionally been trivialized as women's work were suddenly transmuted into fine art, and linked to the larger task of social regeneration.* (Salzman 1987, pp. 90–91, emphasis supplied)

Candace Wheeler, hostess of a main New York literary salon and later one of the country's first professional interior decorators, organized the New York Society of Decorative Art, in which women held all of the official positions: "In a pattern that echoed the format of William Morris' firm, women executed little artistic discretion over the patterns they so diligently stitched, a dichotomy that revealed the depth of feminine insecurities about publicly passing aesthetic judgements in their own name" (Salzman 1987, p. 91).

Auxiliaries were formed in a dozen other cities, downplaying the civic chauvinism characteristic of male control. The Chicago auxiliary was composed entirely of women, and it included classes in Pre-Raphaelite techniques. John Ruskin was their prophet.

Needlework had been almost superseded by the sewing machine when these decorative societies were formed, but

> in the process, traditional feminine symbolism was replaced by less emotionally charged, more naturalistic designs limned by men ... Marshall Field and A. T. Stewart spearheaded the feminization of consumerism. ... By the 1870s, consumer palaces began to dot the American urbanscape, offering a variety of amenities shaped specifically to women's tastes. ... Like women's clubs and societies of decorative art, department stores forged a new definition of feminine terrain. (Salzman 1987)
>
> By the 1890s, women had already begun to move beyond a narrow preoccupation with the aesthetics of the domestic sphere. Supported by Ruskian notions that equated national art with national virtue, women rallied to the cause under the traditional banner of charity and home. Later, when sufficiently self-assured to cast off the rationale of an earlier era, America's patronesses finally came of age. (Salzman 1987)

Fast-Food Chains in France

Much of this account has been speculative. These speculations would require detailed probing of the PRB case to achieve greater certainty. One can also transpose these speculations to other settings to assess generality as well as to further assess robustness.

The speculations concern young artists heralding, with new genre and style, a change in the social stratification of their society. In Chapter 4, on radical change, I make one direct transposition of this thesis—to popular musical art and to the United States in the middle of this century. Try now a yet more extreme transposition, where one may not even at first see participation by artists.

Strong illumination and bright, simple colors are a key to the acceptance of McDonald's and other fast-food chains by youths in France (where one does not see so many of the families with young kids that are prominent in an American McDonald's). These visual design features, along with the "un-Frenchness" of the food, are material from which the young French weave their assertions of identity. This identity runs counter to what they see as rigid and torpid French normality. What these youths are seeking and finding is a decoupling: a freeing of both customers and staff both from the whims of each other and from general French codes of deportment, dress, and taste.

Surely the PRB approach to art had a similar aim of decoupling, though on a more rarified cultural level, both from elders and from social elites. Some of the corresponding artistic changes were similar: bright colors, bold design, invocation of a radically different society, and so on. The main difference is that the artistic realizations for McDonald's are concealed behind a screen of business and professional agency: We aren't informed who the artists hired to create McDonald's in France were. Nor do we know if changes came from initial artistic input to the original McDonald's in California, which were thereafter maintained elsewhere, including France. Nor do we know how conscious those working for McDonald's are of the aesthetic component of the restaurants' identity. We do know that the experiment in adapting McDonald's to Germany through dark colors and lower lighting was a disaster.

GUIDE TO FURTHER READING

Timothy Hilton published his overview of the Pre-Raphaelites simultaneously with John Nicoll's more painterly survey, in the year 1970. This was about when English painting was at last disengaging from its inferiority complex; see Sir John Rothenstein's (1962) overview. All of these volumes have excellent plates and illustrations.

Fredeman as editor (1975) embeds a diary of the first PRB years in an account of the social and aesthetic setting. A one-volume abridgment is now available of John Ruskin's treatises on aesthetics. A recent biographer provides insight: "This restless partnership between the self that lives and learns piecemeal and the self that proposes discrete, whole narratives lies at the center of Ruskin's life and imagination. ... To smooth over the disjunctions, ellipses, the multiplied and parallel endeavors which are endemic to Ruskin's mind and life would be to lose an essential aspect of the subject" (Hunt 1982, pp. 4, 5). On rationalism and romanticism see Campbell's study of consumerism (1987).

Dianne Macleod (1987) describes the growth of art collecting among the Victorian middle class. Elizabeth White (1992) supplies the argument about gender as device masking change in perception of social class. The Jan Marsh book (1988) quoted earlier is wholly devoted to images of femininity in Pre-Raphaelite art.

Leonore Davidoff and Catherine Hall (1987) provide and analyze a great deal of material on the actual relations among men and women in the emerging middle class of Midlands England before 1850. Their argument is that these gender relations were an essential component in even the apparently most public and business aspects of class.

Material in the section on medievalism, relating law to love, comes from the monograph by Howard Bloch (1977).

Poet Kathleen Raine offers both a one-volume modern overview (1970) and a two-volume treatise on Blake, who, like Hogarth (Antal 1962), epitomizes the permeation of English visual arts by literature. Whereas Hogarth, like Dickens, embraced earthly life, Blake, like Milton, fled it; the Pre-Raphaelites were in between.

Material in the section on the view across the Atlantic comes from Kathleen McCarthy's essay in Salzman's 1987 volume. For an extended discussion of influences of Morris and Ruskin in America see Eileen Boris (1986).

Rick Fantasia's study (1992) is the source for McDonald's in France.

FIELDWORK IDEAS

Begin with a simple and direct approach. After thinking through several alternatives for finding a young painter or sculptor, use the one most likely to lead to acquaintanceship so that you can go hang around his or her site for a while. How does the site differ from what you would have seen with a Pre-Raphaelite? Is it a studio? Is she or he a professional? What signs of an art world do you spot? of a style?

Observation is fieldwork. The observer role is a form of agency. As such it can help you to focus your attention and to persist in that focus. Empathy, however necessary, does not supply focus. Guidance from theory is required.

Turn now to develop a line of inquiry that is complex and difficult. Fieldwork need not be confined to learning the perceptions and conceptions, possibly misguided, of those observed! How can the theoretical argument about women and class for the PRB context be transposed to today? Turn back to Speculation 2.1, at the end of that section. What changes might you expect to see in the arts today as part of any such devolution of the middle class and of any such unwinding of nineteenth-century femininity? Think of one or two, and then go out and take a look. This exercise is an example of how theoretical speculations can be useful, whether or not they prove to be well founded, by orienting you to look in fresh ways and spot new phenomena.

Now change the speculation. The new formations in class and gender that developed together in the nineteenth century could, instead of unwinding, happen all over again, but now in some transposed form. Develop a conjecture on the emergence of a new sort of unresolvable polarity, coupled with a new sort of broad change in social stratification. Perhaps the polarity could be gay/lesbian versus straight. Then follows the interesting question of what new stratum or class may be emerging elsewhere in our social formations, a split both energized and concealed by this engrossing struggle. Surely the arts are an apt site for investigating this conjecture. Such furors as that over exhibitions by the gay visual artist Robert Mapplethorpe come to mind as a topic for fieldwork.

The biggest challenges are arguing out possible effects in artworks themselves, as we tried to do earlier around Pre-Raphaelite women. Other sorts of difficulties, more sociological, might beset you in trying to similarly develop the example of fast food in France. No matter—the job of fieldwork in social science is to open up and to suggest, not to resolve. You cannot expect to fully resolve even a simple question or fully observe even a small population.

MEASURES AND MODELS

Aesthetic measure is as important as social model here. Art historians are people who have been trained and become skilled in really looking attentively at particular works of art. Some are also attentive to social historical context.

In his survey of the Pre-Raphaelites, Hilton (1970) supplies tangible detail on both their technique and their social context, with which the preceding account can be fleshed out. He also samples other opinions contemporaneous with the PRB, especially concerning the preeminent Sir Joshua Reynolds. I include here some excerpts, but the entire text deserves study. I supply emphases within these long quotations to signal examples of general points developed earlier in this chapter and in the previous chapter:

> But just as Reynolds ("Sir Sloshua") was looked on by the Brotherhood more as an old buffer than as a malevolent enemy, so too did Millais *regard post-Renaissance art with an amused kind of indifference.* A pleasant sheet from one of his early sketch-books is filled with caricatures of this type of painting. In the centre is a simpering Perugino-Raphaelesque Madonna; at one side of her a Guercinoesque saint, that worst type of excitable foreigner, rolls his eyes in a parody of Baroque ecstasy; in the corner are some low Dutchmen at their asinine junketings. These represent, of course, precisely the types of painting that Ruskin had attacked in the first volumes of *Modern Painters,* but in Millais' satire the intent is more kindly, and has none of the critic's righteous viciousness.
>
> It is sometimes thought that the members of the Pre-Raphaelite Brotherhood met nothing but criticism from the time their work was first placed before the public. This was not the case. *The attacks on their painting date largely from the time when the press first discovered the existence of the semi-secret society itself.* Hunt and Millais had not fared at all badly at the Royal Academy exhi-

bition of 1849 ... Rossetti's *The Girlhood of Mary Virgin*, too, had been very favourably received at the Free Exhibition which took place annually just before that at the Royal Academy, with commendatory and even glowing reports in all the major journals.

The confidence they felt at this stage led to an enlargement of their activities, and in particular to an involvement in literature that went beyond mere enthusiasm for certain writers. As was natural, Rossetti, who had always been more of a poet than a painter, led the way. He proposed that the Brotherhood should publish a magazine. This was to be *The Germ*. Though a paltry thing in itself, *The Germ* occupies a historical niche of some importance in that it was *the first house journal of a self-consciously avant-garde artistic group*, and set the pattern of the many such productions that have succeeded it—a large amount of initial enthusiasm, a dearth of good copy, endless trouble with printers, no sales and a short life. ... But the immediate effect of the activity surrounding *The Germ* was to bring the P.R.B. out into the open. (Hilton 1970, pp. 46–51)

What effects did this bumptious young group have, or at least what developments did it solidify and represent?

By 1850 art was generally felt to be more *important* [Hilton's italics] than in 1840. Ruskin had led the way, asserting that the practice of art had more to it than the mere production of pictures ... the possibility of both good and evil. *... No previous writer on art had ever said this so forcibly, or at such length, or had made so many people believe it.* ... There was more argument and discussion about art. It was no longer the intellectual province only of its practitioners, but a matter for public controversy.

On the actual canvases, there is an obvious insistence on holiness, on deep feeling and on literal truth. ... *The final consolidation of a shift in the patronage of art, from the country houses to the new cities, from an old aristocratic class to a new and bustling bourgeoisie.* Wilkie Collins, a friend of Millais and the brother of the Pre-Raphaelite painter Charles Allston Collins, amusingly describes this change in his novel *A Rogue's Life*, serialized in Dickens's *Household Words* in 1856 ... Collins is very insistent: *paintings should be clean and fresh and genuine. New pictures should look as if they were new*, and they should be colourful.

The pundits of the art world were duly hostile. They objected to two Pre-Raphaelite principles. The first of these was the evenness of working over the whole surface of the canvas, so that subordinate parts of the picture are as fully detailed, as clearly seen, as the central subject. The second was the evenness of light, and the refusal to proceed from dark edges to a light centre. ... These changes can be seen quite clearly by contrasting the paintings that Hunt and Millais did at the Academy before their Pre-Raphaelite days, and those that they painted afterwards. ... *Pre-Raphaelite paintings of the type that depended on mannered imitation of medieval forms are few in number. But it was a stage that had to be passed*, and in a way one feels as if Pre-Raphaelitism needed this sudden dip into historicism in order to slough off connections with the recent past.

The practice of portraiture has always been a staple for artists who earn their living out of art. ... Generally the Pre-Raphaelites did not paint portraits for gain, but because they liked the people they painted. Pre-Raphaelitism completes the process, initiated in Romantic art, whereby *the artist came to regard his sitter as an equal.* (Hilton 1970, pp. 53–57)

3

Narratives and Careers

There are cultural faces to the production of art that are not reducible to the social faces that I have emphasized thus far in the first chapter and much of the second chapter. But art also does not consist in some cultural matter off by itself, subject only to its own intrinsic laws of taste or change. What we call arts today, along with the arts of tribal times, is very much concerned with the interaction of these dual faces, which we think of as cultural and social. Narrative is central to this interaction.

Some Theory for Narrative and Career

A narrative renders a description and/or celebrates an event, in words spoken or written or perhaps in song or statue. A narrative may, but need not, make an argument. But a child recounting a tussle over toys with a sibling is not necessarily engaged in narration: That depends on his or her effort to weave that recounting out of stories familiar to the hearers. Narration selects from a cultural palette according to social and strategic context.

Identities come with and by narration. When conceived of as spread out over time, identities evoke narrations made up out of stylized stories. An identity thus fleshed out over time is what we call a career, constructed out of familiar stories. These identities can be of persons, even of the artist himself or herself, or of various corporate groups, on up through nations.

Careers can be recognized also on much smaller scales. In particular, an artwork is perceived, especially by its creator, as having a career in the sense of an unfolding over time, one that typically includes many backtrackings and merges many influences, physical as well as social and cultural. One can hear from a child who is creating a painting or drawing what amounts to discussing the changing career of that artwork. We go to another extreme in tracing an artwork such as a painting over many centuries, in what is called a provenance.

Narrative aspects of arts express and deal with efforts at control by identities. Narrative when it reports efforts at getting control by identity already formed can, like ceremony, go beyond merely novel performance to assert lasting impact. Shopping for clothes or home furnishings, for example, is constructing narrative in the course of asserting and representing an identity through what we call the applied arts of design, whether these be worked in textiles, in wood, or in glass or metal.

Efforts at control commonly compete with each other and are thus at cross-purposes. Plots derive from and reflect these cross-purposes, but only partially—only in those balanced and emphatic ways perceived as artistic within that social formation. Everyday talk, for example, need not have much structure or much of what we call plot, but talk does tend toward plot when it graduates to conversation. Then one account of everyday happenings is being traded with another, as narrations. In all sorts of ways, the senses of structure guiding such conversational narrative come from arts, for instance through the cumulative watching of plays and movies. And conversely, arts and their plots have evolved over long periods along with habits of conversation and narrative.

It follows that there are narrative aspects to any artwork or art performance within any art. This was taken for granted, for example, by all concerned with oil painting during its classical heyday, in France and Italy a couple of centuries ago. Modern artists for a time tried to sever any tie between story and picture, but their success was always limited: Just look at the interpretations of their works published by art critics, friendly or hostile. Great mimes become famous by presenting narration that can be tragic or comic without explicit words or music.

That program notes, for sonatas and ballets alike, tell stories is no accident. And diverse sorts of narrative can come to be received as arts, be these arts of high gossip or of cartoons as an invidious art. The diversity includes also the picaresque Tom Sawyer tale as popular art along with biography as high art.

Career has come to be seen as central narrative not only by artists in our time for themselves but also by their critics and brokers, who construe it in terms of performance measures. The novel has long been for us the premier high narrative, often as an interweaving of supposed careers, but narrative art keeps evolving into new forms. The latest major one is cinema, to which we shall turn as I build up to a definition of style at chapter's end.

Narrative Creativity and Senses of Identity

Ordinary social life consists mainly in routines that lock actors into various niches, which together make up social organization. But each actor, some of the time, tries for fresh action, for action that breaks routines imposed by ordinary social life. Such attempts at and disruptions of control are where identity comes from originally, just as ties and relations among identities are but negotiated stalemates of contending attempts at control.

Viewing artistic production processes as narratives brings into view—alongside the slick adjustments that mark routine success—failures and misfits and rejects. The result is a better basis for understanding innovation in art, which grows exactly out of misfits and failures and rejects that are grouped together as a fresh start to be valued, whether that be seen as a slight professional improvement or as a stroke of genius.

Identities figure in fury and fear as well as in sweetness and light as part of identity seeking control and thereby becoming creative. The tension between identity and control can be seen in art terms as conformity versus creativity, where the conformity in art may be in approach or medium or theme. Call routine reportage *narrative of a first mode.* Description of creative disruption is then *narrative of a second mode,* or narrative creativity. It can be seen in anthropological terms as the primary and original mode. Narrative creativity corresponds to an additional, a fourth, sense of identity. Identity in the second sense, introduced in Chapter 1, is identity of a whole as the sum of its parts, however intricate its internal architecture. There is also a third sense of identity, which is close to what is usually meant by identity in ordinary talk. This third sense of identity corresponds to an ex post account about identity; it is career seen from the inside.

The fourth sense of identity builds upon the first three. This is identity from frictions and errors across different social settings and disciplines. This additional sense of identity arises from the central fact of social organization: Each human is in more than one social molecule. That is, each of us continues in several different roles that cross distinct realms, such as family and village and job and secret society, so that our actions and thence our selves crosscut these realms. Even as children, we mix with different groups while intermixing our living in different realms. And as adults we do not often try to include all these realms in any one narrative we call career.

There need be nothing unusual or esoteric in this fourth sense of identity. Consider a homely example. A child on a playground may pick up a new way of wearing (or tearing) its clothes as being proper (an aspect of the second sense of identity). But the child finds, upon arriving home, that peer-proper is not family-proper. Such contradictions in life—all the screwups, mistakes, errors, and social noise—are just what bring about establishment of identity in this fourth sense. It is a sense that each of us achieved even as a child, and it is in the fourth and first senses that any identity first comes into existence.

Identity in this fourth sense is urgent, and its expression is urgent; it thus both implodes and explodes with the greatest of energies. These are the energies that generate and call forth artworks along with narrative creativity. This original and crucial sense of identity has no application in utopias because it arises exactly from contradictions across social disciplines impinging on the same actor, from mismatches and social noise. Literary utopias acknowledge the central fact of multiple roles for persons, but they are utopian in imagining individuals to be roles that are combined in consistently prescribed packages.

The fourth sense of identity is the core in any struggle to assert creativity, to celebrate it in artwork. Consider an example. When a William Paley builds a magnificent modern painting collection, he is doing so neither as Paley the MOMA (Museum of Modern Art) trustee, nor as Paley the founder of the CBS network, nor as any other more personal Paley. It is exactly the uneasy intersection of these several Paleys that was his identity in the fourth sense. Riding the irregular combination was what made Paley most Paley and called forth, along with exceptional energies and vitality, a commensurate hunger for its celebration.

Paley was a principal who used enough agents in art matters—and agents sufficiently differentiated from one another—to keep control and to keep getting his own action. Paley was not an artist according to our conventions, yet Paley did create among artworks: He created by putting together. A collector such as he is akin to an artist who does constructions. Paley created rather in the same way as did the director (who was he?) of Guare's play *Six Degrees of Separation* (see Chapter 1). That director created in whatever space was left between star and author. Similarly, Paley created in whatever room he could find between painter and dealer, or painter and MOMA curator.

A farce is also an artwork and also celebrates identities (by somewhat roundabout agencies that we have yet to trace, to be sure). But these are exactly identities in the second sense. That is the import of farce. Farce extracts humor by obvious twists on just those identities that are most confining. These are identities that absolutely straitjacket you because they are enforced by everyday social disciplines in which you take your being. No doubt Paley also could enjoy farce—though there are no chuckling little Klee sketch-oils in his collection of paintings—but the Paley who did so would be Paley in one frame, say, Paley resenting a confining mother-son bond.

Yet all four senses of identity attach to the same constructed reality, for which they weave together layers of expression in all sorts of ways. These are ways that can change. Nor is there any simple correlation between art medium and sense of identity. A painting can reflect a second or third (and boring) sense of identity, and some story or play can reflect the interesting fourth or first senses. But the reverse occurs as well. It would therefore be silly to reify the four senses of identity, to set them up as separate personae. Narrative can weave them together.

A fundamental distinction can be drawn between the kinds of impacts that author and actor may produce upon audience. In each case a story or stories are being given to the audience. The story is taken seriously—it becomes the basis of appraisal by the audience—only when audience and communicator are parts of a system, when they fit together into some larger identity.

The business of narrative is to generate, for the time being, membership in a larger identity, a system embracing both audience and author. There are various possibilities. Credibility may attach not to the story but to the source, so that the relationship that the audience perceives itself to have to the communicator is really the source of credibility. The hallmark of narrative creativity is exactly to attach credibility to the story, to invoke a sort of honorary membership in the story's scene. Yet the business of stage drama is to induce belief in the actor, and the business of biographical narrative is to induce belief in the narrator. In homely terms, the stage actor is salesman whereas the biographer is administrator. Biographical literature, as distinct from creative literature, induces credibility in the author; oral literature induces credibility in the teller. And the creative narrator is genius.

Performance Measures

Narrative accounts are not some luxury that is superfluous except in large-scale embeddings of identity. Narrative accounts are as central to business, both everyday business and strategic business, as they are to high culture. Different institutional realms can have different narrative idioms. In professions, there is a secrecy graded toward the inside and higher. It shapes and adumbrates the stories attended to. This secrecy protects the status quo, including its incompetences, but at the same time it provides an avenue for enacted change beyond what would be likely in less restricted structures of control.

Narrative weighs performances, perhaps many, by choosing which ones and how to string them together. Therefore performance measures are reductions and summaries of narratives. Such measures must embrace the hypothetical and merely possible, as well as the established, so that fiction may be brought alongside fact in narrative form.

Performance as a construct presupposes agency and engenders narrative. This is true of opera, of oil painting, and of business. Performance brings agency. Agency brings measurement. Measurement introduces narrative (both kinds) to performance. By studying the complex interactions of the two modes of narrative in performance measurement, we can come to understand narrative better. First, the narrative of first mode, the ex post mode. Begin with a humanist perspective on performance: "The humanist remains to some extent a guardian of the texts, novelty is not his prime concern. ... The commentary remains subservient to the text. In this respect the humanist as an interpreter of our heritage has something in common with the performer who interprets a text on the stage or in the concert hall" (Gombrich 1973, p. 117).

Artworks reflect tensions between innovation and control in identities and their relations. Each of us looks forward to fresh action but looks backward in rendering accounts of how ordinary social action came about. Such unending tension is demanding and difficult to live through. Art provides help, not least for the paradox of performance measurement.

Performance measurement puzzles and bedevils one in business as in art, and the correspondence can be instructive. Familiar accounting measures such as profit have come under attack lately, as have the financial measures of cash flow and the like that provided the rhetoric of much of the 1980s craze for mergers and spin-offs of American firms. Yet alternative measures, be these measures of human resources or social responsibility or physical efficiency in business, also are hard to calibrate and also are subject to gaming.

Just as an actor learns that a grand exit can cover sins of slurred dialogue, an executive learns that buzzing about quality circles or long-term trends can distract from sogginess in execution. The problematics of performance measure spread further, in art as in business. Aptness of measure depends on audience and is judged differently according to how the audience uses it to allocate rewards among participants. The narrative framing for measures can shift the process being measured, because audiences and actors alike will use a measure as a guide to anticipatory action.

Dimensions of performance can be common across settings. Wall Street firms and manufacturing firms face much the same dilemmas as do the critical fraternity and theatre producers. The price of stock in a company that wins the Malcolm Baldridge award for excellence from the Department of Commerce often has dropped in value shortly thereafter, just as plays that have won awards may close after quite short runs.

Consider parallel difficulties in music: "Those who play Mozart's keyboard concertos on the fortepianos for which they are written are regularly excoriated for their lack of passion and individuality; those who perform these same pieces on Steinway grands, with all the trappings of late-nineteenth century phrasing and pedaling, are pilloried for their insensitivity to historical practice" (Gossett 1992, p. 32).

Picaresque tales are complementary to narrative of the first mode. They exactly concern the unfolding of the unexpected, especially from networks of social relations. Yet picaresque tales come to no resolution, no identity in the fourth sense. Even so, the grotesque, a form of the picaresque, forms an alternative to simple open humor as a foil against officious celebration. Unlike humor, the grotesque does not cast a kindly light.

Humor also offers performance measures, on a less formal basis but often of vast scope. A test case is in order: a tangible yet generalizable case in which to discriminate and show the mix of two modes of narrative in assessing performance. Consider a case of new literature, ostensively narrative, that is an abrupt admixture of popular aspects, across many arts, with high and invidious aspects: "In the Renaissance, laughter in its most radical, universal, and at the same time gay form emerged from the depths of folk culture; it emerged but once in the course of history, over a period of some fifty or sixty years (in various countries and at various times) and entered with its popular (vulgar) language the sphere of great literature and high ideology" (Bakhtin 1968, p. 72).

While a feudal and theocratic order was in the process of crumbling, there was a period of fusion of the official culture with the nonofficial culture of folk humor, which had been shaped over many centuries: "Later in times of absolute monarchy and the formation of a new official order, folk humor descended to the lower level of the genre hierarchy. ... [But] a millennium of folk humor broke into Renaissance literature. ... In Rabelais we see the speech and mask of the medieval clown, folk and carnival gaiety ... [whereas] an intolerant, one-sided tone of seriousness is characteristic of official medieval culture" (Bakhtin 1968, pp. 72–73).

The instant success of *Pantagruel*, which extended to high culture, baffled the next two centuries. It violated the theory of literary genres, which it showed to be a tangible social creation in the service of hierarchy and control. Rabelais was undeniably "high" in that he was immensely learned and encyclopedic; perhaps in this century there is a similarity to James Joyce. But like folk humor and unlike an emerging new canon, Rabelais's tales concerned bodies that had orifices and bulges and births and all the mess of sex and eating and defecation. And Rabelais minted words and created expressions for a language in change.

Folk humor, because it is unofficial, can be radical, free, and ruthless. Yet laughter is an idiom that is never used by violence and authority; open laughter is among equals. Burlesque, with its undertones of irony and degradation, did not figure in Rabelais. It is rather the grotesque—improbable but metaphorically true—and, above all, unexpected and direct naïveté upon which Rabelais drew.

There were recurrent waves of approval and understanding of Rabelais over time; they depended on the state of the social mirror, so to speak. But what is important here analytically is that Rabelais, curiously, is not creating narrative in the previously accepted sense but rather through performance. He is celebrating popular configurations not heretofore accorded such attention.

The sociocultural tone, namely humor, leaches out any possibility of official narrative. Rabelais's humor was exactly the antidote to and antipodes of officious celebration of invidious social discipline. To be so, the humor must itself be celebration, but it is celebration at a higher level. Rabelais's task was that faced by all literary authors seeking great impact: how to combine first and second modes of narrative to recognize and celebrate incoming or heretofore suppressed social formation.

Energy in all literary narrative, not just humor, comes from discovery of what is to happen and so requires presence of the second mode of narrative. The technical challenge for the artist is helping maintain in reception that freshness even after the fact, so as to permit reenactments by others in which they perceive narrative rather than or as well as celebration. There can be many genres of narrative thus conceived. Comic strips in today's newspapers are examples of a genre pioneered by William Blake a century before (see Chapter 2). A long-distinguished form such as poetry can afford examples of narrative creativity, such as poems by Dylan Thomas, but it also will offer examples of ceremonial poems, say those of T. S. Eliot, which celebrate locking into social discipline.

There are curious interactions between criteria of purity, or highness, in art and concerns of social strata, especially during times of social stress. And the interactions can be seen in terms of individual works of art and in arts other than literature. Take just one illustration: the denunciation of George Gershwin's *Porgy and Bess* by noted—and creative—music critic Virgil Thomson in 1935 at its premier. It was followed by his reversal and recantation in 1941 in a rapidly changing social context.

Career and Reputation

Accounts of artistic production processes may be unfolded and woven into some unique narrative story. Turn to the narratives that especially concern today's artists, namely their careers. Biography as narrative is an accounting and celebration of identity in the third sense. Such narrative is primarily concerned with reproduction; it is narrative in a first mode. The third sense of identity is all about rationalization and failures of action. Action and its agency are suppressed in the corresponding first mode of narrative. One contrast is with the first sense of identity, introduced in Chapter 1, which is directly concerned with physical action and in whose layer of expression one might expect to see tics and habitual mannerisms.

Careers, along with innovation, are constant themes in artists' shared talk. What accounts for the skeletons of careers and how do they become fleshed out and interpreted? Careers are a device for handling the future as if it were the past, and so they are a variant of biography. Career can be used as the tag for the first mode of narrative.

Artists must ultimately be recruited from general populations, and they can be seen as replacing earlier artists. Some pattern of succession has to be asserted across and within art worlds to accommodate the claims of career. Opportunity within a social formation goes along with structural equivalence among actors in social network to define succession. Succession thereby can induce and construct social positions and thus invoke artworks, which celebrate the recognition of continuing positions through which succession transpires.

A master theme from Chapter 1 is how agents—as they become defined, specialized, and separated—take over from principals. The key is displacement of those identities that are being celebrated. The underlying general process of social displacement then spirals further out into the reputations of artists and their organizers. Reputations combine and reflect aspects that are both internal and external to art worlds. It is through such spirals of agency that the identities of artists upon whom attention is focused finally combine with the identities of other actors into audiences.

The result is perception of artists as a set of careers. Artworks as well as artists can have careers, which in either case must fit into and yet help shape the material facts over time. Careers of either sort are stories told both before and later so as to rationalize how opportunities chain successions together.

Reputation develops for works of art as well, and that can attach variously to identity of collector, of patron, and so on. An artwork's reputation is generalized by genre and style, and an artist is generalized by school and guild of artist. Reputations help bind all art worlds into a larger universe. In so doing, careers can in turn induce a further level, such as a school or a generation of artists or artworks. These processes can be seen at work in the Pre-Raphaelite and other case studies.

There is a history being constructed through the stringing together of careers; it can yield distinct levels both in social and in cultural action in the arts. In some art in one era, artists' careers may be seen as the main units of production, but in another era they may be disdained for the reputations of performances or the careers (called provenances) of particular objects.

Orchestral music is a setting that provides extreme contrasts between metabolisms. Neither career nor succession is open to modern composers, who are almost dead-ended by this rigid art. Composers have had to function like pure (and little-appreciated) scientists for whom only peers can or do give reputation and to whom no one gives material support. By contrast, the positions of instrumentalists are enhanced by orchestral music: Virtuosi compete to succeed predecessors, and symphony players move up through ranks as in a bureaucracy.

Metabolisms of reputation and career differ among various arts and art worlds. A long run of performances defines success for a Broadway drama. But success for a dramatic artist is a succession of better and better vehicles, so he or she must not drive any one vehicle too long. This is surely a conundrum, just one of the many that constitute artistic life: Classic perfection jostles originality. Performance jostles authorship.

Career can be seen as well on a still broader scale in evolution and succession of more abstract institutions shaped by art. Law briefs and lawyers, like artworks and artists, proclaim identities and account for relations. The practice of law resembles oil painting in that it has arcana and requires technical knowhow and sometimes can constitute a form of art. In some legal systems, such as that of the medieval period idolized by the Pre-Raphaelites, law practice is primarily celebration and announcement. That is to say, celebrations of identity are combined in a rhetoric of law practice by agents who need not be distinguished by skill.

In the first half-century of the new United States of America, searches for and announcements of identity dominated social life, which is not surprising. These searches required narrative and dominated narrative both in law and in literature. It was narrative in the first mode. Narrative had come to be gripped by the amazing new proclamation of career for a new country, in constitutions and the like.

It was in this early period that American literature, including fiction, was the product mainly of persons who were practicing lawyers. This shows how the animus of rhetoric—here which mode of narrative is used—may not derive from workaday practice but instead may depend on the larger sociopolitical and historical context of its application.

After 1850, American law had become firmly ensconced in a new mode that was much more attuned to commerce than to landowning, as it was before. American law entered what was primarily a narrative mode concerned with control and open-ended maneuver, which is to say a second mode. (Curiously enough, the early correlation of literature with lawyer-authors evaporated.) Americans practiced a common-law system derived from England; it always had much of the second mode of narrative mixed in with the first.

Critics and Authors

The Pre-Raphaelites in both their painting and their poetry attempted especially to establish and celebrate new identity of performance; they were thus developing narrative of the first mode. They did not attempt narrative of the second mode, but several of their collectors did. A collector is a buyer who creates a new level of identity by combining to his or her own taste a series of paintings or other artworks. In turn the painter's identity now partakes of some of the identity of this collection. A system of reputations emerges that crosses different levels and distinct art worlds.

The critic is another stand-in for the original patron and thus can be an alternative to the collector as creator of a new level of identity. The critic begins as an ex post teller-of-tales compared to the patron's ex ante specifications. The critic also provides ex ante payments, as contrasted with the patron's payment after the order is filled. Artworks evolve as shadows of these processes in which agency is invoked. Reputation builds along internal network lines, but it is also shaped through broader mechanisms of dissemination to, and critiques for, audiences. Art worlds generally are not isolates but instead overlap and mix, in a given era and place. Thus the critic builds up a reputation that, in a commercial system, is worth some income stream to the artist in the future because of the growing price of his or her artwork.

Critics are like priests to artworks, but the social actors are heroes in place of gods. Critics—along with directors and producers for performing arts—tend the cultural borders. These borders are, however, porous to changing patronage. Patrons may become replaced by audiences composed of "outsiders" who join specialized art worlds only temporarily, as audiences. And the tension may lead to art forms for differentiated classes within an overall community.

Nobles and other politicians pay broad attention to social networks because politicians are trained by the realities of their survival to listen for resonances in networks. Like politicians and sociological observers, critics can train themselves to find resonances by tracing structural equivalences in personal networks and then relating them to networks of perceptions among artworks. Critics come to function on a level of leverage and sophistication held previously by some high aristocrats:

The professional literary historians, publishers, and bureaucrats who installed the canon within the educational system were less concerned with the fame or fate of individual poets than with the larger communal project of creating a plausible narrative for the development of a German national culture, a development supposedly reflected in German literature during the century preceding the establishment of a unified nation. The needs of the narrative, one might say, determined the role and the status of the individual writers within this narrative far more than the verbal artistry or the human concerns that critics attributed to these writers to justify their inclusion in the canon. The overwhelming and singular role assigned to Goethe within this narrative reflected the need for a foundation stone on which all other elements within the story could be built ... Goethe allowed it to compete with such long-standing national literatures as Italian, Spanish, and English. ... The absence of a single author in French with a status comparable to that of Dante, Cervantes, or Shakespeare does not derive from a lack of literary "greatness"—the reputations of ... such as Rabelais, Racine, Voltaire, or Balzac— ... but the unresolved tensions in French cultural life between the so-called classical and romantic, between the political right and left. (Lindenberger 1990, p. 141)

There are many further examples, for complexly overlapping reading audiences, of how critics can induce critical sects, national schools, social class biases, and so on.

A text is not some extrinsic object, but rather it is a construct from many perceptions, a construct for critics to reshape:

> The status of a literary text is not altogether different from that of a historical event such as the French Revolution. ... So the Revolution was not so much an action as a language, and it was in relation to this language, the locus of the consensus, that the ideological machine established differences among men. ... There were no revolutionary circumstances; there was a Revolution that fed on circumstances ... [which] suggests the primacy of plotting much as a literary critic might demonstrate the formative power of plot over character or individual events in a fictional text. ... In studying the rhetoric and symbolism of the Revolution another recent historian, Lynn Hunt, applies Northrop Frye's definitions of comedy, romance and tragedy to analyze the generic plots enacted during diverse stages of the Revolution.
>
> The earlier dramas that speak to us through *Danton's Death* constitute only one set of voices that we can identify. The historical narratives and documents of the French Revolution that Büchner absorbed within his play create still another set. Few literary works ... until the advent, in the 1960s, of documentary drama, itself a form shaped by the example of Büchner's play—are so thoroughly suffused with the material the author read as is this play ... the montage technique that Büchner employed in mixing together his source material. ... In the way that materials drawn from different historical moments are juxtaposed, the play resembles certain European cities in which buildings representing diverse architectural styles from many periods stand unselfconsciously next to one another. (Lindenberger 1990, pp. 125–126)

It is because of the scope for a critic to manipulate sets of narratives into a new creative narrative that one can compare the critic to an art collector, perhaps a Paley. The important question is whether critics of arts have moved beyond exercising influence discretely, in separate bits—whether they have moved to a policy level. Here is a literary critic, Paul A. Bové, on discourse in general:

> The "self-evident" and "common-sensical" are what have the privilege of unnoticed power, and this power produces instruments of control ... control by the power of positive production: that is, a kind of power that generates certain kinds of questions, that includes within its systems all those it produces as agents capable of acting within them. For example, it produces psychiatrists who let people talk and so come to constitute themselves as a certain kind of subject who believes sexuality alone defines his or her identity. ... A general source for this kind of thinking is in the writings of Giambattista Vico, who insisted upon seeing history and society as human productions. (Lentricchia and McLaughlin 1990, p. 54)

Some critics resemble humanists in insisting upon a continuity by their dense texturing of statements from previous works. Other critics and some artists resemble scientists in that their mode of thinking is different: They think in the present, of taking action. They hop and skip around ideas, turning them inside out and every which way. This implies narrative in the second mode. Such critics assert how very general, and how flexibly social, literature has become—at least from the perspective of their enlarged guild of professional critics. Critics, who mine particular literatures, are equated with other social theorists, who view sample surveys or historical archives as wellsprings of insight.

But modern criticism also includes, indeed not so long ago consisted in, a pungent formalism. Listen: "The possession of originality cannot make an artist unconventional: it drives him further into convention, obeying the law of the art itself, which seeks constantly to reshape itself from its own depths, and which works through its geniuses for metamorphosis, as it works through minor talents for mutation" (Frye 1957, p. 132). So much for interplay between tangibly social and tangibly artistic; so much for Rabelais as a resonance chamber for rising social strata in time of social turbulence. And so much for the "author." This critic favors "high art," certainly, but allows very little place for the creators of it. One cannot help but notice the elite and aristocratic tone. It disdains to observe the mere workmen who do the art, who are but hired hands under higher direction, of the spirit of art if not of particular patrons or critics. Such a critic is more remote than any patron.

However divergent and deficient some critics' accounts of social mechanism are, they do not impose on but rather observe and dissect regularities in artworks. Critics carve up literature in many different ways, partitioning by archetypes, by phases, by modes, and by themes, with the term "style" often kept for degree of highness. In 1785, Clara Reeve, in *The Progress of Romance Through Times, Countries, and Manners,* draws conclusions in terms of mode: "The Romance is an heroic fable, which treats of fabulous persons and things. —The Novel is a picture of real life and manners, and of the times in which it is written ... the perfection of it, is to represent every scene, in so easy and natural a manner, and to make them appear so probable, as to deceive us into a persuasion (at least while we are reading) that all is real, until we are affected by the joys or distresses of the persons in the story, as if they were our own." There is a kinship to Svetlana Alpers's view of Dutch painting (1983), wherein she casts Italian painting in the role of the romance as portrayed by Reeves, so that Dutch and Italian paintings are very different genres in this sense. Other critics claim that in a certain period German literature was the romance whereas French literature was the novel.

Then there is the personified genre. Benito Pérez Galdós is the central modern Spanish novelist, the Dickens and Balzac of nineteenth-century Spain who became the focus of another such personalized genre. Around Galdós has grown up a veritable industry of criticism and interpretation— as well as literary imitators and theatre. Galdós "read" Spanish nineteenth-century social complexities as effectively as the Elizabethan dramatists read their time, and he thereby induced a resonant mix of audiences and critical apparatus sufficient to sustain a whole genre. Even today he has devotees called *galdosistas,* and even in the United States they maintain journals such as *Anales Galdosianos.* Art is about identity at many levels, and Galdós, like Shakespeare, has come to express an overall identity of a society at the same time that he celebrates more limited clusters of identities and relations.

Earlier I pointed to a critic who was celebrator of rigid identity. In his brand of so-called new criticism, styles in one art influence styles in another without benefit of social mechanism, of tangible human agency. Poetry talks to music. Writing talks straight to painting (but not to science). He does not speak of or talk to social forces. But Galdós parallels him on an abstract level, for neither is attempting narrative creativity. Moreover, neither is attempting to push still further toward becoming a collector-melder of literature.

There are important social aspects within literary authorship that remain hidden from most critics. Begin with extensive quotes from a serious editor (notably of Keats poems) on the omnipresence of multiple authorship. These quotes downgrade lonely genius myths. They can also be used to assimilate literary to other artistic production. Stillinger fights not only the banishments of the author as mere instrument, such as by the French critics Barthes and Foucault, but also the opposite apotheosis of the author as the only source of the text's meaning. Jack Stillinger focuses on

> *the joint, or composite, or collaborative production of literary works that we usually think of as written by a single author* ... by the nominal author and a friend, a spouse, a ghost, an agent, an editor, a translator, a publisher, a censor, a transcriber, a printer, or—what is more often the case—several of these acting together or in succession. ... The reality of what authors actually do and how works are actually produced is often—perhaps usually—much more complex than our theories and practices allow. (Stillinger 1991, p. 191)

Stillinger gives popular art examples such as Jacqueline Susann's *Valley of the Dolls* and Grace Metalious's *Peyton Place* to go along with such examples of editing in high culture as Maxwell Perkins on Thomas Wolfe manuscripts. Stillinger assimilates narrative to prose literature in general, as can be seen in his meticulous identification of how Harriet Mill heavily shaped philosopher John Stuart Mill's rhetoric, if not his ideas per se.

Stillinger comments on Susan Wolfson's formulation of authorial revision as a continual process of self-reading, self-reconstruction such that a poem, for example, is constituted by all its successive versions taken together. He starts with the Greg-Bowers theory of using the first edition or manuscript for authorial intention and then turns to the Thorpe counterargument of each version as real and then finally to the McGann socialized concept of authorship. It is clear that the concept or construct of "authorship" is no simple, univocal affair in literature.

Yet even so, a clear distinction can be drawn with respect to these fundamentals. Actor carries performance; author carries narrative of the first mode, and narrative of the second mode carries author. These distinctions are not restricted to artworks in language. They apply equally for cinema.

Cinema

The camera in cinema parallels the narrator in narrative. Go way back, to the technological roots of literature in Mesopotamia:

> Cylinder seals from this "abstract" group could be made in a fraction of the time it would take to prepare a "figurative" seal. ... For the first time, we see the emergence of flat clay slabs with the oblong signs for numbers on their surfaces, which may be completely covered by impressions of cylinder seals ... a much simpler way than with the use of sealed balls. ... And with the help of simple incised lines such clay tablets could be subdivided into compart-

ments ... what was actually being counted and the time, place, and so forth still had either to be retained in the memory or distinguished by the use of particular storage places for the tablets. After so many attempts to expand, in so many directions, the extent of what could be recorded ... finally a universal means of control—writing [was] invented, with the help of which everything could be recorded that seemed worth recording. (Nissen 1988, pp. 78, 87)

This passage reminds us that writing is a protean form that can be used for performance and storage as well as for narrative. In extreme cases such as the Ottoman Imperial Porte or Peking mandarins, the literal mechanics of writing (which was a symbol of authority) may be turned into an aesthetic of visual art, much as there are today cults of angles and cuts in use of the movie camera.

Writing presages cinema. The film shows only what the camera eye sees. The narrative need not have a narrator, because there are other important options such as omniscient observer for framing narrative. But the eye of the narrator, once ensconced, is the eye through which the tale is perceived. Camera and narrator eyes alike can postulate widely different modes of perception: The story may be told in jagged contrasts with abrupt changes of scene and tone and meaning, or the story may flow smoothly as if in rational discourse.

Cinema can be adjoined to literature in narrative. With narrative folded into cinema, philosophers' arguments that narrative constructs our meanings of time in social life extend to cinema as well. The implication is that cinema has or will eventually shift our whole sense of time. Books have long since done so, and perhaps that will also prove true of television.

Cinema counts as a new art form because of the *combination* of enhanced memory and enhanced editing, along with an apparently continuous flow of actions from many actors that is shared with theatre. All else, such as illusion of three-dimensionality, is secondary. Directing, which combines preediting of action with editing of film shot, focuses control activity to an unusual extent, comparable to the fabled control of author over narrative characters.

Relations between visual and written arts are clarified through cinema. There was long a dogma in high Western art that pictures should be controlled by the expression of literary, poetic meanings. The greatness of French academic art was founded on this dogma as exemplified in the paintings of Poussin and interpreted by LeBrun. Art historians along with much of modern art seem to argue the opposite—that image is utterly unlike word. Cinema art has come to show that the truth lies in between: There are more degrees of freedom both in written and in visual imaging than had been suspected. In a memo quoted in Chapter 7, a working artist points out, quite unself-consciously, how she achieves narrative linear form in her paintings, just as current novelists can assert to the contextual richness of a picture plane. And the distinction between theatre language and drama language from Chapter 6 is also apposite.

Cinema is, however, multiplex to a degree that written narrative can only simulate. A film provides multiple, parallel narratives in the artwork itself, the diversity of which is multiplied by distinct audiences and critics and the like. Within the visual track, multiple points of view can be presented by a director or editor. The soundtrack parallels the visual sequence as yet another narrative. And the soundtrack is usually split among background music and dialogue as well as other "natural" sounds.

Because of these distinctions, an unusually staccato social world of art has come into being around the production of cinema. The center of Hollywood is sievings and matchings that are very expensive, multidimensional, and very uncertain. What should in the long run be more important is that cinema has greater potential scope for narrative of the second mode than does literature.

Narrative helps to construct social time and compare different possible social realities, especially but not only in cinema.

Style as Juncture

Variability across examples thus is requisite to a style, just as human perception of the physical world has been shown to build itself around variability. Human perception clusters physical stimuli as signals of variability and change. Just so, particular changes in artwork, social and cultural, are packaged so as to have recognizable stability and thereby constitute a style. A style is a style because of the richness of its potential membership.

Take an example. The blockbuster has come to be associated with the style of American book publishing. Much of total readings, and hence sales and profits, come from a sprinkling of a few titles a year. Which entries will succeed is very important to publishers because the real profits come from the big print runs. Yet the difficulty of prediction leads via anxieties to an apparatus of editorial guidance and to huge advances and the like to shape potential entries in what seem the likeliest directions for commercial success. In this ambience apparently abstract formal aspects of the stream of submissions shift: Now romanticism is in, now the neoclassic tale. This is a style-of-juncture that cuts across continuing particular genres of mysteries, romances, and even cookbooks, the mix of which supplies enough variety and variability of examples to sustain a style. Critics and agents and all the other sorts of players in the publishing game orient around this style, if only in attempted opposition. Very similar was the style of American popular songs before the rock'n'roll revolution.

A style implies a formula or prescription, an envelope for its examples, whether or not made explicit. How could one go about characterizing a style just in its cultural aspect? Say an artwork is classic if it depends on its formal organization to evoke emotion; "classic" can be a style. But one appreciates a work as classic only against the latent vision of its being romantic; such latent mixtures will be invoked by the social facets of a style because the actors are highly concerned with relative ratings by this and that social layer, or faction of critics. Such judgments are the stuff of controversy, first because they play into invidious distinctions and second because they compound with new layerings of agency, in criticism. It is not sufficient to speak of cultural aspects, in medium and technique, off on their own.

Or one could differentiate an artwork in allover style from an artwork in focused style. An allover painting, say Monet water lilies, would maintain equal visual interest across the whole canvas, right up to the edges; a focused painting, say a Poussin history painting or a recreation of antique legend, would draw the viewer into a balanced set of central figures composed so as to focus attention. An analogous contrast from literature would be one between the mellifluous rounded periods of a Trollope novel focused on some bishop or prime minister and the jagged incantations of a modernist story. Again, social facets will invoke more than one cultural facet.

There is a social side to a style, a side fully embroiled in its controversies. Is sentimentality a style? Sentimentality is hard to abstract in cultural perspective but one can point out social network correlates. Sentimentality is not found in all historic periods and contexts, but neither are romanticism or classicism. So a style can be partially characterized also just from its social embedding. I argue that style is best defined by interweaving social with cultural aspects.

A style goes with certain profiles of interaction as it inculcates distinctive perceptions of its cultural pattern in audiences. A particular style in current painting, for example, requires both social resonance (through a set of galleries and collectors) and art-historical resonance (a cultural provenance) to establish itself. A style is also subject to broader critical commentaries, which interpolate them into a broader context of styles across art worlds.

Any work of art, however tangible and permanent, can be seen as a performance. Style emerges and becomes recognized as the in-system specification of standard against which performance is judged. It is judged by the population that has been induced as its familiars, its audience. This justifies the operationalization of style as some sort of social profile. Pre-Raphaelitism is exactly this kind of style. Such style is still a black box, a construct that we recognize in its impact but for whose mechanism and operation we cannot yet account.

Once formed, the peculiar hybrid I call a style is very stable. This is so because of the interlocking friction between cultural and social. It is also so because a style does not establish itself neatly and separately in one particular art or art world. Styles develop as by-products of evolutions that unfold through networks and do not stop at the boundaries of any one art world.

New York music concerts and New York dance performances both spring from art worlds analogous to those in the national theatre system sketched in Chapters 1 and 6. Such distinct worlds of art production interleave together in cultural space like fish scales to yield the overall art scene of our experience. It is in this broader art scene that styles can get established, and there too is where separate arts establish themselves and spin off. Each such style as identity is spread out as profile in use across social actors in diverse art worlds.

Performance and perception specify identities and frame efforts at control, whether these be liminal or stereotyped, whether they be in business or in art. But they slide by the massively historical and the deeply hierarchical social orders that result. Narrative is required to bridge performance and perception over toward the invidiously social. Thereby narrative gets built into style.

The second mode of narrative, creative narrative, seems the obvious source for continuing change and innovation. Creative narrative breeds more of itself, to the net effect of sustaining style, having brought it to more sophistication. Yet this discourse is unpredictable in incidence. Creative narrative in social life will already come in company with many other instances of itself and go on to generate yet further instances. The overarching result is to permit and actually support a massive inertia of style. Struggles for creative narrative help generate the very frame that holds them back. That is a crucial aspect of why style is so hard to change.

Artists, like audiences, define their own identities and site them in ties with other artists' identities exactly through cultural aspects of styles. This utilization can be of a relatively pure style or of a mixture of styles, and it can come about from rejection of certain styles. Reciprocally, styles, to be more than ethereal emanations from critics' brains, must be realized in concrete works by artists. This dual process never ends, as both style and artist shift in the course of the continuing reenactments that are their substance.

By following a style, actions, in the stochastic environment of social life, become ordered and recognized with respect to one another. Yet at the same time such actions are being decoupled from the actions in other styles. The net result is that social ties can be maintained in regular patterns at the cost of crossing styles, and conversely. Greater certainty in tangible social relations comes from an increase in cultural ambiguity, and conversely. This latter increase comes, despite rigidity within a particular style, from that style's low correlation to other styles. For example, this flexibility in combination permits artists to define themselves by style and yet concurrently continue a pattern of tangible relations to other artists with other definitions. Any artwork is an instance both of a style, or a combination of styles, and of an artist or set of artists.

Styles are triggered in complex overlappings among networks of meanings. In that sense, styles are cultural analogues to identities, with canons being the norms among styles. A style presupposes some continuing larger context in a range of styles seen to link differently to various populations and historical periods. This larger context of styles defines and reproduces itself only on a stochastic basis; an example on a small scale is styles of conversation within a network population. The social environment in which a style becomes established embraces, as a system, stochastic incident and process among actors, as we saw for the band of young Pre-Raphaelite artists.

Styles come in nestings, as successions of less and less minutely prescribed characteristics. So style can be specified by a series, in which the more general kind, such as romantic, would be easier to transpose than would be the more specific varieties, such as Dickensian. Then there is a different kind of specificity that is more explicit and deliberate, in content and social form. This other kind can be seen as contracts in performances—call them *genres.* One example is the genre of royal portraits in oil painting; another example is hard-boiled detective stories.

One could say that each of these genres is the concrete deposit of a style among works from a particular art world, recognized through repeated revival in a larger social setting. But genres evolve first, with styles being recognized as more abstract similarities that hold across genres. Style can be recognized, at least partially, across different sensory modes and art worlds. A genre, in contrast, is always tied to a particular vehicle (such as drawing-room comedies) and to some related art world (such as the pre-1950 London professional theatre). Performances are not isolated atoms but tend to evolve as packages of what have come to be accepted as natural variations, which we call genres. Genres are groupings that are smaller and more tangible than styles. They are portable because they presuppose

only a limited and stereotyped art world that can be maintained or reproduced deliberately.

I want to keep the term *genre* distinct in your mind from *style* and to
keep both distinct from the term *narrative*. Genre is the nitty-gritty term
describing the tangible agreement between—the contract between—artist
and audience that gets set in an art world: "I have called this book *The
Narrative Contract*, but I could simply have called it *Genre*, for genre is the
narrative contract between author and reader, the framework of norms
and expectations shaping both the composition and the reception of the
text" (Damrosch 1987, p. 2). The last section of Chapter 6 develops in
depth examples of genres for the theatre.

GUIDE TO FURTHER READING

In a brilliant but difficult book, Bryson (1981) develops how closely
bound up with verbal narrative a visual art (French classical painting) can
be. Gardner (1982) analyzes how and why children create art.

Some social theorists, such as Talcott Parsons and Claude Lévi-Strauss,
have come close to arguing that the real world is itself like a utopia.

Eccles (1991) and Meyer (1992) taken together bring out the paradoxes
of performance measurement in current American business.

Burns (1977) probes how the bureaucratic and professional involution
of ideas and careers that are characteristic of a major media institution affect its rhetorics. For the musical arts, Bodinger-deUriarte (1989) and
Faulkner (1971) dissect how the building of reputation interacts with commercial aspects of applied art. I wrote a book about how careers depended
upon chains of movement by vacancies (White 1970a). Abbott (1988)
spells out how networks of agency build into the social institution of the
professions.

Scholes and Kellogg (1966) are good on early forms of literature that
trace to the present, as is also discussed by Northrop Frye (1957). Auerbach (1953) interrelates two narrative modes, the jagged contraposition of
the Old Testament and the classically smooth flow from Rome.

Ferguson (1984) discusses law in relation to literature for the early
United States, which parallels the work on France in medieval times
quoted in Chapter 2 from Bloch (1977). Horwitz (1977) traces the shift of
American law toward commercial use in the period after Ferguson's first
half-century.

Becker (1982, Chapter 7) is eloquent on editing as a general activity in
all art production, not just literature. As Robert Ferguson (1984) argues,
there is much similarity between the tasks of the literary critic and those of
judicial interpretation. Culler (1983, p. 183) is notable for arguing the

merger of literary analysis both with general social analysis and commentary and with painting criticism. For an overview of Galdós by an American, see Goldman (1977).

Modern Hollywood filmmaking is treated in terms of social networks and combinatorics of production by Faulkner (1983), Baker and Faulkner (1991), and Faulkner and Anderson (1987).

Hebdige (1979) uses the concept of style in much the way I argue for in this chapter. Whiteside (1981) sketches the blockbuster style in publishing. Gibson (1950, 1979) establishes that human visual perception evolved through the clustering of endlessly variable cues, especially from continuing movements by the subject, so as to induce a stable context. Baxandall (1975) lays out the issue of how physical perception and social context and formulations interact and analyzes how the emergence of Western perspective was bound up with the burgeoning mercantile life of Renaissance Florence.

FIELDWORK IDEAS

1. Locate and study some personal or corporate actor who is evolving from being a mere purchaser of artworks into becoming a collector. Or, if you can spend time at the Museum of Modern Art (MOMA) and want to enlarge your scope, develop a study of the posthumous evolution of Paley as creator. Paley willed his entire collection of paintings to the MOMA, which proceeded to display it, magnificently, in 1991 and 1992; see the thoughtful review by Roberta Smith on page C1 of the *New York Times*, January 31, 1992. But now what? No museum would destroy a painting (or, these days, even sell—"de-accession"— it), but surely the MOMA will not be able to maintain the collection as is. Will it even be kept together in the basement? Or will it be put back together from time to time and sent on tour? In any case, what does this do to Paley as creator? Perhaps his role was prefigured in the happenings of the previous generation.

2. Look for some offbeat art worlds where narrative excuses and efforts at control are more transparent. For example, a student at Columbia University did a field report of tattoo parlors in Manhattan from which many of the ideas presented in this chapter can be illustrated. At the other end of the social hierarchy, you could look at luxury, elite furniture as an art world; for guidance consult the intelligent and elegantly illustrated book by Praz (1964). One can see the use of art objects for reputation building and for disparagement of others.

MEASURES AND MODELS

1. The curious erosion of the connection between law and literature in America after 1850 calls for investigation that requires some difficult anal-

ysis and assessment of hypothetical alternatives. It seems established that American literature was stunted during the nineteenth century by the absence of copyright protection for British authors. It could be that as narrative shifted toward the second mode, it became in its literary embodiment less requiring of local adaptation. But probing this requires some sort of explicit measurement.

Attempts are now being made to measure and identify authorship in narrative literature with much more precision and impersonality. For example, the relative frequencies of a dozen apparently innocuous short words (pronouns and connectives) in Jane Austen novels have now been tabulated (by computer, of course). The result is a profile of occurrence, with which to identify style. So defined, the style does change between novels that already had been established by consensus of qualitative criticism as having different styles. A still more ambitious approach is that of English sociologist Peter Abell (1987) to render narrative structure and process in explicit algebra of networks.

2. Interviewing is a social interaction, and an interview is a narrative. To gain a valid answer to a question, and a valid measure of a process, requires attuning to the context, both social and cultural. I can do no better than quote a poet introducing a collection of elegant interviews of poets:

> We live in the age of the interview. ... Everywhere one turns, everyone is busy interviewing everyone else. ... All this talk talk talk talk talk must come from some very deep insecurity at the heart of things. And of course there is the danger that charisma may take the place of character, and chatter may take the place of matter.
>
> So it is no wonder if the practicing poet, caught up in an unreal world of words, may seek to keep his own counsel. For he alone knows that whatever is deeply intuitive cannot really be revealed except in rhythms and images. ... As Thoreau wrote in *Walden:* "Speech is for the hard of hearing." ... Even so: there will always be a good deal of legitimate curiosity about poetry. ... Very well then, but what kind of interview? There are interviews and there are interviews. ... Finally [after the professorial, the opinionated, and the gossipy] there would be the craft interview. This line of questioning would try to discuss the circumstances of an artist's work and not the work itself. And it would try to restrict the questions to those which might occur to a practicing writer. ... Usually they are grateful that we are interested in their true identity as craftsmen poets. ... Following are guidelines we have been using. ... *Ideally this discussion should be more in the form of an intercourse than a "question and answer" approach which sometimes feels more like a game of ping-pong. ... As poems progress what do you do with the worksheets that you no longer need? ... Do you carry a notebook with you? ... What would you say about revision? ... Do you ever play games with the craft of poetry, prosody, for the fun of it, or for what it might lead to? Anagrams, palindromes, etc.? ... What do you feel about the*

need for isolation in the life of a writer? … Have you ever received lines of poetry
which you were unable to incorporate into a poem? (Packard 1974, pp. ix–xii)

Each of the interviews was incisive, and together they were disciplined by
the specified framework of verbal probes just excerpted. Each of seventeen poets was interviewed by one to four specified persons, altogether
eighteen of them, who were used a total of thirty-four times. (The cham-
pion, Mary Jane Fortunato, was used eight times.)

From the first names of the interviewers, the reader can tell that nine
were women and eight were men (one could have been either). Of the
seventeen poets, five were women. Four of these women were interviewed only by women; Anne Sexton was interviewed by Thomas Victor
and by Packard (who participated in three other interviews, with poets W.
H. Auden, Stanley Kunitz, and James Dickey). This suggests a bit of sex-
ism, whether it be from Packard, from interviewees, or from interviewers.
Because half the interviewers were men, you'd expect two or three of the
five women poets, instead of one, to be interviewed by men. However, of
the thirty-four interviewer *slots,* as opposed to the eighteen persons, only
eleven slots, or one-third, were filled by men. The two men who interviewed women poets made up nearly one-quarter of the nine slots for interviewing women poets.

Look up *palindrome* or another unfamiliar word in the good dictionary
you should always have on hand if you are serious about measurement,
which includes word and meaning as much as number and counting.

4

Six Major Shifts of Style

Artworks celebrate identities and relations, either directly or at some remove, and they play into efforts at control over others and the world. Art's reception depends upon social channels of communication and influence, just as art's production relies on positioning in cultural rhetoric; the converse is true as well. So construction of artworks is social and cultural, and artworks in their reception are as much perceived as performed. All this is so whether the artwork is object or process, visual or aural.

Thus a style must signal mutually sustainable reinforcement between the social and cultural aspects of art, in physical terms, and also signal identity in social terms. Such definition is consistent with accounts from other analysts attentive to social contexts of art. For example: "A new style was formed in the clustering of developments from several realms, and could only have occurred in its peculiar form at that time. ... While the styles emerged from the art tradition, their realization was intimately molded by this broader ideological, emotional and economic basis" (Pelles 1963, p. 149).

How and why do major shifts in arts come about? When I began writing this book, I wished to avoid the before-and-after syndrome of explanation in which a shift is rationalized by what its function and/or cultural motive was and is rationalized only in hindsight, after change is noticed. This book almost wrote itself once I saw that the social situation of art and its cultural content can change only together and hence must go together in a style.

From time to time, whole arts do appear; they do split or merge or evaporate, but not easily. The development and recognition (and inculcation) of a change in artworks may be brief, but it is never some instantaneous inspiration divorced from art world apparatus. Styles are social constructions with cultural content, so a major shift in style is itself difficult.

Propositions One and Two

Four propositions about major shifts will be tested by examination of six major cases that are spread out in time, art, and location. The first proposition is suggested by the analysis thus far:

Proposition 4.1. Innovation in style involves change in social organization coordinate with cultural change across art worlds.

This is true not least because clear separations, among art worlds and also between cultural arrangement and social arrangement, prove elusive. This will be illustrated by the "scoring" of a premier for the Metropolitan Opera Company (compare Proposition 5.1). Certainly there is a duality between cultural and social, but determining which end is cultural and which is social becomes a matter of contention, subject to tricks of perspective and rhetoric.

Innovation in style is thus a social construction, so that one stands forewarned to be cautious in interpreting the evidence. A shift in style that is able to sustain itself will attract and require much and prolonged attention from participants. A major shift thus depends also on shift in the social organization through art worlds that frame and sustain recognition of style.

Proposition 4.2. Similar causal mechanisms may underlie diverse shifts in style.

A master theme across six cases in recent centuries is the change to a focus on individual artists. In earlier eras, when artists were workmen or artisans, the focus was the work of art, which was thought to be conceived, as it was controlled, by the principal or patron or other audience. The artwork represented the patron's identity and ties rather than the artist's. A corporate body was often the patron, and an individual patron often was seeking identity and precedence within such a body.

Producing artists—or critics or directors—may substitute their own selves for artworks as the focus in style, so that change in style may come to be coded in terms of rise and fall of individual artists. This was true of German religious sculpture in the Renaissance, and it also occurred in Italian opera. It applies for the impressionists in Paris and subsequently with the abstract expressionists in New York. We will see it yet again from teenage fans of bands and star performers in an American revolution in popular music as well as in the emergence of modern dance. So call it the *modernist theme.*

The Pre-Raphaelites of Victorian London were an intermediate example, between medieval and modernist. Particular identity, such as Dante Rossetti's, and particular relations, as of Rossetti to his shop-girl fiancée, become represented, accounted, and celebrated in particular artworks, but other themes emerged, including medievalism, which couples the young men's identities with Victorian England's emerging class dynamics. Across the Atlantic, much the same themes and fervors as in the PRB circles of Ruskin and Morris were activated a generation later in the United States, where they were especially associated with the increasing roles of women in the arts.

Others besides artists can enter the identity sweepstakes of art worlds in new ways as artists' preeminence becomes established. Back in the Pre-Raphaelite era, one T. Butts became the devoted patron of William Blake despite his own humble station in life and limited income, and much the same was found among the impressionist crowd. The collector Daniel Schacter, described in the next chapter, is another prototype.

Who Were the Impressionists?

There were Manet and Monet, of course; then Degas, balletomane and scion of a banking family, comes to mind; also Cézanne; and of course you remember Renoir for his wonderfully decorative canvases (he, like Diaz and other earlier painters, began as an artisan painting teacups). The list goes on to include an American or two and a woman or two, Berthe Morisot, Mary Cassatt ...

But is that the right sort of answer? Isn't the question really who they were *artistically?*

Did the Impressionists-to-be Train and Paint Together? Monet and Bazille early on (and later Pissarro, Renoir, and others) painted together outdoors in the country, quite a lot, in a tradition just emerging among earlier painters such as Corot and Daubigny and Rousseau, who wandered the Barbizon forest upstream from Paris. Paths of impressionists-to-be crossed and recrossed as they bounced through training studios, one after another. These studios ranged from the official *académie* in which Manet started, to private training studios of academicians such as Couture or Gleyre or Ingres (who in today's estimation range from awful to great), on to threadbare commercial operations like the Academy Suisse and even to exuberant nonsense such as the huge studio complete with a live bull as a model in which the megalomaniac realist painter Courbet pontificated for a few months in 1862.

But then many other painters trained and painted together—painters of many tendencies in style plus technique and who had various sorts of personal and political and emotional interconnections with the impressionists-to-be.

Did Each Appreciate the Others' Work? Sometimes one bought another's work, or received it as gift. A young Pissarro received a delicate forest-scape from Corot, perhaps as a hint to moderate devices of stridency imitated from realist master Courbet.

Sometimes they exhibited jointly. Quite often they did in fact get into the official yearly Salon, but erratically enough so that, for example, when Manet was in, Monet was out. And of course the Salon was enormous, a mountain of thousands of paintings even though so many were rejected (no matter how that year's jury had been devised). To be rejected was a disaster commercially, if not in some artists' own critical views, and a key step was the move toward the novel institution of an independent group show. (In the first of these, in 1874, Degas cannily made sure that a number of Salon-accepted painters were also included.)

But one can't live just on the appreciation and fellowship of professional peers.

Did They Find Their Works Grouped Together by Critics? The wish to be grouped together was a matter of negative identity being better than no identity. Baudelaire, the poet, and Zola, the writer (and childhood chum of Cézanne in Provence) had considerable influence over opinion among artists, intellectuals, and hangers-on, but not much elsewhere. The few weighty conservative critics had to follow more than call the official tune.

Sometimes their works were grouped together, but sometimes not. When they were, it was by any sort of critic, the sorts being numerous enough to vitiate the combined impact.

Were They Recognized by the French Government? French governments, whether royal or republican, always aimed at Paris being the arts capital of the world, so recognizing outstanding artists was important business. The Academy of Painting, like the parallel academies for literature and sciences, had enormous prestige. It was the backbone of *the* system: of training, purchase, and publicity and of recognition in all its many facets. And to say it was French is to know that it was in Paris and dominated the lattice of academies and art schools in the provinces.

But recognition came on strict terms: The highest art was to be "history painting"—huge set pieces of battles, Greek gods, biblical figures, and other "serious" topics conducive to respect for authority. At least some of those painterly qualities were to be carried over into worthy though more common paintings of landscapes, portraits, domestic incidents, and so on. And because there was a Truth, there was a Beauty, but there was no room for the notion of recognizing as legitimately outstanding various groups of artists with differing idioms. An increasing fraction of the production by artists in France was diverging from this doctrine, yet to recognize many of the resulting tendencies and factions and clusters would subvert the existing rationalization for government recognition of artists and art.

Were Their Paintings Bought by the Same Discerning Buyers? Conventional buyers referred different canvases to the academic criteria, not to reputed relations emerging among aspiring artists. There were discerning buyers who bought numerous canvases from several impressionists-to-be, such as the Cohn sisters of Baltimore, unmarried women of limited means whose magnificent collection now has a gallery to itself in the fine arts museum. But as likely as not, purchasers were as enamored of the Barbizon school, or Boudin or Delacroix.

Durand-Ruel and the New System

My own answer to this question of who the impressionists were artistically centers on Paul Durand-Ruel, who to a sociologist seems as predominant a genius in one way as was Cézanne in the painterly dimension among the impressionists-to-be. Subsequent recognition of "them" as the impressionists, I argue, was accomplished by Durand-Ruel's agency, not by some immanent painterly style. Daubigny, a somewhat older landscape painter, could well have claimed title as creator of exactly that style, which is the "impressionist" rendering of what actually is seen—if such were indeed the core.

The real core of a new style, however, always is dual: It consists in an evolving interaction between its couching in social organization on the one hand and painterly transformations on the other. Durand-Ruel was central to just such dual realization of the impressionists. In so doing, he can be called the father of a whole new system of art world, a system at first counter to and soon thereafter largely displacing the long-lived academic system of France.

Some perspective can be achieved by crossing the Channel to view again the striking, though small-scale, development within British painting during the decade before the impressionists. The socioeconomic setting of Victorian England, laid out in Chapter 2 on the Pre-Raphaelites, somewhat resembled that in France. The Pre-Raphaelites appeared as innovators, mostly outside an academy: At first blush they were like the impressionists. But it was a feeble academy and from the beginning some of the PRB members achieved striking success, selling paintings at impressive prices to Midlands industrialists who were totally unimpressed by academic imprimatur and not concerned with speculation. The PRB did not confront a well-established and institutionalized art world.

Durand-Ruel created a new social category rather than merely assuming an already defined role. Durand-Ruel had inherited from his father a dealership of conventional scope and terms, which is to say a jumped-up art supplier, framer, and shopkeeper for minor canvases. You could argue that Durand-Ruel had already fathered one revolution in style before he became involved with impressionists-to-be (which was only in London while he and several of them were in self-exile during the Prussian siege of Paris in 1870). Durand-Ruel had already nursed along, with both material support and help of recognition, the earlier Barbizon group of landscapists—and a good thing he had made of it for himself!

But in 1850 the academic system was only bursting at the seams; it was not yet drowning in the flood of aspiring artists inundating Paris exactly because of the academic system's enormous prestige and success. Today the painterly magnificence of more and more of the academic favorites is more widely recognized, as Salon "machines" come out of museum basements following generations of storage. Only against the rich tapestry of the academic system can one make sense of new developments exemplified by the impressionists-to-be. In the words of an art historian, "Unless we have a better picture of the official and Academic art world, we can know little about any other kind of art world that existed within its boundaries, and our claim to be historians—as opposed to connoisseurs— rest on somewhat shaky grounds. ... The revisionism represented here can be seen as centrifugal, linking art even more strongly to the external world" (Mainardi 1989, p. 7).

Call the emerging new system, in Durand-Ruel's honor, the *dealer-critic system*. It was Durand-Ruel especially who came to see, and persuade others, of the speculative potential in buying works by unknown painters who might then rise to the same astonishing prices that even still-living academicians fetched (equivalent to Madison Avenue gallery prices of up to six figures today). It took nerve, and Durand-Ruel had inherited only a modest dealership. The payoff could be enormous, especially as he often sought monopoly over all the works from an artist.

Generosity was there, too, in the odd painting bought outright from and other aid extended to a painter in a frantic mood—when repugnance rather than purchase was as yet to be expected from customer-clients. Durand-Ruel treated young painters with respect and even deference, as he came to believe in these constructs of avant-garde and genius that were dimly emerging as central to new art, in part through his own efforts and arguments. And no one understood better how vital publicity was. Favorable publicity was preferred, but any notice of what could be conceived as a movement was important.

The point was that at last the ultimate receiver was delegating judgment to the artist(s) as to what—in style, technique, size, theme, everything—should count, now, for greatness in art. This was a switch in agency. Formerly, a patron, whether a noble or a cardinal or of "old money," might judge for himself, but the thrust of the academic system was that a state savant was the agent. In the dealer-critic system, the receiver was one of the "public"—the newly cultured (and well-off) public—as was exactly being confirmed and certified by the public's having the taste to support *this* new art through choosing *this* painter. And, it should be added, the art was being chosen with help perhaps from a dealer, less apparent than the influence from a critic—not that the roles were kept all that distinct.

Thereafter, to an extent that no one could have foreseen, the new system became predominant worldwide, despite stubborn resistance from various provincial imitations of the academic system that have kept niches to this day. Unquestionably (in hindsight), this success owed much to compatibility between the dealer-critic system and growing encroachment internationally by modern commercial and capitalist activities and attendant prestige ordering.

Many features are important to the new system besides the two of dealership and critics' branding of genius. Painting had to come to be seen differently, as a set of careers that were each laid out in a set of canvases. The vision of the *artist* had become primary. Now canvases were to be taken home, not to be hung in palaces and museums; this made turnover through dealers and exhibits all the more important. As some new style came in, one could consider replacement for obsolescence—although that interfered with a hope for one's early purchases becoming enshrined as masterpieces. Most paintings were of size and price modest enough to fit into ordinary bourgeois homes. Most paintings were for decoration and amusement, even though a core of avant-gardism was crucial to the overall dealer-critic system.

This new creature—a public—had to have been constructed already in the growth and turbulence of that society. There had to be at least the raw material of a cultured public for a Durand-Ruel, together with a Baudelaire or Zola as critic, to knead toward a new idea of high art. And still further publics should be induced—for example, across the Channel and across the Atlantic—which Durand-Ruel sought through establishing branches in both New York and London.

One can look for analogues in other arts and sites and times and thereby explore what combinations of features might be essential or sufficient to observe a major shift in style, which is marked by emergence of a new from an old institutional system in arts. From this case, neither individual genius in artists nor remarkable change in technique and technology need accompany major shift. To be applicable to further cases, a model must abstract from specific features of the dealer-critic system and its academic predecessor.

From Artisanry to Art
in Limewood Sculpture

Judged on their social face, revolutions in art are biggest when they mark transitions from artisanry to art. Impressionism signaled a revolution, true, yet visual art and artists both retained high status throughout: One could, for example, quite naturally discuss painting together with science and literature in the salons of Parisian hostesses both in Republican times and in earlier imperial eras. (Such had been the achievement of the academic system.)

An analogue to the artisan-artist transition would be when a mere plumber becomes a sanitary engineer because of technique and conceptualization taking off in complexity. Free, commercial cities were at the core of all such transitions in the West. These transitions were only occasional, and each was hard fought: "The free craft substructure of the Renaissance cities, where manual labor in the guilds was never tainted with servile degradation, produced a civilization in which the plastic and visual arts of painting, sculpture and architecture occupied an absolutely predominant position [whereas] the nine muses of the classical world of antiquity had significantly omitted the visual arts altogether" (Anderson 1974, p. 153).

Cross the Rhine, and four centuries, to tiny cities within the sprawl of principalities and dukedoms that constituted what is now Germany, at the time of great growth and commercial activity during the Renaissance just before the Reformation. Sculpture in limewood became distinctive of Germany, although it had been influenced by French limestone sculpture. Effects from edges and coils were emphasized in Germany, whereas Italians' work was concerned with space.

Sculptors had moved away from itinerant work on huge cathedrals:

> More and more sculptors set up independent workshops in the cities, combining into guilds like the masters of other crafts. ... The fourteenth-century sculptor had typically been producing stone architectural sculpture on a great church as a direct employee. ... The craft guild's first priority had always been to protect craftsmen from the newly aggressive type of merchant, wanting a great role in financing and organizing ... the sculptors were a vulnerable little group. (Baxandall 1980, pp. 12, 107)

There could be more than a dozen journeymen in a master's shop, but the gap in earnings might not be more than a factor of two or three.

Sculpture joined other expert crafts concentrated in scores of small, free cities, each with just a few thousand inhabitants. Each city was girded both by masonry walls and by hard-won rights to limited self-government for its merchant class. The cities were bound together by networks of commerce, some of which, such as the Hanseatic League, were active in far-flung international trade, and each city was active beyond the immediate rural locale that it controlled directly.

Within a city one guild had jurisdiction over limewood sculpture (combined variously with other sculpture, gilding, or other work, depending on struggles with rival guilds). Carved pieces for the home were mostly trinkets, such as Tirolese toys. The basic demand was for statues for churches. This is still pre-Reformation, just the one Catholic church. In these small cities, where landed grandees did not dominate local churches, the churches were the prime locales for proclaiming and celebrating identities of all sorts.

More common than individual statues were groups of figures posed together in a shallow vertical box, called a retable, behind an altar. A retable identified the saint for that altar and often had side boxes as wings hinged onto the center, providing for complex displays. Buyers sometimes would come from other cities, even far away, in part because there was some specialization between cities in types of sculpture, with subcontracting as one result. And there was cooperation, especially along lines of kinship connection, among guilds from different cities in coping with large orders. One of these orders would be costed in advance, much as we might cost a new car depending on what features were desired.

There were regional traditions and masters, such as the itinerant Gerhaert's florid works, Multscher's classical artworks (his early works being from Ulm), and an evangelical purism common in the north. Altogether, it was a highly localized system that was attuned to provide a guaranteed level of craftsmanship, but no more. When art historians look back on these works, they notice astonishing variations in quality by our standards, but these variations were not socially activated by that guild system and so were not significant within it.

Even before 1500, this basic system was diversifying. There was much coming and going, with net migration into a city and quite frequent upward social mobility within it. As part of these social dynamics, various corporate and kinship groups came to identify with different churches and also with distinct masses and activities within a given church:

> In 1488 a book in praise of Ulm ... makes much of the great Minister's number of altars—fifty-one of them, all endowed and maintained by burghers ... these altars went with the proliferation of an under-educated and wretchedly underpaid class of chaplains attached to the altars for the saying of Masses ... the retables on these side-altars seem a concrete projection of the will among well-to-do people to secure their own souls, in groups of fraternity or family. ... The obvious contrast is with high altar retables ... which were commissions from communities—as with Veit Stoss's retable at Cra-

cow, which is something like forty feet high ... or Riemenschneider at Rothenburg ... Pacher at St. Wolfgang or Erhart at Blaubeuren. (Baxandall 1980, pp. 62–67)

Many new churches were organized, and many German traders who were setting up new colonies in Eastern Europe were wealthy and eager to proclaim it.

The pressure toward system change was not just from proliferation in the number of altars. Newly prosperous buying groups are not content with works that merely meet the existing standard; they are attracted by, and thence competing groups also seek, more distinguished, more elaborate, truly finer works with which to pronounce their status. And an increase in sheer size of works, as in Stoss's altarpiece for the expansive German colony in Polish Cracow, meant closer connections with other crafts, which brought new ideas and materials as well as vivifying threats of encroachment.

Above all, it was intense competitiveness in identity announcements that helped to induce changes in both social and artistic aspects. A system of protected local productions with standard quality, even though made for diverse ensembles, was pulled apart. The increased demand for sculptures in a boom period also attracted numerous new aspirant sculptors. A journeyman from here could try to set up his own shop there. So competition among sculptors was increased by prosperity.

A breaking out of differentiated authorship under new commercial pressures and opportunities pried open the guild system of cities. Artistic tensions resulted: "a particular problem of the period, a tension between the sense of group and the sense of individual prowess which arises. ... Both 'German art' and the individual style were being discovered at the time and both notions seem registered in the style of the carvings" (Baxandall 1980, p. vii). But there were artistic expansions also. Hans Leinberger and other preeminent sculptors learned to control viewers' perceptions by controlling relative placements of statues, and of figures within retables, within the church and by integrating both with the poses of figures, especially the figures' eyes and draperies. With this increasing sophistication came a shift in perceptions that anointed the high sculptors, who were formerly mere artisans, as artists.

Put in economic terms, a preceding fair-trade regime was challenged by a regime of monopolistic competition. In the latter, each market does have distinct claims of jurisdiction, but the dynamics are such as to induce members to joust for special niches within that market. Now demand is differentiated so that matching up with production is a more fluid and aggregate process. Skilled but previously anonymous masters become show-offs, each both artist and entrepreneur.

Much the same developments seem to have marked the rise of arts in Greco-Roman city-states. These states, too, were small individually but in continuous interaction as trading nexuses for their various hinterlands. Some goods and materials were distinctive to a region. And makers of luxury goods aimed for the wealthy and for merchants' own trade by deliberately differentiating their output within the category of good. Let us venture a small theorem:

Lemma 4.1. Commercialization can break artisanal constraints on craftsmen and petty merchants and induce individuation in artists and their works.

Being guild craftsmen was itself, in systemic terms, a step above being venal dependents, as scientists and scholars then were, and much above being mere servants or hired hands.

This breaking free socially and politically through commercialization was wrapped up with creating the notions of individuality, genius, and creativity, to which we have since become accustomed to deferring. The paradox is that these very notions tended to erode the legitimacy of the process of commercialization that objectively made room for them. Today we see the paradox once again in the disdain for so-called mass or low or popular art, and yet in the ancient Hellenic civilization that we so much admire, there was a bold vulgarism in reception of visual arts by elites, who gloried in yet more gilt and bright colors.

For many years, both old and new sculpture systems continued side by side in Germany, around 1500. Even though these systems were walled off by regional effects and the like, their cohabitation was not easy. A likely final outcome was separation into three: (1) the earlier guild system, reasserted for certain kinds of traditional work; (2) the cosmopolitan wave, stimulated from abroad, which resulted in moving on to another art or phase of art; and (3) a continuing new art of high sculpture in limewood that was flamboyantly individual. Before all this could play out fully, however, the Reformation arrived, bringing icon smashing. Sculpture is not a Protestant art! Whereas impressionism has come to be universally cited as a revolutionary change, the change in limewood sculpture was not formulated as revolutionary in its own era.

Propositions Three and Four

The first two cases together suggest:

Proposition 4.3. The key to innovation in arts is flexibility in reception; that is, a field of alternative receptions must be feasible not only culturally but also in material and social technology.

Flexible reception is here being set off against originality in individual creators. Proposition 4.3 thus downgrades the causal significance of the modernist theme identified at the chapter's beginning, namely, the theme of artist as focus. It thereby excuses our omission of the most original artists from Shakespeare, Dostoevsky, Beethoven, and perhaps Wagner, on to Picasso.

Proposition 4.3 brings the focus to a brief period of actual change. Durand-Ruel's significance, this proposition argues, is primarily in his inculcation of reaching out to new audiences. And similarly it argues that the German diaspora in Poland, rooted in commercial expansion, has to loom larger in the account of limewood sculpture's transition.

Specification of process mechanism is called for:

Proposition 4.4. A new style results from an intermediate period of overlay and melding between one style and another in both social and cultural infrastructures; the new style is followed by rejection of the separate styles that went into its formation and then again became separate.

It seems fair to characterize this theorem in shorthand by the aphorism "styles mate to change." According to this theorem, a new style emerges from the superposition, for a time, of two or more existing styles, with attendant institutions, and then only if there follows an untangling and rejection between them.

Proposition 4.1 simply holds that changes in artworks go with changes in social matrix, because style has dual faces. Proposition 4.4 specifies a process mechanism, and Proposition 4.3 identifies the necessary context. These first two cases of major shifts in style, among painters and sculptors, fit this theorem of Proposition 4.4 and it in turn casts new light upon them. Especially singled out is the overlay, the coexistence phase, between a previous and an emergent system in processes that were both social and cultural.

Opera

Investigate the applicability of the preceding theorem and propositions to a third case, for a different art and period: opera in the seventeenth century. Begin with an appreciation of opera in the present century by an aficionado:

This book starts from the notion that opera is the last remaining refuge of the high style. ... In view of the suspicion of formal structures and lofty modes of expression that characterizes the consumers of art in a democratic age, it seems genuinely surprising that a form such as opera, with its penchant for exaggeration and its overt artifice, should still play to enthusiastic audiences willing to support it with an extravagance commensurate with the extravagance of deed and expression they witness on stage. (Lindenberger 1984, p. 15)

He goes on to point out a striking change:

> Throughout most of operatic history ... before World War I, audiences eagerly awaited the first production—most often, as it turned out, the last—of new works. ... Throughout most of our century the opera house could be called a museum exhibiting what its audiences accepted as the great monuments of the operatic past. The classical age was over, and the creative activity of opera had shifted from the composition of the new to the reinterpretation and rediscovery of the old. ... To imagine the situation of opera at an earlier time, we have only to glance at cinema, whose audiences expect constantly new products—and quickly discard most of the old ones. (Lindenberger 1984, p. 16)

But this devotee makes only grudging concession to general social contexts and art worlds surrounding opera production. Instead he blames arrival of a fairy—"modernism as the new aesthetic of difficulty"—for opera's premature closure. On the next page he helps mystify opera as recondite culture: "It is no wonder that its academic study demands knowledge and skill that no single specialist ordinarily possesses ... certain thinkers whom we have enshrined as central to modern intellectual history have used opera to work out major ideas."

Opera's origins were in the same period as Shakespeare, but under much less popular conditions: in a noble academy (*ridotto*) in Florence.

> Opera in the beginning was the outgrowth of a limited musical theory applied to an artificial, stylized poetic form. There were no first-rate musicians among the founders but only noble amateurs, poets, and singers, all actuated by an enthusiastic misconception of antiquity. They have often been compared to Columbus, who set out to find the East Indies and accidentally discovered a new continent: so the Florentines, seeking to revive Greek drama, opened the way to modern opera ... they were soon outdistanced. ... The first composer fully to realize its possibilities was Monteverdi ... up to the end of the eighteenth century some operas continued to be produced that were primarily for the delectation or glorification of rulers, nobles, or other wealthy patrons and only incidentally if at all for the entertainment of the public. ... Most of them, like the earlier operas at Florence and Mantua, were created as special events for festal occasions, and hence were mounted with little regard for expense. (Grout 1965, pp. 49, 61)

However, there came a Venetian revolution of popularization both in audience and performance:

> The popularity of the new form of entertainment at Venice was amazing. Between 1637 and the end of the century, 388 operas were produced in seventeen theatres in Venice itself and probably at least as many more by Venetian composers in other cities ... for the last two decades of the century this city of 125,000 people supported six opera troupes continuously, the usual season filling from twelve to thirty weeks of the year ... only the shell of classical subject matter remained, and even this was frequently abandoned in favor of episodes from medieval romances. ... The Aristotelian unities gave way before a bewildering succession of scenes, sometimes as many as fifteen or twenty in a single act, full of strong feeling and suspense ... lavish scenic backgrounds ... ingenious mechanical contrivances for the production of sudden miraculous changes ... broad effects by simple means ... tuneful melodies, unmistakable major-minor harmonies, strong rhythms in easily grasped patterns—these became the elements of a new operatic style. (Grout 1965, pp. 79–81)

The crucial brief flowering in Venice of Florentine opera, as overlaid with commedia dell'arte, was the birth of Italian opera. Grout (1965) sets the background:

> The prevalence of solo singing in sixteenth-century Italy has the character of a national reaction against the Netherlands polyphony which had been implanted there in the early part of the century. It is a manifestation of certain deep-rooted Italian traits which have remained constant throughout the musical history of that nation: hatred of complexity and obscurity, a profound feeling for melody as constituting the essence of music, and a preference for the individual artist as against the communal group represented by the church choir or madrigal vocal ensemble. (p. 34)
>
> There were no comic scenes in the earliest operas. Italian popular comedy at this period was represented by the commedia dell'arte, which found its musical counterpart in the madrigal comedies ... [which] show clearly in their plots, character types, and the use of dialect, their derivation from the *commedia dell'arte*. (p. 72)
>
> The music of the comic characters is mostly in simple note-against-note style, with a fine sense of the animation of comic dialogue. On the other hand, some of the five-voice pieces are beautiful examples of the serious Italian madrigal style. The madrigal comedies were an early attempt to combine farce comedy with music, to exploit the lively, popular commedia dell'arte as against the languid, aristocratic pastorales. (p. 33)
>
> Although the beginning of opera is commonly reckoned from the Florentine performances of 1600, it would almost be more appropriate to date it from the opening of the first public opera house in Venice in 1637. Itinerant troupes of singers, rivaling the troupes of the commedia dell'arte and bor-

rowing from them many features of both libretto and music, had begun to circulate in Italy before this date; but the destined center of the new kind of musical drama, based on a combination of broad popular support and prestige appeal to the upper social classes, was Venice. (p. 78)

Learned and abstruse efforts akin to the original Florentine opera continue on, with little impact now on opera as a living art. And commedia dell'arte has continued on to this day, little changed since the feverish period of overlap. At least in this early era, prima donnas do not seem crucial, but the enormous importance of Monteverdi as composer is enough to keep the modernist theme in the running. The principal assertion, Proposition 4.4, appears fully applicable. We shall explore further its applicability to revolutions in two further arts, but first turn to changes in a very different musical art.

Rock'n'roll

The same sociocultural mechanism can underlie change in both high and popular art. This transposability is made vivid through an extreme contrast within musical arts that center on singing. Turn from revolution in opera to revolution in American popular music.

The appearance of rock'n'roll as a new style within American popular music is illuminated by the four propositions. This striking shift in singing depended on simultaneous changes across several popular music genres and art worlds as well as in the broader audience. Divergent streams of black and white art and artists were pulled together by brokers in the media, who depended on drawing a whole new population into the audience. Then the emerging shift broadens into a fuller canon and thus is no longer confined for audience to the newly mobilized group of preteens that gave it that initial burst of energy that can come only from exclusive identity.

There is an abundance of archival material: Philip Ennis, a longtime observer and analyst of the popular music scene, was able to quiz still-living participants rather than be, like Grout, forced to reconstruct a remote scene. Around 1950, there were six preexisting streams or general styles of popular music, each with its own base of audience, producers, performers, and disseminators, with some overlaps.

Three streams were for black Americans: black popular, gospel, and blues/jazz. They had distinguishable but intertwined and supportive networks of performance, audience, and creator. Their listeners were segregated from their counterparts in the other cluster of three streams, as were their radio stations, recording companies, agents, critics, playing clubs, and performers.

Call these three the black cluster; the other cluster was that of whites. This too had three streams: mainstream disc jockey (earlier called Tin Pan Alley), country and western, and folk. In the early 1950s, quite suddenly, a few songs and music pieces in one cluster began to attract attention in the other. White borrowed from black. The values as well as the music, the lyrics of one genre as well as the tunes, for a bit obtained a foothold in the other cluster's social networks of attention and appreciation.

At first a song crossed over only after being arranged and resung according to conventions and by performers familiar in the other cluster. But even in the first period, the early 1950s, the original performance and recording earned a place—even a place on the hit chart of the other stream (though probably on the bottom). The real causal nexus, Ennis claims, was differential attention to the crossovers by outlets that were each relatively marginal and localized within its home steam. Outlets and networks in Memphis, Tennessee, happened to be prominent enough on the black as well as white sides to be catalytic in the overlay. The main key was radio stations small in the national picture but plugged into regional networks of playing clubs and also into networks of smaller record companies. A crucial catalytic role was played by the disc jockeys, whose interest was development of distinctive new combinations.

A particular performer, Elvis Presley, became the seed for the hailstorm that was the truly new style that was to come out of the temporary overlay of white and black styles. He was the seed not simply because of his musical talent but because of his audience. Presley specialized in a hitherto unattended-to fringe: preteens, who were present alongside each of the initial six streams but were disdained.

No single theme in the Presley message was different from ones in the mainstreams, but Presley's combination of themes was very different. Moreover, it was explicitly tagged as different and as tied to a particular population, the preteens. The commercial potential had been recognized by clever agents since the preteen mob scenes around the young Frank Sinatra. What was required to realize potential was not a single gimmick but a retuning and a regrowing of social and performance networks.

There soon followed renewed rejection between the six preexisting streams/styles. There was no enlargement of each canon; instead there was a retreat. But out of the overlay had come this new style for a new audience.

An unfailing indicator of the newness of a style is rejection by established critics. When rock'n'roll began to get established and make inroads, there was a veritable frenzy of critical attack. Rarely has there been such a universal shower of opprobrium, presumably because of the peculiarly segregated—yet related—status of the preteens in the general population.

There was a resonating crescendo of denunciation of the new style as being perverse in content and inane in form. Later, much later, a Leonard Bernstein would rhapsodize about the creative aspects of the new music (in the Beatles).

The principal and fourth proposition is seen to be applicable, along with the other three propositions. Study of the history suggests that most of the stars were more a by-product than a cause of the revolution, which owed at least as much to intermediary figures analogous to Durand-Ruel.

Modern Dance

Modern dance in its early days probed the grounding of art in the sacred (in religious ceremonies), as discussed in earlier chapters. Modern dance reached its fullest expression in America, but in the early period after 1900 European appreciation of touring American groups was indispensable to its survival. To begin with, there was no public funding for dance in America and precious little patronage; instead there was the box office, and even there Europe was more supportive: "In 1909 Diaghilev's Russian Ballet took Paris by storm with dances that at times violated the traditions of ballet. ... Isadora Duncan also first danced in Paris in 1909 to wide acclaim as well as some mockery" (Lynton 1980, p. 34). Thus "it was possible to step aside from [ballet conventions], as did Loie Fuller with great success in the 1890's in Paris, and develop an abstract dance ... an art of expressive bodily action, without narrative or props and with the body scarcely veiled" (Lynton 1980, p. 17).

Modern dance in America also was a creation of the excluded, the denigrated, the shunned in America: first women, then gay men, and, crosscutting both, blacks. The proportion of blacks grew steadily, a direct influence of European support, and blacks became intertwined with arts other than modern dance:

> In Paris, 1925 ... a tall gangly black dancer named Josephine Baker, a graduate of Sissle and Blake's Broadway revue Shuffle Along, now a performer in the Harlem-sprung La Revue Negre, dazzled Paris in a free-form, flapping Charleston. ... Bringing real Harlem dancers to Paris was the idea of Fernand Léger, the Cubist painter and designer of ballets; he thought of it after writing a scenario for a Ballet Negre and then realizing it already existed in New York. ... Josephine became a further catalyst to the picture-making process of the time, especially the Cubist-influenced theatrical posters. (Kendall 1984, p. 198)

Among all these swirling crosscurrents, relations of American theatrical dance to ballet and its European social-cultural forms are the crux. "It was the Europeans and especially the Russians who analyzed and built upon the dance inventions of Loie Fuller and Isadora Duncan" (Kendall 1979, p. 85). It was only after encounter and overlaps with ballet that what we in hindsight call modern dance even came to think of itself as a movement. Out of the superposition for a time in the 1920s of this American movement and European ballet came, through a subsequent split, the art form we have come to know as modern dance. It was a crossbreed of a state-supported, indeed aristocratic, high art and a yearning middle-class art. The latter supported itself as needed by burlesque and vulgar, verging on pornographic, dance "art."

The crossbreed came to be regarded as legitimate through establishment at universities (Wisconsin University was first, followed by Bennington College and Connecticut College) as well as in many other middle-class fora. The earlier image of ballet girls and chorines alike as, socially speaking, unclean creatures, was banished. Although ballet was hierarchical and early modern dance was positively monarchical (from Isadora Duncan on through Martha Graham and beyond), the crossbreed was doctrinally egalitarian in its companies of performers. Perhaps as a result, these companies were all small, with between two and thirty members—numbers lower than ballet corps yet higher than most theatrical dance acts of the old days. Whether as further effect or as an additional cause, there was a one-choreographer, one-company tendency, which tended to give different companies different modes of performance as well as distinct repertoires.

Flavors continued to be contributed by otherwise excluded groups. Overweight women, for whom ballet was impossible, were from the beginning prominent in modern dance in America. They continue to contribute innovations through successive new social movements in dance, from eurhythmics on through the free-to-touch dance forms of the 1980s.

Modern dance in its postwar revolution became further intertwined with changes in other arts: "Rejected by his fellow musicians, Cage deliberately sought contact with artists in other art forms. He was an early member of the Abstract Expressionists' 'Club.' Under his influence and that of his long-time collaborator, dancer Merce Cunningham, a group of dancers, painters and poets participated in radically innovative dance programs and 'Happenings' at the Judson Memorial Church in Greenwich Village" (Crane 1987, p. 65). Indeed, Robert Rauschenberg, who was best known, and paid, as a post–abstract expressionist painter, has a three-page description in Don McDonagh's encyclopedia of modern dance: "Like his paintings and constructions these pieces were a combination of elements with great and provocative diversity. As an early member of the Judson Dance Theater, he first showed his work there. In the following de-

cade he continued to make pieces and also to become associated with the
Merce Cunningham company as its designer. In addition to his dance
pieces he also created 'happenings' of a stronger dramatic character"
(McDonagh 1981, p. 532). Much the same conclusion—that a turbulent
merging of old styles yields a new style—can be drawn as from the preceding case of rock'n'roll.

Abstract Expressionism

Many find a striking parallel between the rise of the impressionists and
the rise of abstract expressionism, which has been described in terms of
the same dealer-critic system identified for the impressionists. At least in
the arts, postwar New York seemed as predominant in the United States
as Paris was in France.

Impacts of technology in arts commonly come all mixed up in subtle
ways with social context. For example, the meanings of space, time, and
rhythm, especially as shaped in our cities by architecture and design arts,
have been shifted by new regimes of locomotion that were made possible
by material and social technology. Perhaps similar influences impinged
on shifts in pictorial space during the rise of abstract impressionism and
accounts in part for its location in New York, as, for example, the Dutch
artist Mondrian suggests in his abstract composition *Broadway Boogie-
Woogie*. This would be consistent with Proposition 4.4.

Certainly New York's preeminence was not because of state control
and influence, so there was no American analogue to the academic system. One can instead propose, as an establishment to be fought, some
nexus of private patrons and museums devoted to a predominant American school. According to this theorem, one can expect to find some preexisting sociocultural infrastructure interacting with the nascent movement
to generate turbulence out of which a new style gets established.

One obvious candidate is realist painting grouped around such prewar
figures as Charles Sheeler and Charles Demuth, who were dubbed *precisionists* for their scenes of modern industry that did not include people or
trees. They hung out, in the ambience of the collector Walter Arensberg,
with dancer Isadora Duncan, poet William Williams, and émigrés like the
iconoclast Marcel Duchamp. Their eerily realist paintings may have influenced Edward Hopper, Arthur Dove, Stuart Davis, and other Americans.
The truth is that there was never a predominant American school that
gained mutually reinforcing streams of patronage and support and emu-
lation.

The reason was Europe. Up through the war, American society was
profoundly insecure about the value of its culture; indeed, it had the colo-

nial's suspicion that it had no culture. Arrival of European émigrés in the early days before and during World War II was epochal. It made the Paris school a presence just during that school's own wartime suspended animation. It brought major talents who also had intimate familiarity with the preceding avant-garde waves. These waves had been dubbed "surrealism," "expressionism," and the like and followed cubism and the fauves. Modern art is often dated from the christening of the fauves ("wild beasts")—an assortment of French and later some German painters claiming to push beyond the impressionists—at a 1905 exhibit in Paris and the subsequent 1913 Armory Show in New York.

Sheeler, Dove, Hopper, and other American originals of course already knew about, and some followed, these European innovations, but they did so from the cultural periphery, as outsiders. Americans had to undergo a wrenching discovery of self-worth and an assertion of it as challenge that were analogous to what had faced the impressionists—and all the other outsiders to the academic system. Galleries would not proliferate; nor would dealers and critics and curators bestir themselves into some dominant system except in accompaniment to a multiplying assertion of artistic predominance. The Museum of Modern Art and its allies were more in a struggle against the hegemony of Europe than against any pallid American establishment.

The magical period of the mid-1940s was when for a few years the Paris school and its attendant ways of organizing and construing art worlds was overlaid onto the scatter of American art continuities. Even the physical sense of a Left Bank was imported onto the existing Manhattan loft districts that were becoming known as successive bohemias for struggling artists and small galleries—East Village and SoHo and TriBeCa. Recruits came in plenty, not just artists but also the equally indispensable talkers and writers of galleries and journals and museums as well as new postwar streams of income and wealth-holders available to be made into collectors.

The well-known glory days of abstract expressionism followed, on into the 1960s. Social construction of a world movement was enabled out of the infrastructures of overlaid art worlds, European and American, combined with the self-regenerating energy of new artistic direction. As in Paris a century before, there were many new directions visible in canvases that could be, and were, clustered and eulogized and energized in many and competing ways by commentators and artists. Among the latter, Clement Greenberg and Harold Rosenberg were predominant on painterly matters. Their fundamental theme, of painting becoming expressive action by an artist upon a canvas rather than being a portrayal, was foreshadowed in other arts, notably modern dance, as well as in preceding European art as far back as Cézanne:

This distinction between form and content is the legacy of an earlier generation of scholars. ... My interest lies in the interaction of theory and practice.
In particular, I study the attempt to "represent" originality through the medium of painting as if linked to a unique and immediate experience. Artistic
originality emerges within a painting that seems to have no definite model,
despite its references to art and nature. Painting becomes self-referential and
self-expressive. (Shiff 1984, p. xiii)

Other American materials for the social construction of a revolution
were on hand besides precisionism. There were various tendencies toward regionalisms, both painterly and social, and toward radical social
commentary associated with depression-era government arts programs. It
was important to reject these directions to move to a subjective, individual
expressionism. In these rejections, the new movement, unlike the preceding American abstract artist group of the 1930s, asserted its own preeminent authority rather than appealing to the modernism of European art as
a defense against Babbittry.

American painter Jackson Pollock, painter-commentator Charles
Motherwell, and sculptor David Smith were central artists, along with expatriate painters Franz Kline and Willem DeKooning, as the core of networks with perhaps eight other Americans and fewer expatriates as further subsidiary foci. A hundred or so galleries sprang up and died,
quickly. Of these, twenty were predominant, the same number as of predominant painters, but there was no neat matching of one painter to one
gallery.

Not surprisingly, there was enough momentum to generate successor
waves within what had become the American art establishment, the ethos
of which was to fight an establishment that in sober fact was merely the
artists and galleries that just preceded in seniority as a wave. Minimalism,
photorealism, pop art, figurative expressionism, and several others followed, but with skimpy ties in networks that had fewer internationally
visible foci.

Control shifted back and forth in the social mechanism. For example, it
was the support of collectors that pushed pop art to preeminence over
objections and indifference on the part of critics and curators. More generally, as prices of works tend to go up, the influence of critics goes down.
As prices were seen to keep rising, there was a turn toward the old Parisian tendencies to purchase for later speculative sale rather than for willing collections to museums, with corresponding diminution of curatorial
influence. Nor were all the artists naive and powerless in commercial and
critical aspects any more than Monet had been half a century earlier in deliberately bringing out his canvases as staged series: "He possessed a superb sense of the art market in which he was operating ... subscribed to

two clipping services ... had a 600 book library" (Tucker 1989, p. 9). With the aid of a variety of expedients, Monet maneuvered the average prices of these series up from 3,000 francs for the original series, *Grainstacks*, to 5,000 for the *Poplars* and on to 15,000 francs for the *Cathedrals*.

In all this there is some parallel to the rock'n'roll story, suggesting a homology between the systems of high art and popular art despite the obvious surface differences. In the words of a British art historian:

> Dogma invites counter-dogma. ... As a process it is very wasteful of talent and ideas. ... The support system of modern art, in many respects most highly developed and commanding in the United States, encourages and disdains, feeds and starves, picks up and drops artists of all sorts, including artists of great and precious ability. The best, the most powerfully motivated and self-critical artists probably survive, but the public is encouraged in its lust for new stars and new slogans. (Lynton 1980, p. 256)

In Chapter 7, I chronicle an artist being roller-coastered in this fashion by a system that, like impressionism's system earlier, induced huge numbers of new entrants. This glut of newcomers led to a proportion of canvases being able to achieve sale, real arm's-length sale, that was perhaps as low as 1 percent.

Once again the propositions do well. Proposition 4.2, that the same causal mechanisms underlie these six diverse revolutions in style, seems confirmed. But it is to the original abstract expressionist revolution that the propositions apply. The successor waves in Manhattan painting do not achieve the stature of a major shift able to sustain themselves. But the modernist theme is certainly more applicable to the successor waves than to the abstract expressionists.

GUIDE TO FURTHER READING

On the logic of case studies, see the recent volume edited by Ragin and Becker (1992). In a monograph on the social psychology of art, Pelles (1963, Chapter 2) argues for Britain and France from 1750 to 1850 as the incubation site of what I call the modernist theme. Her account is excellent as background to both Chapter 2 and the impressionist sections of this chapter.

The standard sociological account of the emergence of the impressionist movement is White and White (1965). Rewald's massive and magnificent book (1946; revised editions 1955, 1961, 1973) is, though not written in French, the authoritative account of the impressionists and their interrelations as individuals and has copious, excellent illustrations. What Rewald does not look at is twofold: the explosive pressures on the academic system and the great number and variety of new painterly movements that were, or could have been conceived, perhaps around other individuals marginal to the academic system, such as Puvis de Chavannes or Gustav Moreau.

Professor Patricia Mainardi gives an overview of uses made by art historians of new approaches through the sociology of art in her "Editor's Statement: Nineteenth-Century French Art Institutions," in the Spring 1989 issue of *Art Journal,* which is devoted entirely to that topic. The account in White and White ([1965] 1993) can be supplemented by Bryson (1981) for the academic system, by Green (1989) for dealers, and by P. Ferguson (1984) for the literary ambiance that was closely intertwined socially, not just through critics.

Baxandall's account (1980) of limewood sculptors in early Renaissance Germany is the classic rendition of that transition from artisanry to art. On the emergence of new styles, Baxandall is definitive because he combines economic with sociological and historical perspectives while developing incisive aesthetic assessments.

Whiteside (1981) and Hirsch (1972) expound the style of big hits, for book publishing and record publishing respectively.

On opera, Grout (1965) is definitive. Lindenberger (1984) and Schmidgall (1990) are interesting. I became aware of Ellen Rosand's 1990 monumental work on Venetian opera (*Opera in Seventeenth-Century Venice: The Creation of a Genre*) too late to incorporate.

Ennis (1993) is the definitive account from a sociological perspective of rock'n'roll's emergence, and Belz (1973) is an interesting attempt to consciously avoid the sociological dimensions. Hirsch (1972) probes the commercial context of popular music more generally.

Kendall (1984) lays out the pursuit of ancient myth by the founders of modern dance around 1900. McDonagh (1990) also tells about the creation of modern dance; for alternative accounts, see McDonagh (1981 and 1990). Novack (1990) cites the literature on body movement in a fascinating account of the uses of improvisational dance in communication.

Crane's monograph (1987) is the definitive sociological account of the emergence of abstract expressionism and six subsequent movements in New York. She uses much the same categories as in the analysis of the impressionist revolution by White and White (1965, Chapter 2); so does Moulin (1987) in a study based on extensive interviews with participants of the postwar French art scene, which resembles the early postwar scene in New York. The Shapiros (1990) provide an excellent selection of writings on abstract expressionism, most from the postwar period. For the broader New York arts scene of that era see Wallock (1988).

Lynton's account of abstract expressionism (1980, Chapter 7) builds upon his descriptions of earlier international modern movements beginning with the fauves. Tucker's monograph (1989) on Monet's late paintings weaves together commercial and artistic themes for those years when modern art was originating. Surveys of American art before World War II, and of the precisionists in particular, are offered by Rose (1975) and Doezma (1980), but to see plates of many works or to get much detail one must search out catalogs of major museum exhibits. McKinzie (1975) is thorough on the Works Progress Administration (WPA) arts project.

The critics Rosenberg (1969, 1972, 1982) and Greenberg (1986) provide mutually hostile assessments of follow-on movements. Their essays were themselves part of the tendency (argued in Chapter 3 and again in Chapter 6 as the modernist theme) for social construction of a group around some artist and that artist's work as core, a group that shares in the resulting suprapersonal identity. Perhaps this is one source of rapid changes in styles. Lucie-Smith (1985) is trenchant on the revived challenge to Manhattan's predominance among American regions that goes along with the new movements.

FIELDWORK IDEAS

Major shifts are rare. Read Becker (1982, Chapters 10, 8) on drift in art worlds and on mavericks for leads to spotting change on a much smaller scale.

MEASURES AND MODELS

Baxandall (1980) is exemplary in his deployment of economic models. Ennis (1993) shows how to weave together numerical and tabular data with aesthetic debates and assessments of broad social class and generational changes, all while keeping attention on the shifting use of social networks in the revolution in popular music. Crane (1987) demonstrates the usefulness of cross-classification tables.

The standard dance encyclopedia (McDonagh 1981) documents a shifting gender balance: Four or five forerunners were women, as were five of eight founders, whereas among the followers there were twenty-four women to twenty-five men. Then all five of the key innovators of the postwar generation were men (Merce Cunningham, Erick Hawkins, Alwin Nikolais, Paul Taylor, and James Waring), but in turn women predominated among their followers, by thirty to eighteen.

5

Creativity and Agency

Style as juncture of social and cultural faces is a product of history. These histories get concretized in particular art worlds, as we have just seen. These art worlds are not neatly separate bubbles, but rather each spills over into others through all sorts of social and cultural networks. But such histories also interlace with one another in what we call a civilization, which leads to recognizable species of art worlds as well as overlaps among them. On a finer scale, such historical elaboration comes along with specialization, which presupposes delegation to agents. We can't paint our own Mona Lisas. It is on this finer scale that art by agency comes to dominate.

Creativity

The agents include many sorts of brokers, from critics and producers to editors, but all these depend on the producing artists to generate continuing streams of art. Focusing on the production situations for art enables one to sidestep debate on competing metaphysics of arts, such as figural versus image, form versus content, or high art versus mass art. These are metaphysics that each overemphasize either the cultural or the social face of art—to the interest of one or another sort of broker. Such focus on production and agency excludes neither commonalities across the arts, such as in their funding and recruitment, nor differences among arts, be they in technology or theme.

Production of what we have come to see as art begins as announcements of identities, in visual or other images portraying attributes of actors, living or dead. In such an announcement, any process of specialization in production, technological or social, already is inducing and creating agency in art. Agency is the business of any person or other actor being empowered to act for another, alive or dead. Agency is there from the beginning.

Production through agency is not just a matter of efficiency through specialization. It also has an impact on cultural contents. Overlaps among and within art worlds ensure such impact. One example is when modern high composer Philip Glass listens to and adapts rock music; another is when the Beatles compose music to take advantage of new technological devices for mixing and shifting sound.

It follows that what we come to call creativity—that is, originality in composition or performance that perhaps contributes to shift in style—is to a large extent a by-product of agency. There are, after all, astronomical numbers of possible combinations among agents in and across art worlds. Chance has much to with which combinations get realized for a while. Each new combination exposes creators to a new set of templates and notions.

Aesthetics

The very notion of beauty is late in coming. Artwork in earlier eras was available only to the people of those who created it, and it was created without alienation: A tribe then truly and exclusively owned its art. And then came in high arts, along with an elite, which in origin is the tribe that is master over other, interpenetrating tribes. High arts are for overawing. Beauty comes later.

Beauty presupposes the loss of signification in celebration or accounting that is specific to a particular setting:

> The aesthetic consciousness had hardly troubled the Greek mind in the fifth century at all ... [instead] give to later Hellenistic Greece and Imperial Rome the credit of being the homes of true and genuine aesthetic feelings, such as the modern mind can understand. ... It is appropriate that the first flicker of aesthetics should have been struck by the rationalist Euripides. The genius of fifth century Greece was truly medieval. ... In decadent, irreligious Rome and Alexandria aesthetic feelings flourished as never before. (Chambers 1928, p. 104)

The invention of beauty as a construct presupposes social classes and sophistication in trade and exchange. It also presupposes the loss of those celebrations and accountings of identity that are specific to a particular setting. Beauty, once invented, becomes available, in place of sacredness, to mark identity in the hands of agents other than priests (cf. Dauber 1992). In extreme cases such as the mandarins of traditional China or the Ottoman Porte, the literal mechanics of writing—which is symbolic of authority—may be turned into a visual art much like ancient Mesopotamian seal impressions and thus into an aesthetic topic.

Already with the pre-Raphaelite band of very young English one begins to see the artist slipping the noose of agency held by some patron or by some more remote principal such as a buyer or collector and instead moving the artist's own self into the seat of signification. Until then only religious and political and military heroes were accepted and legitimate as displacements and alienations of identities. The identities of larger collectives indeed often were originally built around such heroes. It was a real coup to establish the idea that a beholder could gain benefit in his or her own identity by deferring to an artist's expression of that artist's own identity. That is what the avant-garde myth and the genius myth are really all about.

That was a first but only partial reversal of agency as we define it. The Pre-Raphaelites are but a halfway point on the way to the avant-garde. It was not so much their own identities as artists that were put at the focus (with the exception of an odd figure of working-class origin, painter-poet-printmaker William Blake). Rather the focus became new ideas of beauty and truth, reflected through renderings of the medieval era—of long-necked beauties and free-standing spirituality—and realized in their own persona. We see slippage more easily in this case because the English painting world was so tenuous and the Pre-Raphaelites were so naive, and there was neither curator nor dealer nor collector of note around.

There was, however, an ideologue of generalities for the PRB. With John Ruskin we begin to see a new sort of critic emerge. The half-displacement from viewers' own identities was aided and abetted by Ruskin's endless offerings of hyperbole to viewers. Drawing out perceptions of and meanings from particular artworks is delicate business, just as is assessing particular souls, and broad assessments are drawn from such particularities.

Ruskin aimed high. He moved criticism into new prominence and invaded the very production of art, as if in lieu of the patron. The critic became a new sort of agent because of action, on behalf of a new sort of principal: a compound patron, a fictional compound of a host of viewers. There was a sort of double slippage of agency and thus a double displacement of meaning. A self-conscious aesthetics appeared, resonating from and for broad new strata.

A political scientist recently pointed out that "there is deep antagonism between organizational concerns [of our art museums] and the aesthetic mission" (Banfield 1984, p. 92). Yet aesthetics itself is imposed as an anachronism from the Victorian era of the Pre-Raphaelites. In judging beauty in others' art one is not just imposing, from one's own art experience, particular criteria that are foreign to that art. The foreignness is in the very idea of rendering such abstract judgment—as opposed to other judgments more tangibly tied to particular needs. Beauty can be conceived differently, as agreement in critical assessment by committed viewers, and then no fixed objective standard of beauty is argued as aesthetics.

Any full-blown aesthetics, a philosophy of art, has to build across many art worlds and particular rhetorics. In pragmatism as a philosophy, a philosophy distinctive to America, the aesthetic is seen as a transformation and refinement of experienced emotion that goes beyond ritual reenactment and symbolic duplication. This is indeed reminiscent of the nineteenth-century views of Ruskin and the PRB, which built upon identity taken in the third sense. Beauty, and its exploitation as aesthetics, is itself then presupposed by advertising, which is directed to large modern populations. And the Pre-Raphaelite movement helped to apotheosize beauty as one reverberation of a new class thrusting into existence in Victorian England—along with modern advertising.

Aesthetics is some replacement for theology. Science also became a partial stand-in for theology about then. Truth replaced the beauty of aesthetics. Each science, and each of its invisible colleges of active researchers, presuppose and rely on and encourage stories, founding myths, heroes: dramatic narratives, if not yet songs and dances. In order to continue, each invisible college of science must advertise itself through audiences to potential sponsors. It is no accident that the author of the major sociological study of New York avant-garde art (Diana Crane, see the end of the previous chapter) was earlier, in 1972, the author of a well-known study of sciences.

There are different stances to doing science and these correlate to stances of doing art. Turn to farce in drama, which goes back very far, as to the cornball bawdiness of Plautus's comedies in ancient Rome. Farce is like tragedy in its mode of relation to the audience, the ironic mode: The audience already knows, and savors knowing, what the actors will do. This is exactly the ex post stance of positivist science, the currently official science of the schoolbooks. But reading James Watson on his discovery of DNA with Frances Crick reminds one that science in process may more resemble happenings, or paperback romances, depending on who composes the narrative.

The use of agency in art can suggest inadequacy exactly where one wants to be a "presence." Religion and science also involve agency, but the former exhibits agency glorified whereas the latter exhibits agency as remote. And both are associated with forms of engineering such that imitation does not diminish the celebration but instead enhances it. Artworks are replacing these other agencies and, to assuage anxiety in doing so, some stereotyping and rigidity are essential.

Technology and Ecology

All works of arts are associated in content and in medium with particular technologies as well as with social themes from their respective periods and contexts. This was illustrated in the earlier chapter on the Pre-Raphaelites, whose themes and technical choices were shown to extend to the London theatre and to pictorial arts in Germany of that era. A little later in the century, a similar association of thematic content with technology was exemplified by the stage designer Gordon Craig. As a leader in German expressionism around 1900, he introduced extremes in lighting and staging to capture the heavily symbolic and mythical such as in Strindberg plays and Pre-Raphaelite painting.

Craig's thematic and technical associations have continued down through subsequent decades in avant-garde theatre, from Alfred Jarry to Grotowski. Several of its thematics are mentioned in the next chapter. The oddity is that this avant-garde is ritualistic, but in ways suggestive of the scientific laboratory as envisioned by outsiders (although Grotowski explicitly denies any such similarity).

Avant-garde effects can come from materials, perhaps borrowed: "[The fauve artists] learned from African sculpture the value of working in direct response to the nature of the material. The European sculptural tradition depended almost entirely on overcoming the limitations of the materials; here was an alternative tradition" (Lynton 1980, p. 30).

Even thousands of years ago, material technology itself had a major impact on style expressed in pottery:

> A very important innovation was the introduction of a pivoted working surface. ... The skillful painting of pots in different fields or sections, which had been the usual practice up until then, gradually gave way to simpler styles of painting, which are, on the whole, based on concentric bands round the pots ... created simply by pressing a color-soaked brush against the rotating pot ... by moving the brush up and down, garlands, wavy lines, or herringbone patterns could very easily be applied. Both the production and the painting of pots could therefore be carried out in a fraction of the time. ... Under the influence of the new technique, earlier, more localized, types of decoration underwent such uniform change.
>
> The next technical innovation was setting the wheel's axle in bearings and hence the creation of an actual potter's wheel. ... The potential of the potter's wheel can only be fully exploited if the clay is pliable ... could be enhanced by the use of additives, and ... the finished vessels might look totally different, basic yellowish color replaced by a reddish-brown background color. ... Painting was discontinued, apart from a very few examples, and, aside from particular shapes that were given an incised pattern, the pottery is undecorated. An ever-greater role was played by vessels whose shapes indicate that they were used for specialized purposes. Unlike the rotating work surface, the potter's wheel did not spread rapidly over large areas of the Near East. It could only make a breakthrough in the more highly developed regions. (Nissen 1988, pp. 46, 62)

The evolution of fresco art and the introduction of new materials for painting and sculpture in recent centuries also are clear examples of the direct impact of material technology upon style. And there is a modeling effect upon artistic vision from conceptual as well as material accomplishments in sciences and technology.

In nineteenth-century visual arts there was a shift away from portraiture and realism. Does one account for this materially, by reactions to the invention and dissemination of photography? Or could it be the emergence then, with modernism, of further levels of identity, removed from the person as conceived in previous portraiture? In the present decade, computer-aided design (CAD) seems likely not only to revolutionize the practical side of architecture and other applied design fields but also to shift visual artists' ideas of what designs are interesting. Combinations of standard colors in patterns may supersede hunts for exact tone and shade.

One can compare copies in literature to copies in visual arts, in each case for high versus popular forms, to explore the impacts of technology on two issues: When is art a stock and when is it a flow? Second, under what circumstances is art perceived without artists and under what circumstances is it conceived as without critics?

An example from a different art is Bob Dylan's adoption in 1956 of electric instruments, followed by many others. Within the preexisting world of folk music, which is a "genuine" hands-on music from and for the people, a general value was no doubt violated, and indeed there was a ruckus if not a schism. But among the active members of a world, operative values concern matters much more specific than such an abstraction. The change to electric instruments violated some but not others of the set of specific values, so that one could encompass it, cognitively, with rather small adjustments in the set. The shift also at the same time had an impact on social relations, particularly relations among performers and among them and new sorts of technicians, which would be reflected in shifts in the specific values. Like observers, those participating are reading values as much out of accomplished actions, shaped by technology, as out of explicit guides.

Ancient Rome offers a striking example. It is one that speaks both to the importance of technology for realization of art and to how inextricably intertwined its effects are with socioeconomic issues and cultural history. I refer to the near-universal use of large fresco paintings to decorate Roman private homes. Not just one room but all rooms of any size had these wall paintings. The whole sense of current art worlds of painting would be turned topsy-turvy: The Romans could not speculate in paintings because they were permanently fixed; their artists had to follow the patron's right to guide the theme and contents of paintings; they would not understand the point of a museum or a gallery or even what a critic would be. But one could well imagine the importance that a strict academic system of training would have for them.

Art worlds can support dual mappings: social rhetoric into perception and, conversely, physical perception into rhetoric. One mapping predominates in the art of ancient Egypt, which possessed a sharply defined set of social grades. This is an art in which social perception dominates: Views that are socially related, even though physically disjunct, are combined into the same planar figures. Many of Picasso's paintings resemble Egyptian ones in this respect. This is presumably not because of similarity between modern French and ancient Egyptian class structures but rather because of choice by an artist decoupled from larger society.

Dutch paintings contrast with this: They are positive statements of identity by itself rather than as played off against or aligned with views of and from other identities. Pluralism in religion could have much the same effect. Another contrast is with the Renaissance painting of Italy, which is totally committed to unitary visual projection from a fixed physical point. At this fixed point is the observer, who thereby is helped to become the famous individual person of the Renaissance tradition, which continues to enfold us.

Witnessing Identity

The McDonald's example at the end of Chapter 2 reminds us of the impact of technology and that observable influences can spread from, and to, an art world through long and involuted chains of agency. To witness is to attest particular formations and celebrations of identities. A witness is a specialization of the "others" in agency, the general viewers. Thus witness introduces a fourth party to the triad of principal, agent, and public. Attesting takes place as commonly to announce ties (as in marriage or in joining a secret society) as to celebrate and announce actors (as by attending someone's graduation ceremony). Witnessing operationalizes boundary.

Witnessing may be a preliminary and summons to embedding into a further identity, into a further level of social actors, to which agency itself is a first step. The unease of agency relations helps to ease transition from interplay of agency and witnessing into a mutually disciplining configuration, a further identity. Artist, critic, distributor, and audience describe not only formal roles in large institutions but also tendencies evident in small-scale encounters witnessed by those interested in arts.

By starting with the Pre-Raphaelites, we began with embedding on a broad scale, of new class identity. Now consider embedding into literal tribal identities. A given ethnicity, such as Amerindian, is a social construction of identity, or congeries of identities, to which artworks can contribute.

> Once largely a conceptual and cultural construct, defined for Indians in terms of a sense of peoplehood and shared cultural practice, the tribe became a political and legal construct of the relationship to the institutions of American society. ... The process has been consolidational: the creation of formal political unities in place of multiple autonomous units. ... Especially in the reservation years there tended to be a decline of older, subtribal identities in favor of more comprehensive self-concepts. ... At the same time [there was] a process of fragmentation. The cultural and conceptual content of tribal identity was then largely the same for all members of the tribe, but is no longer so. Change in the focus of identity has been convergent: the tribe. But change in the content of identity has been divergent. Originally, autonomous political units were bound together in the conceptual framework of a single people. Now the roles are reversed: diverse concepts of peoplehood are bound together in a single political framework. ... In the twentieth century another, parallel development was taking place, different from tribalization but with equally profound political consequences: the gradual emergence and growth of a supratribal American Indian consciousness. The survival of the tribe required an *Indian* consciousness, the ability to act as Indians and thus confront federal policy on its own terms. ... At the same time, via peyotism and other movements, powwows, and networks of inter-tribal visiting, marriage and exchange, a "pan-Indian culture" had appeared: a set of symbols and activities, often derived from plains cultures ... ceremonies, styles of dress and dance, social events. ... But the identity embedded in "pan-Indian" cultural and social life ... often had the effect, even as it fostered a sense of Indianness, of reinforcing tribalism: the interaction itself sensitized groups to each other's distinctions. (Cornell 1988, pp. 102–105, 126)

One accessible artistic manifestation is the American Indian Dance Theatre, founded in 1987, which tours with a company of as many as thirty dancers and musicians from a dozen or more tribes. It presents traditional dances—including ceremonial and seasonal dances, spiritual and social dances—from many regions, which influence one another. One also encounters dances of individual expression. These performances are strikingly original with respect to ballet and other Euro-American dance and also afford scope for innovation and individual expression. Similarly, one encounters in the plastic art of Great Lakes tribes many themes and symbols of prairie and southwestern tribes.

Such rapid embedding of tribal identities goes on even though such embedding of identities through artworks and culture is neither an obvious nor an easily transferable process: "The 'artist' as the creative perceptor or interpreter of social situation is very much a historically determined figure in European society and is very difficult—and probably impossible—to define or find cross-culturally" (Greenhalgh and Megaw 1978, p. xviii). Nor is the embedding in this country of new identities with artworks confined to aboriginal tribes. In the 1930s a school of midwestern painters and muralists strove hard to project one or more identities for that region. One of them was Thomas Hart Benton, instructor of Jackson Pollock, who catapulted into the very different identity of abstract expressionism in postwar New York (examined at the end of Chapter 4). And southern writers continue to generate identity for that region, generation after generation.

Taste arises as outcome of and venue for witnessing. It presupposes and induces an overarching genre. Showing taste in a wedding gift is an example. Livery for servitors of nobles was another early form of taste in witnessing, within genre noted for invidious ostentation. Taste invokes boundaries.

Boundaries

Artworks are used widely in connection with boundary formation of all sorts. Social boundaries are always having to be constructed and negotiated and maintained, and artworks can contribute to this. Boundaries require and induce some further form of agency. Boundaries can mark rejection from but also embedding into larger social organization. Popular versus high art, and associated rhetorics, are a matter of boundaries.

Multiethnic situations are also partly translations out of, and back into, multiclass situations. And production of mural art can be, and most commonly is, on behalf of an elite rather than as agency from below. One finds examples in other multiethnic contexts, such as the ancient Assyrian empire, and multiclass contexts, such as Renaissance Italy.

A boundary for a population is a theory, or collection of theories, rather than some singular outcome, and it needs proclamation. One boundary gets recognized from, and as a frequency distribution of, sets of social actions. Another boundary is constructed out of stories to dampen impacts of network. One identity's boundary is another's neighborhood. Boundaries are not a free good, handily available to participant or observer.

A major shift of boundary for arts is when the audience itself becomes professional. This shift is as big as the earlier steps, when the performance factored out into being a specialized group once there was an audience. Art worlds result from such involutions. Boundary maintenance is as strict against amateurs as it is concerning separation from the laity-audience.

Specialization of art through agency into art worlds generates conundrums in the form of borders that depend on viewpoint. An art world looks different to differently situated artists inside. More subtle is network as population, as context for rather than mere juxtaposition of ties. The social fact of an art is mediated by its coming in definite art worlds that not only have memberships but also have locations and interconnections in networks among each other. Argument about the edges of memberships is of course not only possible but is half the fun for the people involved. And just who are involved—in particular who are artists versus who are critics or whatever across various worlds—is a good deal fuzzier around the edges than which artworks are involved.

The undoubted insight from the cruise ship as metaphor for art world, in Chapter 1, is only partial and can be misleading because it suggests sharp, clear boundaries. A better metaphor for production in arts may be the complex artworks one can see in New York art galleries today. These are constructions that collage together materials from very different realms—street scraps with velvet fustians—and thus produce tapestries whose constituents are themselves complex fabrics woven from diverse materials.

There are no neat boundaries to, or tidy rules about, art worlds. Consider an example. In New Mexico pueblos in 1900, making pottery was just a part of practical life for Pueblo people, who threw on some customary decoration. Art for identity was elsewhere, in ceremonial dance and costume. Then, beginning in the 1920s, tourism and its entrepreneurs reconceived and reconstrued not pottery as such, but rather the construct or idea of pottery. Doing pottery was to change from artisan production of objects, but it was not to change into production of a standard commodity. Rather, pottery was to become a live and evolving art, an expression of identities and creation. This is the converse of the earlier example of Indians supplying artworks to embed tribal identity into pan-Indian identity.

Pottery production became all tied up into an art world—or rather with a set of art worlds—along with painting and jewelry and other sorts of art production, which also were being induced and expanded as tourists were being lured to the region. The resulting mix owed little to aesthetics—even though many of the outputs of these art worlds are stunning. The resulting mix owed much both to historical accident and to social climbing.

Incoming new Anglos, only some from elite backgrounds, sought high standing alongside, or replacing, an existing landed and traditional elite, much of which was Hispanic. Introducing high art, as in pottery, is a vehicle for such social climbing. On the other side, local Pueblo potters had about then been facing disastrous competition from outside, from metal and later plastic as well as mass-produced ceramic pots and bowls. The more nimble of the potters responded to the chance to reconstrue pottery into art, high art for others' eyes. That is one example of how art world as agent may develop via narrative for control as a cause of rather than as a result of artistic production.

Arts in the Streets

Style establishes and defines itself in dual cultural and social profile. This conclusion from Chapter 3 is supported by the following dialogue about boundaries between leaders of an American street mural artist movement and a predecessor group. This dialogue also makes clear how much the art depends on the particular artists-as-agents even when they are fervently committed to the idea that they but reflect a people (a class, nation, ethnicity, whatever) in representing them:

> How could a foreword written by a veteran of the Mexican mural renaissance add anything worthwhile to this vibrant recital of the present deeds of American muralists? What we wrought in faith and hope happened half a century ago. .... I was moved as I scanned these pages, by the undeniable zest of youth.
>
> We too started on a crusade bent on toppling ivory towers once and for all. We too disdained the twin myths of personality and art for art. We would, through communal effort create anonymous masterpieces beamed to the people at large. ... Our youthful dread—and, as I gather, yours also—was that, come a potbellied middle age, some of us would weaken, shed anonymity, meekly take their place in the stable of artists of some art dealer.
>
> Up went our scaffolds. Up went masons and painters, troweling, frescoing, desecrating these hallowed places—or so opined men of taste. The revolution, even before the end of the shooting affray, had found its image.
>
> Both our groups violently broke loose from orthodox modern styles. In our day that was Cubism. The Mexicans were well versed in it, but a different language had to be forged to plead Mexico's case before the world. ... I now realize that Parisian Cubism remains at the core of our murals, its angles softened mostly by the deep respect in which we held the taste of our own brand of street critics, mostly Indian villagers come to the capital to sell their handmade wares.
>
> The official art you are reacting against is quite unlike the one we knew. New York has now replaced Paris, so it is said, as the navel of the art world. Splashes and blobs are "in." Sophisticated Happenings partake of the ballet. ... This thinning of the boundaries between the fine arts and the performing arts plays a role in your apparently casual concern as regards the preservation of your murals.
>
> Clear though your motives are to yourselves, a time may come when onlookers will have lost the key to their meaning. For the very reason that your murals document strictly contemporary attitudes, they deserve to last and enter history, as medieval shrines did, as Mexican murals do. (Cockcroft, Weber, and Cockcroft 1977, pp. xv–xviii)

Art worlds increasingly emerge and fission (and fuse) along lines of ethnicity or class or gender rather than of sensory modality or aesthetic dogma. Street murals in Chicago were an early and forceful example:

> This vital movement ... has produced hundreds upon hundreds of large-scale wall paintings in less than a decade. ... The mural movement has been a unique experiment in the possibility of a democratic mass culture that is public, authentic, and activist, in opposition to the manipulative culture of alienated spectator-consumers produced by the commercial bourgeois media and the equally alienated obscurantist "high" culture of the elite institutions. ... Only a handful of established art critics have given the community murals attention. ...
>
> The vitality of the contemporary mural movement casts a new light on the central problem of twentieth-century art. This central problem is not the destruction of the collectible art object by non-salability, by environmental scale, or by participatory creation, all of which are characteristics that the new murals share with Minimal and kinetic art, Conceptual art and Happenings, etc. It is the problem of the audience. Despite the promotion of art as spectacle, status symbol, and hobby, visual art has persistently lacked a true audience in this country. (Cockcroft, Weber, and Cockcroft 1977, pp. xix–xxii)

Weber, of this trio of authors, had been a founder in 1970 of the Chicago Mural Group, the formation of which had been inspired by the *Wall of Respect*, created in Chicago's South Side in 1967 on a derelict building by twenty-odd black artists of the Organization for Black American Culture.

> Much of their work peeled badly after a year or two. Some sections simply grouped rows of portraits and photos, whereas others were filled with fully developed compositions. To facilitate the work, figures were grouped by fields of accomplishment. (Cockcroft, Weber, and Cockcroft 1977, p. 2)
>
> It was not exactly a mural, nor was it simply a gallery in the streets. Its purpose was not to bring aesthetic enlightenment to an area too poor to support even a nominal art fair, but to use art publicly to express the experience of a people. It was a collective act, an event. (p. 3)

Both similar and different are the themes, colors, and symbolism of the public murals produced under sponsorship by Chicano groups in the Southwest:

> George died of an overdose. It was in his memory that his brothers Samuel, Albert, and Carlos Leyba painted a children's mural and organized Artes Guadalupanos de Aztlán ... a contract was entered into with one of the *barrio* organizations in charge of distributing federal appeasement money while local government did its thing with urban renewal. Six weeks, $3,600, nineteen addicts, and four murals later ... an exhibit of canvases, furniture,

leathercrafts, tinwork, needle-point, clothes, quilts, and sculpture to show what we had uncovered in the *barrios*. Gone were the frantic days of getting it together when people painted what seemed right; now we needed a god-damned philosophy. ... One thing was clear: We couldn't go on doing pretty pictures of zoo animals and pastel Aztec gods ... an independent slate was thrown together to run in the upcoming city elections ... our next piece of money came from their campaign funds. ... The site for this mural was a tool shed owned by Roman Salazar, who was running for mayor, on Canyon Road ... *the* "arts and crafts road" in Santa Fe. ... Suddenly, we Chicanos ... *we* had come around and decided to let these devils know we were still alive.

It's been argued that our murals are American art in fact because we're Americans, and that my statements on art in America don't make sense. But then again, we've never been known to call ourselves Americans; that nationality was laid on us by the existence of imaginary borders created by war-mongering colonists. We are, as a matter of cultural fact, Mexicans. (Geronimo Garduño, quoted in Cockcroft, Weber, and Cockcroft 1977, pp. 203–208)

This mural art is very much bound up with proclamation of identity as ethnicity, if not nationality; it is not supposed to be about career and liveli-hood as a painter. Such proclamations are, however, contested, as when Garduño tells of their projected mural on the Student Union of New Mex-ico Highlands University being blocked by the art teacher who rallied art students to preempt with their own work these outsiders who hadn't paid tuition. Mural art does in fact contribute to career as organizer and in poli-tics.

African American Arts and Literature

The most significant task of embedding in the United States is of Afri-can Americans, and there will be found the greatest scope for narrative creativity and witnessing identity. A few diverse efforts will be surveyed. Art historians may begin with cultural roots in Africa:

Most African carvings are in sharp contrast to the traditions of European art. Whoever it was who first saw, and made his fellow artists see, the power of this strange, remote and in a sense timeless art opened up a rich vein in the world's goldmine of creative art—to all of us, in due course. And it looks as though Matisse and Vlaminck, two very different men, share the honours in France. In Germany it was the painter Kirchner, also in 1904. (The first book to discuss African carvings as art was *Negerplastik* by the German art critic Carl Einstein, published in 1915. In 1916 in New York, Alfred Stieglitz's mag-azine *291* printed an essay on "African Negro Art: its influence on modern art," written by Marius de Zayas. Stieglitz had shown African sculpture at the "291" Gallery in 1914; de Zayas was presenting New York's second African exhibition at his recently opened Modern Gallery.) (Lynton 1980, pp. 29–30)

But more commonly in such art discussions in the United States one begins from race, as in the 1920s era of the Harlem Renaissance:

> What I have wanted to do in this book is to illuminate, through a searching look at this one instance of Negro self-consciousness, that essential condition of American life which has caused such periodic racial identity crises ... Afro-Americans have inhabited a special ethnic province within provincial America. They have been perplexed by the desire to emulate the European-entranced white Americans. ... For both black and white Americans art has been the more problematic because of these provincial uncertainties. ... One thing is very curious, except for Langston Hughes, none of them took jazz—the new music—seriously ... most Harlem intellectuals aspired to *high* culture. (Huggins 1972, pp. 8–9, 5)

The Harlem Renaissance centered on writing (prose and poetry), but I want to turn from that and jazz, touched on again later, to the less well known black presence in visual art.

The decline of Harlem leaves no unambiguous center for black cultural life, which handicaps visual arts more than others. Even now, not every major American city has a gallery devoted to black art. New York has had one, Cinque, for two decades; it was brought into being through the narrative creativity of three black artists. Boston has had one for as long or longer than has New York because of the enterprise of a pair of Radcliffe College friends, one black and one white, now married respectively to a federal judge and a Harvard Law School professor. The latter's Cambridge home, at 17 Wendell Street, a quiet, shady street, has become a significant gallery—by appointment only—for black artists and their collectors. This gallery embodies a narrative creativity.

As in the Isabella Stewart Gardner Museum on the Fenway in Boston, artworks are shown here in a setting familiar to us—that of a lived-in home. At openings, the new paintings are proudly placed in the living room, dining room, and entryway, but many other pieces are fitted in on staircase walls, upstairs halls, and, in clement weather, on easels in the gardens. And you can always pull aside Jane Shapiro or Connie Brown to show you some prints from great horizontal drawers in the study.

Yes, the ambiance is one not only of culture but of luxury, even down to the canapés at the receptions (by written invitation only). And many of the paintings will surprise you. Some are social realism, some are superb Haitian primitives, and I have from there a wonderful watercolor of a great blues singer performing at Harlem's Apollo Theatre. But one show at 17 Wendell was entirely of high artworks depicting high society among African Americans: They wore nothing but tuxedos and long gowns, at balls and in champagne receptions on estates, just where one should expect to find an elite crowd.

The painter of this socialite show, a young man named Rob Freeman, had moved from being a full-time public school art teacher to being a part-time private school teacher as his success rose. Indeed his success rose to the point where he accepted a better-known gallery as an agent, which was hard on the initial gallery. Connie Brown gave me her view of the basic economics: Monotype, prints, silkscreens, and so on, which are not much less expensive than watercolors, do not make much money. Paintings are the real payoff—a given painting can quadruple or even go up tenfold or more in price the minute it has been shown in a museum.

Conundrums from competitive striving create stress for black artists too. Here are comments written to me concerning a 17 Wendell Street show by a course student, Michael Goodwin, who had showed keen analytic intelligence and who himself was developing into a painter of considerable accomplishment: "Small watercolors by Bearden were selling for $4,000. A new painter at the gallery was represented by three large oil paintings, major-sized canvases according to current standards. These large oils sold for, at most, $850. I would be tempted to make aesthetic judgments and say that the oils by the new painter were better than Bearden's playful watercolors."

17 Wendell Street is an upscale gallery. It doesn't have the constant struggle of raising the huge monthly nut to pay for commercial space in an accessible location, as the gallery Cinque does. A different narrative creativity was required for Cinque. Aside from one part-time place way up in Harlem, Cinque is the only gallery in Manhattan entirely for African-American art, even though hundreds of galleries dot SoHo, TriBeCa, and nearby neighborhoods, not to mention the dozens of sleek midtown Madison Avenue galleries. (There is an African-American gallery or two in Brooklyn plus two over in New Jersey exurbs.)

The very name "Cinque" is an insider name: Cinque was a successful black mutineer of yore. The triumvirate who founded it includes one painter whose works any museum would delight to acquire, Romare Bearden (who was also represented by 17 Wendell Street and a number of other galleries in Houston and Los Angeles and abroad). Cinque's present location, on the fifth floor of 560 Broadway at Prince Street, costs about $3,000 a month, and yet their prices can be as low as $100 for a monoprint and they take much less than the usual 40 or 50 percent gallery commission. In the words of the brochure: "After twenty years of existence, there is still a great need for Cinque gallery. In spite of the proliferation of art galleries and museums, too often minority artists are totally excluded from the mainstream art market. It is painful to read in the New York Times that an artist of the caliber of Mel Edwards has not had a major New York Gallery show."

There are signs that the exclusion is declining along with preoccupation with same-race subjects and race-oriented topics. During the time that I was taking my sociology of art students on visits to 17 Wendell Street, one of their longtime artists, Benny Andrews, who does soft sculpture reminiscent of Claes Oldenberg, became head of visual arts for the National Endowment for the Arts. From 17 Wendell Street I acquired two studies of elderly women by Edward McCluney, and I treasure an abstract monoprint by JoAnne McFarland, acquired from Cinque. After the latter acquisition, I was able to go see more of McFarland's work at another gallery in SoHo.

In literature it may remain harder to separate art from social content and racial background. Reception may be experienced more in terms of groups. In particular, reviewing may work differently, and it is easier to analyze reviewing according to social content. I quote one study, by a black prelaw student, that contrasted reviews of novels on racial themes published in the 1950s, half before the Brown decision and half later. A total of 161 books (out of 400) that were reviewed by at least two of five white journals and four black journals regarded as elite were coded into nine thematic categories as well as to favorability of the review:

> The percentage figures indicate the special interest that black periodicals accorded race novels. ... Black reviews collectively demonstrate greatest interest in those novels in which the black characters have the greatest autonomous control. ... White publications concentrated on books about altruistic white characters, martyred for the cause of integration. ... Whites reviewed slavery novels more frequently than integration novels in which Blacks share at least an equal part in the process. ... Each racial set of publications gave most favorable reviews to a category of particular interest to members of the other race: black publications favored the White Epics, and the white periodicals championed the Black Epics. And yet, each institution devoted very little column space to the literature in its "most favored" category. In black publications, for example, the average novel within the White Epics category received less than a quarter of the coverage it could possibly have received. ... Relative to the other categories, the black reviewers evaluation deems White Epics superb, while the white reviewers quality score indicates that it is mediocre. ... Yet, there is evidence which suggest the influence of "empathy" in the appraisal of white critics as well. ... Before 1954 white critics rated novels about race higher than black critics. ... Towards the end of the decade, the white reviewer means increased for novels primarily concerning black lifestyles, and decreased radically for novels primarily about white life-

styles. ... Overall, black authors received more favorable treatment from the white critics. ... The black evaluations indicate that there was a great deal of controversy among black reviewers about the merits of Confrontation novels. The degree of controversy manifested by black critical response, compared to the striking agreement suggested by white response, may again be evidence of the schism in the black community. ... The level of controversy indicated by black response may also be linked to the apparent inconsistency in the quality of the novels encompassed by this category. ... Perhaps, then, whatever peculiarities of this theme which render writing about it difficult also render appraising it difficult. ... Yet, white response indicates improvement in the consistency of the novels and fuller accord among the reviewers toward the end of the decade. Moreover, white critics evidently witnessed a positive change in the quality of "protest" literature while Blacks noted a negative change. A good case might be made, then, for the suggestion that *Brown* and all of its attendant consequences for Blacks, actually deepened the schism in the black community. (Robinson 1979, pp. 50–67)

Analyses of African or of Caribbean writing, and of its appraisal by reviewers, even in England, suggest that in America race may more pervade writing and its appraisal.

Storage and Canons

Canonical measures—which truly measure what is agreed to be of central value—are a dream in business as in art, but they are a necessary dream. Some resulting paradoxes were already discussed in Chapter 3 around measures of performance. Canons are all the more important just because they are necessarily flawed and changing. It is only in the scaffolding provided by canons that particular lines of artwork can generalize, that whole genres and schools of art arise, and new arts factor out.

Transformations of arts into art worlds became possible only after the development of storage for production, whether it be with oral or written or physical embodiment. Only together with storage, for a given art and social context, does the notion of choosing what to perform arise. Only then can one perceive art as a stock of possibilities as well as a flow of reproductions and thereby induce criticism. "Storage" is really just shorthand for enlarged kinds of agency.

Memory is insufficient to buttress choice, even within a lifetime and even when developed in a specialized way, as for music or poetic declamation. Storage for art is in symbols, and it ranges from entirely physical, as in a statue, to a remembered pattern of signification. Throughout the range, art storage requires socially understood coding. It is choice of what to perform that right away leads, via invidious orderings, to the appearance of authorship and composition as constructs.

Thus appears the background for canons of excellence to evolve. And the other face of such a canon is reputation, both of individual artworks and of artists. Reputation implies full recognition of a duality between, on the one hand, artists—whether author of the stored version or performer of the live ceremony—and, on the other hand, artworks. Codification, when turned into transmissible, storable enactment, is the key to arts that can be both widespread and serious.

Turn to a study of Renaissance revivals on the London stage (developed further in the next chapter):

> The creation and re-creation of meaning is possible because of the formal properties of cultural objects. An artist formally organizes individual and social experience, embodying it in a symbolic medium that will enable it to be communicated to others. Such formal embodiment gives cultural works a fixed quality, a permanence, that does not exist in real-life experience. ... In "real life," experiences appear to be random, continuous, inexplicable, and morally unsatisfying. Cultural objects, in contrast, seem purposeful, have clearly delineated beginnings and outcomes, satisfy expectations, and hence are immensely pleasing. ... Literary quality depends in large part on the elegant articulation of archetypes, as when Vindici uses the silkworm to express the vanity of human life. Such striking and multivocal images helped ensure the preservation of certain Renaissance plays in the literary canon, after their topicality helped them to be popular and get published in the first place. ...
>
> While society poses questions that culture addresses, the cultural archive is not ransacked for the best possible answer to some current question. Instead, preservation, and then accessibility arrange the cultural archive in such a way that certain cultural works will be encountered more readily than others. *This stacking of the deck is what characterizes a canon.* (Griswold 1986, pp. 208–210, emphasis supplied)

The Bible is an example of a canon made fixed. More commonly there is some continuing exit and entry to a canon, as a sort of rolling library. Dance (like drama) and to some extent music have remained especially arts of performance, whose principal result is to define audience, but some change is at hand. Because first music, and then more recently dance, acquired reproducible and transmissible codings, they can be stored better. They thus become possessed of tighter canons and can be taken seriously across a broader horizon.

A canon is cultural counterpart to a theatre revival in that it is a response to specific pressures from larger social formations. In Europe the long and difficult evolution of artistic imagery for the theological construct of purgatory is one example. Another is the Pre-Raphaelite search for earlier canons that they could take over and adapt to a new situation, thus attempting revivals in visual arts and poetry.

Storage, the possibility of storing and reproducing art performance, has differential impacts on various species of artworks and artists. The most important is that the more rigid the canon and limited the array of choices for performance, the more significant is the performer. With Shakespearean drama, the actor is all. With the symphony orchestra institution, with its narrow and fixed menu of classics, the conductor is all.

Proposition 5.1. The tighter the scoring in music—the more rigid the conventions—the more the composer loses control and the more, paradoxically, the performer gains status through control.

A vivid characterization of the complexities that this proposition addresses can be found in opera. Along with storage must come scholars, who compound relations between composer and performer (and conductor, librettist, and a host of others). A case in point is the Metropolitan Opera's revival in 1990 of *Semiramide,* a noncomic opera composed in 1820 by Rossini and based on a play by Voltaire. A distinguished music scholar defends his aid with the opera's score from rebuke by the *New York Times*'s music critic:

> The Metropolitan Opera needed a full score for the conductor (one containing all orchestral and vocal parts), piano-vocal scores for singers and rehearsal pianists, and individual orchestral parts from which violinists, bassoonists and timpanists could play. ... In the nineteenth century only piano-vocal scores were printed. [In the intervening years] as each new performance made different demands, extra pages were added to (or omitted from) the La Scala score, and orchestral parts were ... pasted together in new configurations. ... When an opera composer expects his score to circulate in manuscript, as Rossini did, he tends to be less precise, since copyists' manuscripts are prepared in haste and rarely reflect accurately the composer's text. ... Although a great deal of ornamentation used in *Semiramide* by early nineteenth-century singers survives, none was adopted by the cast, all of whom developed, either by themselves or with the help of their coaches, ornamentation they considered suitable for their own voices. ...
>
> The crucial element for the Metropolitan's budget was to get the theatre emptied before midnight ... between fifteen minutes and a half hour of music needed to be eliminated. ... We can identify four categories of cuts: (1) Many of the recitative cuts taken at the Metropolitan were already being made in the 1820s. (2) The massive choral interventions ... lend an air of solemnity and monumentality to the opera. Dramatic needs, scenic needs, and judgments about musical value were invoked. As a result, three identically constructed choruses were handled in three different ways. ... A listener familiar with Rossini's style but not with this particular composition would have had no reason to think the score was anything but intact. (3) Conductor, scholar, administrators: all of us looked longingly at Idreno's first-act aria, a full eight minutes toward our temporal goal. The role of Idreno, however, marked the

debut at the Metropolitan Opera of Chris Merritt, a fine Rossini tenor. He was hired on the understanding that he would sing both arias, and he was going to sing both arias. (4) Ultimately, we settled for a series of internal cuts in each piece. Some cuts of repeated passages were made in duets, largely in recognition of the sheer endurance required for the soprano, mezzo-soprano and bass to perform this score. ... Opera is about people as well as about art; the singer's will could not simply be ignored. ... The world of the theater is not a place where one pays obeisance to a written score—and musicologists who truly love opera would have it no other way. ... A certain puzzlement at the formal (even static) dramaturgy ... in such sharp contrast with the precepts of the Romantic theater underlying most nineteenth-century Italian opera. (Gossett 1992, pp. 32–51)

One can illustrate Proposition 5.1 in college teaching also: The standardized introductory, large lecture course puts a premium on rhetorical variation to the detriment of the innovative scientist or scholar who may shine in seminar format, where the conventions are looser because the material is less known. In music an application is comparisons of music within Manhattan: midtown (big symphony), downtown (avant-garde), and uptown (in-between academic).

Agency in Networks

Any agency itself can be proclaimed and celebrated through artworks: This may be a king asserting his presence in a plenipotentiary through the latter's royal robes. It may, on the contrary, be when the agent asserts self-identity, as being, say, the agent for the greatest concert pianists.

Art worlds themselves have evolved through these specializations in artworks by which they announce others' identities and agencies. Sets of art producers become reified, as do sets of consumers; altogether they make up an art world. Artists often struggle within, yet also depend upon, several overlapping art worlds in order to create or perform.

Agency thus is effected through networks of relations. Each artist gets involved through ties into many networks, which thus become art worlds themselves. Social networks link artists not only to each other, and to various patrons, but also to a variety of other lay organizations and communities quite aside from kinship and business ties that may have little bearing on artwork.

During this process, artistic agents, in turn, take to acquiring agents of their own. But agents, over time, may also band together to arrogate to themselves much of the independence that their principals started off with. The major impact of this continuing transformation of agency is still further erosion in the coding of meaning into and from some particular, tangible social formation.

Meanings become more labile. Packages of alternative artworks supplant fixed folk themes. The paradox is that agency, which is conceived and reported as a matter of coupling, in fact is a primary decoupler, as in separating actresses from the shaping of a play as artwork.

Agency is shaped within the networks of a population by and in terms of the principle of structural equivalence. Obviously, those who need agents of some particular kind come to be structurally equivalent in the social position of being principals and may use the same concrete agent—as when several kings use a Velázquez to paint their portraits—and the very term *agents* denotes a converse position of structural equivalence, say, as portrait painters. The real point about structural equivalence, however, is that the common desire for some agency arises from the structural equivalence of your positions in networks, *not* from your closeness.

A king is much closer to his prime minister, his generals, and his huntmaster than he is to other kings, but it is only the other kings who seek out fabulous portrait painters. This is exactly because the kings are in—within some broader interacting context such as medieval Europe or Mughal India—the same sort of network position from which they seek to induce awe and admiration in all the others in their respective portions of the networks. Or take a homelier example: Teenage girls resemble one another, not their mothers, in desiring poetic exaltations.

Uncovering and tracing agency is an activity that forces identity back into focus. Who the presidential candidate is becomes shaped by writers or videographers locating his agents, for speechwriting or for play. Artworks can help agency seize hold as a construct in the minds of actors, whether they are involved or just watching the given celebration. Agency can be transposed in many ways such that there is displacement of the identity being expressed and celebrated in artworks. Such displacement is the central theme common to what is called "modern" across our spectrum of art worlds since the late nineteenth century, particularly avant-garde work.

Agency can lead to transference and reflecting of identity. Agency is confined, from the principal's perspective, to the third or fourth senses of identity, whereas, from the agent's perspective, agency concerns either the second or the third senses of identity (see Chapters 1 and 3). When some set of agents captures control, when agents wrest control away from their principals, the anatomy of agency is changed thereby: The agents tend to move into identities of the fourth sense, whereas the principals are being put back on the interpretive shelf in being confined to the third sense of identity.

Artists–including critics or directors—may also become the art products. That is, artists themselves may become icons in terms of which to cel-

ebrate and account identities. Thus artists within an art world may be sur-
rogate identities, and in that sense agents, for quite various outside actors
and social formations. This is seen all the time for teenagers and their favorite performing groups in the media. And everyone experiences this in
seeing advertising representations of identities and ties that derive from
art worlds of one sort and another. The producing artist, whether of objects or performances, also may herself or himself become an indirect producer such as a critic or director. Agency gets involved. Such transformations happen during the cumulation and amalgamation of chains of
agency that go into an art world.

Alliances, as well as divisions, over recognition and over content get
expressed in these networks of agency. These are alliances and divisions
that cross over into the artists' audiences. Stories and their rhetorics
emerge within social networks from interacting control projects. Seeking
control is the source of the energies of identities spinning out social networks and coping with each other and ecology. Stereotyped stories
emerge as part of relations settling down enough to yield any social network. Once art through agency enters, more possibilities are generated for
the sets of stories that can be used. The contracts called genres (Chapter 3)
evolve between audience and artists as to the vocabulary of celebration;
examples in theatre are developed at the end of the next chapter.

GUIDE TO FURTHER READING

Campbell (1987) develops how in the Victorian era romanticism and rationalism played off each other in a new aesthetics of individualism.
Rostovtzeff's views on aesthetics for ancient art (1930) and Runciman's for
Byzantine art (1971) bracket those of Chambers (1928) for Roman and
Greek art. A very different aesthetics of riches is argued by Schama (1987)
for the Dutch in their own hegemonic period. Boime (1987) complements
for visual arts Williams (1977) on the Marxist class approach to aesthetics.

John Dewey long ago devoted a whole volume, *Art as Experience,* to aes-
theticism as pragmatic philosophy.

Waddington (1970) is wonderfully specific on the interrelations between modern painting and the sciences in the twentieth century.

Nissen (1988) surveys early pottery.

A Metropolitan Museum of Art catalogue (1968) surveys fresco technique and so also gives background to the survey of Roman painting by
Ling (1991).

Richard Sennett (e.g., 1977) comments on the effects of New York's architecture and ecology on visual impressions, as does Huxtable (1986).
And Zukin (1989) provides a trenchant analysis of the interaction of com-

mercial real estate pressures and city ordinances in the SoHo and neighboring loft districts as mediated through social activism by artists and
their supporters.

Cornell (1988) is definitive on the current American Indian resurgence.
Christian (1981) illuminates religious expressions of local identities of an
earlier era. The ancient Inca culture and its arts sustained an elaborate empire of subordinate ethnic groups, yet it did not even have wheels or writing. Their records were kept as knottings in strings of various colors,
called *quipu*, which perhaps they saw as art along with their ornaments of
gold (Ascher and Ascher 1981).

Dauber (1990) traces the "invention" of pottery as high art in the Southwest.

Cockcroft, Weber, and Cockcroft (1977) provide a brilliantly illustrated
account of the War on Poverty heyday of street murals. Lachmann (1988)
explores how street graffiti in New York became assimilated into the
dealer-critic system of Chapter 6.

The reader edited by Addison Gayle (1972) includes views other than
Huggins's (1972) on the Harlem Renaissance and many views on blacks in
theatre. Charles Robinson reported his findings in a thesis (1979), which
won the Albert Fulton Prize of his department. A parallel methodology is
shown, though with less detailed tabular reports, in a study of cross-
national reviewing published by the Swedish sociologist Rosengren
(1968). Griswold (1981) has analyzed Caribbean and West African novels
and critical reactions thereto.

Gilmore (1987) lays out the interaction of locational and musical conventions in the Manhattan music world.

My own recent book, *Identity and Control* (1992a), develops a systematic
approach to identities and social networks within institutions, and it is
generous with references and examples. I also recently published a short
account of agency as control in social networks (1992b).

FIELDWORK IDEAS

It is time to take a more abstract and analytic look at fieldwork. The key
difficulties come from interviewing and otherwise learning about the people involved. Alienation is the core requirement for effectiveness in such
fieldwork. You are already, and have long been, steeped in common sense,
that is, in hegemonic understandings of the social around you. That
greatly detracts from the possibility of fresh observation guided by a new
and presumably more independent and scientific frame of constructs.

Just going to a scene foreign to your immediate experience—say, a
painting studio—is some help because it is a form of alienation. Adopting

an explicit role as observer is the next step in alienation. This step offers some sense of liberation, as you have discovered if you served as reporter for a school paper—or perhaps even took on your principal for a story.

The conscious assumption of a role, and even the mere use of the term *observer*, give protection both vis-à-vis imprecations from others and vis-à-vis your own insecurities. It helps further when the role is assigned to you—"I'm doing a course exercise." An observer role can surround you with a protective bubble in other people's eyes, and at the same time it can unleash some unexplored aspects of your own self.

Some alienation is necessary for fieldwork, but so is some empathy, some ability to perceive through others' perceptions. To reach some balance of empathy and alienation, you need to bring ingenuity and flexibility to the role. Exactly what that means should develop around your own style as a person—brashness for the exposé reporter, quietness for the participant-observer. What that means depends as well on the details of the situation.

Go find out by trying.

1. Begin with a simple example from your own past. Try digging out your high school yearbook. How do the themes of this chapter bear on it? Develop some speculations and then (if it is spring) go watch and talk to some yearbook student staff and faculty advisers about their use of arts. (Hints: Surely both photography and layout are arts, and many of the composite identities in the yearbook may be from art worlds.)

2. If you can find two street murals, describe and contrast them with two outdoor sculptures. (Hints: In New York head for lower Manhattan, and in other cities head for a ghetto area or look for graffiti on a large scale.)

3. Take a stab at how processes of differentiation and disdain affect production and reception of artworks by developing an account of graffiti as art in your locale. Lachmann (1988) gives valuable guidance.

MEASURES AND MODELS

It is helpful to have models for description by narrative combined with quantitative measures. A number of case studies relevant to art production can be ordered from the Harvard Graduate School of Business Administration. They supply, besides a number of ideas on techniques of fieldwork and how to measure, a sensible introduction to thinking about commercial aspects of art worlds. These studies range from a Danish pottery (cite Intercollegiate Case Clearinghouse 9-371-288) to an American architecture firm (9-582-061) and a symphony orchestra (9-375-340) and a repertory theatre (9-580-133).

6

Paths Through Broadway

I turn to fine-grained analysis of one system of interlinked artistic productions, American theatre. The central problematic for any performance art is the audience, a construct that is shaped by critics and other observers out of myriad concrete audiences. Or rather, some hierarchical levels of such audiences become recognized, each level being, in different ways and to differing extents, an arbiter of reputational success and material support. Such differentiation plays back into the ranks of art world members, performers, and others. This differentiation seems to me better established and more fine-grained for theatre systems than for the cinema systems touched on in Chapter 3.

The point is that narratives and other artworks grow out of and, to be heard, must interleave with tangible social mechanisms such as audiences. And such mechanisms breed and require larger systems of social agency and support, which may reach beyond particular art worlds. This chapter maps out one such institutional system, the one for current American theatre. As this example will make clear, these are not tidy systems designed as consciously and explicitly as is, say, a new subway system. History and accident and particular larger social contexts are prime influences.

I begin with the evolution of theatre more generally, before and outside of Broadway and America.

From Sacred to Market

Sacred performance and art come into being together. A tribe owns and holds as sacred to itself not just the products of art but their very meanings. The same was still true with temples as they and their priests came to represent the religious life of different ethnic groups, within early city-states in Mesopotamia and elsewhere. Evolution into performance came about as the specialization of sacredness. Specialization leads on from ceremonial by priests on into more sophisticated use of art in religion as well as on into freestanding arts of performance.

For archaic times the distinction between priest and king is hard to make, and both statuses grow out of sacred performances of tribes. A king

is there as much to define and celebrate communal identity as to formulate, much less have any apparatus to carry out, "rational" policy. At the
same time, a priest often is an organizer and effector, whose ministrations
are effective steps toward achieving control as, and for, a joint communal-
ity. Director and actor are in this same line of descent. Sacred and profane
become intertwined in performance art as in social life, with which it
shares many social mechanisms of agency.

Take as a starting point the drama of Attic Greece. Put into today's
terms, it combined religious ceremony with opera, which in turn equals
drama + chorus + dance + orchestra. The equation becomes:

PERFORMANCE = MASKS + PLOT + CEREMONY

Such performance is a basis and training for coordination into social organization of some complexity. Indeed, such performance inhibits innovation, inhibits creation of new work; instead it typically provides setting
and occasion for the virtuoso performer.

Somehow, however, possibly through carryover from stylized sports
competitions, Greek drama came to use competitions to encourage new
stagings. Eventually the composition of new plays was not only allowed
but encouraged, although these competitions always retained a flavor of
religion. The modern successors of Attic drama include opera and musical
comedy as well as theatre.

Theatre in modern times has assimilated to the idioms of market economy and competition. Jean-Christophe Agnew writes: "Market and Theater. What different meaning these words evoke ... ledger books (versus)
gallant heroes ... every sort of material need (versus) more symbolic, less
tangible human longings. Markets and Theaters have stood as worlds
apart. ... Theatricality is to the serious person of business what
commerciality is to the serious person of the theater: a threat to the foundation of trust on which each enterprise stands" (Agnew 1986, p. ix). Thus
begins an analysis of the evolution of our theatre since its Elizabethan beginnings. But in fact, "What bound the market and theater together were
the same peculiar experiential properties that set them apart from other
kinds of exchange. Owing to the special and often implicit conditions of
belief and accountability that operate within their bounds, the two institutions have for long periods of time stood at some remove from the rules
and rituals of ordinary social intercourse" (Agnew 1986, p. x).

Agnew goes on to argue a change since 1550 in how theatre and market
stood apart, *together*.

Commercial and legal inventions did little to resolve (and much to aggra-
vate) the larger, more refractory questions of personal identity and accountability arising within an increasingly placeless and timeless market process.

... How one's self, one's motives, and one's relations were to be represented in a world where traditional reference points were increasingly subject to the market's overarching rule of full commensurability. ... How or where human acts of representation were to be anchored in the face of such detached and impersonal abstractions as exchange value. These were social and cultural problems and as such were left to the theater (among other institutions) to take up during this period. It is thus in the evolution of the theater and *its* conventions or representation—its theatricality—that I trace a protracted struggle.

The early modern stage did more than reflect relations occurring elsewhere; it modeled and in important respects materialized those relations. ... I am concerned above all to chart the changing formal and informal resemblances between commercial and theatrical convention over time. (Agnew 1986, pp. x–xii)

Agnew pays little heed to the insides of drama art worlds, which in their intricacies resemble facets of the worlds of industrial markets. Look behind the curtain for organization principles that hold also in business firms. For example:

Proposition 6.1. Alternate generations are allies.

The prototype here is grandparents doting on their grandchildren and all conspiring to evade the parents' discipline, just as department heads and presidents may gang up on vice-presidents. One can transpose this proposition to any ladder of rungs in standings. There are endless illustrations in theatre lore. One ladder in our commercial theatre is angels—producers—directors—stars—leads—cast—and audience or backstage. There is always some arbitrariness in distinguishing levels or rungs. For example, why need directors be separated from producers, and where do brokers, or costumers, or the orchestra fit in? But this is as true for business.

Within American commercial theatre, reputations and income are distributed far more unequally than in large industry because the organization of theatre more resembles that of an earlier era of short-lived entrepreneurial firms in rapidly changing markets. Our world of symphony orchestras exhibits hierarchies as in firms, but the star system has a toehold for soloists and conductors and seems to also be penetrating further and further into the subsidized worlds of performance arts in Europe.

Audience and Performance

The processes by which arts evolve and an art develops are charged with anxiety. Performance is a celebration of identities and is an accounting of relations between identities. The second evolutionary step into what today we call art worlds is when performance first factored out to a specialized group. But prior to this second step toward recognizing artists was the creation of an audience.

The older and continuing alternative to audience in tribal times was when those receiving were just everybody and thus anybody. The alternative is when performers were also and simultaneously the audience. Audiences came into being as independent formations particularly in multiethnic and multitribal situations and often with recognition of homelier divisions by age, by kin group, by gender, and by hamlet. Many such manifestations combined to bring about this basic step in evolution of art worlds, of specialization to audience as a distinct role.

Then longer practice and rehearsal efforts are stimulated, such effort being sustained through material contributions by others. These are further intermediate steps on the path to artists in permanently specialized groups. Performance comes to evoke and demand more than passive reception. One of today's end points to this evolution is artists having their peers as the audience. This is the notion, dear to professionals, of artists being best able to appreciate artists, much as it is scientists who now are the audience for scientists, doctors for doctors, lawyers for lawyers, and so on.

Recognition comes in arts today according to what distinct audiences watch and hear, once they recognize themselves as so watching and hearing. Success is not registered until artworks get separated out by audiences' recognition, as that spreads around through social networks. Audience requires some sense of duty (still so, as in parents attending a school play). Audience requires some sense of aptness (it is for the young to watch puppets).

Specialization into audience thus precedes and controls specialization of performance, a truth that is not a favorite of performers. The fascination of performance is immediacy—the intensity of present involvement that it brings about in audience as well as performer. This is also immediacy in a historical sense. That is, the fascination need not depend on or be changed by sophistication in experience, by learned knowledge of the past, whether local or general.

When one probes this immediacy, its root seems to be the paradox that performance embodies, which is the basic contradiction of human action: the contradiction between taking action and enacting social pattern. Performance is enactment of something preset. This truth begins in the religious ceremony, which is ancestor to all performance. But performance is also fresh action in that it is new creation of the social. The contradiction is unresolvable, which is exactly where it gets its energy.

Theatre can be seen as practical theory of human social life, purely social life. There is no acting without audience so that acting is a social ceremony, in which the audience itself is dramatized. In detail we can observe that body movement (body language) is of decisive importance in acting. Exits and entrances are central to theatre technique, part of creating the symbolic mask that replaces the literal mask of Attic drama.

This suggests why stage theatre continues to be more significant for the actor than any film or television work. It is no surprise that the theory of director as author, and more generally director as central figure in the art, comes in with cinema. The cinema director is the person who "does" the entrances and exits. Theatre is closer to dance than to cinema or literature.

Since stage drama in modern society has moved far down the road of agency, the actor has become the he or she who seeks and wrestles with identity. No longer is the actor a mere hired hand—whether priest or workman—to carry out some celebration of identity and relation as one's agent. The agents have each specialized and together solidified themselves as a guild or profession. The result is our acceding to their being the principals in wrestling with identity.

The actor as seen in the theory of Bertolt Brecht, who was a great playwright and director, is the explicit realization of this modern situation. For Brecht the acting occurs at three levels: actor and character and audience. From a more social perspective, this can be seen as actor-in-cast, actor-in-script, actor-in-theatre-with-audience.

Just last night I saw a vehicle, a vehicle for star actor Tony Randall. It was called *A Little Hotel on the Side*. Being a farce, it required, and received, exquisite timing, with cops and unclad beauties bouncing in and out of doorways, up and down staircases. With the curtain raised at intermission, we all could inspect the two parallel sets that had cleverly been placed on rotating merry-go-rounds. If now they made up the apartment setting, next they turned into the hotel setting, and so on.

There were a great many small parts in the play, for this was the National Actors Theatre, which is a showcase for actors. It is seen as a theatre for actors in some sort of corporatist sense—for actors as a body—rather than as a theatre trying to show a profit for the producer or theatre of, say, the Sherry-Nederlander chain. In fact, the building that actually houses this National Actors Theatre construct is the "Belasco Theatre: A Shubert Organization Theatre—Gerald Schoenfeld, Chairman; Bernard B. Jacobs, President," according to the *Playbill* notes.

Lynn Redgrave was superb as the viraginous wife of Tony Randall, yet the part seemed to offer her little scope. Did Redgrave have a choice? Perhaps not, because there are so many more actors, gifted and committed actors, than there are plays. This imbalance remains true whether plays are counted in distinct productions or by scripts offered. Does this mean that there is a shortage of playwrights, a shortage of audiences, or both? How

and how well do all the streams of talent and support fit together into theatre in the United States as some system of art worlds connected through
networks of production and appreciation? Those are the principal questions of this chapter.

Production Packages Among Arts

Connections among different arts are matters of history and of mutual
social construction, much like any one art world is itself. External developments, whether in technology or in wartime disruptions or in shifts of
social classes, play into relations among arts, as well as into some arts directly. The current theatre world in the United States is more oriented to
neighboring art worlds, especially of dramatic performance in cinema and
television, than to the broader society and its changes.

What are these other arts of music, dance, literature, painting? Such a
listing in the abstract is misleading because it imposes a cultural gram-
mar, one that ostensibly discriminates between sense modalities. In fact,
these other arts are whatever worlds have been able to establish themselves as tangible social constructions interleaved with acknowledged
menu of cultural product. There are issues of overlap and nesting: For example, opera surely is a separate world, but what do we do with German
lieder singing and with barbershop quartets and with madrigal groups
and with singers of modern atonal compositions? Do we recognize musical comedy as a separate world of its own or is it within opera or within
drama or other? There are no neat answers.

Process in art worlds brings in packaging, which is variously into stories and pictures and on into operas and literatures. Packagings often
move between and reach across art worlds. An illustration is the explosion
of Happenings upon the visual arts scene in Manhattan of the 1960s,
which fed off the new wave of experimental Off-Off-Broadway theatre.

Process in an art world is all about combinations. Getting the play *Six
Degrees of Separation* (Chapter 1) on stage rested on a dizzying succession
of sievings and matchings. So would just getting a new playscript as far as
a reading—especially if this script be for a musical, which has so many
subscripts seeking combination. Every *Playbill* tells me that today's actors
(and directors, designers, and others) see themselves in montage, in the
succession of such realized combinations—combinations in which they
appeared long enough for it to count, for it to be a "run."

The most realistic criteria for a drama art world are such conventions
buttressing it. We must be able to observe institutions like leagues, unions,
trade journals, and so on as well as conventions of behavior. Much research would be required in terms of such criteria before proclaiming a

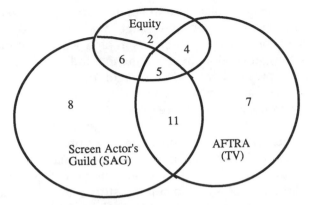

Figure 6.1 Venn diagram: Overlaps of union memberships (in thousands) among actors, c. 1975.

map of drama worlds in America. Instead we will limp along with a crude first outline. An initial step is the Venn diagram of union memberships in Figure 6.1 (explained more fully later and at the end, in "Measures and Models").

Popular and Professional

Theatre is representative of all American art worlds in having to live with the tensions between art that is perceived as commercial and that which is not. This tension often is formulated as being between high, or pure, art on the one hand and low, or popular, art on the other hand. One can try to list art worlds in accordance with this split, but many of our arts, such as cinema, are not neatly segregated into high and low art worlds, either in their production or reception. Nor does professional coincide with commercial, though the correlation is high.

Perhaps we are moving back into an era in which alcohol consumption, not drugs, can be used as a litmus test for high versus low in drama worlds. Dinner theatre, which verges on older forms such as cabaret and nightclub, does not put on Ibsen or Sartre scripts, but it does do drama and does give valuable experience to professional actors. Summer stock is harder to locate, but its offspring, the musical tent theatre in the suburban summer, is surely popular art and surely is as lubricated by beer as its cousin, the classical—but popular—circus.

The professional and the amateur in theatre do not relate to each other as bread and butter, but they are symbiotic, more like airplane and auto in transportation. There is an enormous disparity in size. You yourself almost certainly have acted in a play as amateur, though perhaps not since third grade. Within any ten-year period in this country, at least one-and-a-half million amateur actors appear on stage in ticketed performances. The amateurs are of course mostly teenagers in high school, but then several occupations (burglary and modeling come to mind) are restricted almost entirely to a narrow band of youth. (This and the following estimates are detailed in the section at chapter's end entitled "Measures and Models".)

How many professional actors are there altogether, viewed against that background of a million or more amateurs? Trade union memberships provide realistic, social-constructivist criteria of professionalism. In theatre, as in other worlds such as medicine or real estate, professionalism starts with getting paid, but it embraces much more. Professionalism refers to social in-group-ness and to cultural story lines about training and talent, but above all it refers to (at least partially) enforceable claim to turf, to exclusive control of certain kinds of performance of service. Unions stand for such claims. Drama union members' reports tend to support my interpretation: Between 68 percent and 80 percent of the members of these unions say that acting is their chief profession.

To act as a professional in the United States requires membership in one of three unions. From union memberships one can estimate that there are 43,000 professional actors in the United States, of whom somewhat less than half concern themselves with the "legitimate" stage, as shown by membership in Equity. But at a given date, only about 2,000 professional actors are being employed full time in this country at full Equity salary! The core is the Venn diagram of Figure 6.1. Altogether there are 74,000 memberships in the three principal acting unions: Actors Equity, for stage; the American Federation of Television and Radio Actors (AFTRA), for TV; and the Screen Actors Guild (SAG), for cinema. The Venn diagram shows the membership of each of these three unions split into four parts, with seven parts altogether: (1) the purists (in that union only), (2) those who mix with just one of the other unions, and (3) the whole-hog actors who belong to all three unions—of whom there are fully 5,000! If every actor was a whole-hog actor, there would of course be only a bit under 25,000 actors represented by the 74,000 memberships. If there were no overlaps at all then there would be a full 74,000 actors.

The actual total of 43,000 is closer to the lower than the upper bound; so overlap is indeed very heavy. Notice, however, that this heavy overlap is not even. There is more intense overlap (allowing for different total sizes) between SAG and AFTRA than there is between either of them and Equity. Yet the overlap may be more crucial for Equity members: With only 2,000 of the 17,000 membership working full-scale at a given time, it seems obvious that they must depend on some employment in TV (perhaps making commercials) and film (perhaps making company promo or training films). No doubt Tony Randall in *A Little Hotel on the Side* was making but a pittance by his movie and TV standards. Yet surely it was more fun for him than sitting around in house trailers while some director decided whether to make a sixth take of some six-second snippet, with only bored insiders hanging around, no one with whom to resonate.

Only professional theatre can validate a new play, can install it in the repertoire that is thereafter drawn upon by amateur and professional productions alike. There are in fact concrete organizations that maintain this repertoire, making scripts available and dealing with royalties and the like. The professional theatre in this country is also the chief channel of intercourse with theatre in other countries. Professional companies are the ones that tour abroad, enshrining European or other plays in the repertoire upon which our high school and college and community and neighborhood amateur theatres draw.

The National Endowment for the Arts

A new era for the arts, particularly drama, was made official by the creation of and then the substantial national funding for the National Endowment for the Arts (NEA). In this country such recognition usually follows prior private pioneering. NcNeil Lowry of the Ford Foundation induced a sense of American drama as a national field of interacting regional and specialty theatres: This was in the 1960s in the course of throwing millions of dollars into support of resident regional theatres. Within the foundation Lowry also established the Theatre Communication Group as a sort of command center and support group for innovative theatre of many sorts. Its subsequent support as a sort of trade association by the NEA signaled the NEA's recognition of drama as a major concern (along with symphony orchestras, dance troupes, and so on).

No totally new institutions appeared with NEA support, but there was a major reweighting of different sectors of theatre. Particular innovations appeared that otherwise might not have been tried. These included some, such as dinner theater, that had no direct connection to NEA programs but were undoubtedly still beneficiaries of spin-offs from the general infusion of activity from NEA money.

Pay levels certainly rose, but they rose more than employment did, more than live activities. This was a pattern across many arts. This pattern raises unpleasant and confusing issues about audiences and communities and tastes, issues to which we return in later chapters.

Before the NEA, there had been repertory theatre (a theatre that rotated among a menu of plays), which is often associated with permanent residence in a particular provincial city, such as Pittsburgh or Minneapolis.

With NEA largesse there came into healthy existence a widespread League of Resident Theaters (LORT), for heavy action on a Broadway scale. There also arose, alongside the Theatre Communication Group, various associations of non–New York theatres that were on an Off-Broadway or Off-Off-Broadway scale.

At the same time, theatre on the college level—university drama departments in particular—developed a new sense of importance. This was in part perhaps because their products could sense possible careers in nearby newly strengthened theatre more readily than in the one and only Manhattan. This was also because there was now far more support, in New York as well as elsewhere, for theatre that was experimental. Often this was not direct NEA support, but surely the glow of possible federal funding was crucial.

Above all, the change was toward a revision, a broadening of the definition of professionalism in drama. Making money, real money, on Broadway (or elsewhere) remained. However, commitment to stage unions and such artisan-guild devices declined. For the first time, drama people could begin to think like academic scientists or scholars in terms of the reaction of peers. That is the magic step: when your primary audience, literally as well as figuratively, becomes your professional peers. This step can, incidentally, also be taken by professions ostensibly defined by individual service—as when the surgeon or internist attends primarily to an audience of his or her peers.

There is a more analytic way to contrast popular with pure, in terms of agency. In the previous chapter I show agency leading to specialization and thence often to turnover of control to agent, which may be followed by displacement of the identity being celebrated. At the heart of much modern art, including high drama, is identification of the viewer with identity problematics as seen by the artist's own self. But there is also a different sort of displacement: that of escapism, where one "uses" the artist-agent to transport oneself to a pretend land of one's own desire—as on most of Broadway.

The outcome of this development can be approximated as a split of professional theatre into two parts: *commercial* and *institutional*. Each part cuts across existing categories. For example, repertories of many of the larger theatres in LORT came to resemble each other and commercial Broadway, whereas smaller and less-established regional theatres were more experimental—and had shorter lives. The two parts tend to relate differently to other arts: Commercial tends toward the popular and the performance arts, whereas the institutional side tends more toward the high and the literary arts.

Now imagine yourself transported back to the 1970s. That is the last time a full-scale empirical study of the American theatre scene was made.

It was a time of perceived crisis by the self-designated "theatre community." Was this new era, the NEA era, really proving viable? Would Broadway survive? (This was a question that, incidentally, had been asked decade by decade back into the previous century!) The perceived crisis was serious enough so that top Broadway figures like producer Harold Prince and playwright-songwriter Stephen Sondheim took the lead in a broad-based study. The National Endowment for the Arts commissioned extensive surveys. All the numerical estimates given earlier and hereafter refer to this period, the only one with reliable and comprehensive data.

Networks of Sieving and Matching

Figure 6.2 is a chart that opens up the two portmanteau trunks, *commercial* and *institutional*, to show flows within each as well as between them. The primary criterion is audiences. Several of American drama's subworlds fit together into a system. It is a rough-and-ready system, not one neatly planned out. Figure 6.2 is very schematic, for the system is built from a multiplicity of flows. There are many sorts of flows—scripts, actors, audiences, set ideas, and so on. And the key aspect of this system is internal differentiation within each category by prestige.

Combination theatre is the basic Broadway (which even in 1981 should include Los Angeles mainline) commercial theatre. A Broadway producer combines. He combines money from different angels and theatre chains, and he combines script, or playwright, with director, who combines actors into a cast, and so on. ("She" would apply toward the end of this period, but only for the Liz McCann and Nelle Nugent pair.) It's all a bit like combining pieces from a giant Lego set into some artifact, drawing on the various pools of actors, set designers, dancers, and others according to reputations and specialties and network contacts. And on a larger scale the system as a whole is a combination system.

Think of the theatre system as a gigantic system of sieves. First, take plays. Perhaps 10,000 scripts are written in this country per year. Most are sieved first by community and college companies, and they are possibly routed to the professional theatre world. More of the new professional plays come from playwrights who have already established some reputation, of whom there are about 100. Many playwrights cluster in New York, where they can hope for showcases and tryouts in Off-Off-Broadway and semiprofessional contexts.

Suppose 1,000 promptbooks result in a year, that is, playscripts taken seriously enough to have full apparatus of staging directions included. Approximately 150 of such scripts are optioned each year for professional theatre. A whole distinct apparatus comes into view here: There are approximately 20 agents handling playwrights, and there are about 200

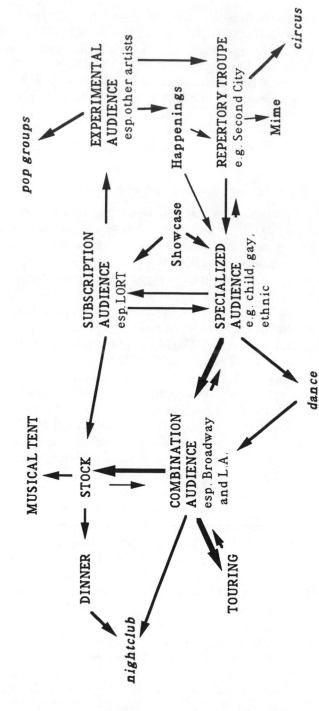

Figure 6.2 Flow diagram of influences among sectors of American professional theatre, c. 1975.

producers-to-be around, including about 10 established producer companies. That is the commercial side. There are about 30 major regional and
specialty institutional theatres, plus 150-odd experimental theatres together with a few clearinghouses run by the trade associations.

Only a few plays get through the sieves even into a dry-run rehearsal or
showcase, much less a professional production or the ultimate accolade
(albeit informal and shifting) of being in the repertoire. Now we can start
over, with actors, say. Perhaps 3,000 a year are making serious professional bids from the amateur world. They face 150 stock companies, 50 regional theatres, and 100 experimental theatres as likely conduits—places
big enough to hire but not established enough to be drowning in applications from fully established professionals.

Success comes when they get into Equity—which, of course, they can
do only when they have already appeared in an Equity production, for
which Equity membership is required! This is not just a sieve but is a conundrum that would-be actors must solve. Solutions often come at the
edges and margins—say, a sudden need to replace cast in an obscure, but
Equity, summer production in Maine.

Money talks. Turn to backers. For Broadway there are perhaps 200
would-be angels in a year, comparable to the number of producers-to-be.
Somehow some sift into actual productions, perhaps ten mainline ones
and thirty specialty ones. On the institutional side are the backers we'll
call "theatre buffs": Although much devoted to theatre, they are not necessarily in a position to, or are needed to, put in much personal money.
They may be NEA board or committee members able to control the public
disbursements. They may be leading citizens whose prominent participation makes going to the local LORT theatre "the thing to do." There may
be 150 of these per year, heading toward the boards of theatres—and toward committees of about ten major foundations.

It is already clear that besides sieving into fewer numbers according to
some labelings of prestige and talent there must be matchings of all sorts
and on various scales going on. Start on the periphery. There are about ten
law firms, besides the agents for playwrights and actors, working to broker deals and combinations for the commercial theatre. They have to cope
with about five principal theatre chain (building) owners as well as the
producers, the backers, the directors, established stars, and others through
the many specialties of lighting, costume, and so on. And there are then
matchings on lower and more detailed levels.

The matchings are loose enough that there is more freedom from exter-
nally imposed choice of plays in the commercial sector than in the experimental theatres, which depend on interviews with foundations. Personal

networks loom large throughout the entire system of sieving and matching.

What end-form emerges from survival in these networks of professional theatre in America? In commercial theatre, reputation is the key. The core of this reputation may be among fellow professionals, but they refer to, communicate to, and are influenced by popular opinion when it exists (it does on stars, does not on stage sets). Reputations must above all be periodically stoked by renewed contributions. Perhaps a star can remain such three years after the end of a long run in a hit. A production company needs more than one hit within some multiyear period, but then its prestigious reputation can survive more than one flop and for as long as five years, I should think. A new play in New York may stay alive on critical acclaim also for as long as five years without further performance, whereas directors, who need critical acclaim for more than one play, cannot survive two years without real work, leave aside summer stock and the like.

In institutional theatre the form is different. Career is the basic unit, and promotion within some sort of graded tier of positions is at least the ideal. Actors in repertory theatre can be very strong performers, but their trajectory is in career, not stardom. They too develop reputations, but they are reputations within the frame of career, within institutions and bureaucracies rather than within combination arenas. In Europe this institutional theatre is the norm around which dramatic artists shape their expectations; so in Europe careers are the center. In America commercial theatre remains the norm so that reputation and fame are the center.

Research and Development

Rather than focusing on audiences and numbers of productions and on careers and reputations, one can turn to the process by which plays are created and then adapted and adjusted. Think of this process in analogy with the research and development (R&D) activities of production industries. As in innovation there, exceptions and freaky beginnings occur, yet there is some system. In the old days, the development half of R&D for Broadway often was accomplished in New Haven and Philadelphia and other provincial locations. These places were for initial runs of plays, usually accompanied by script rewritings and recastings in those cities' commercial theatres.

There are truths from the old days that seem peculiar to drama, but research often can be generalized:

Proposition 6.2. It takes a "flop" to launch a new wave.

This proposition points back to Chapter 4. It derives from the fourth sense of identity, which is a general follow-on to turbulence and which can apply as well to other settings such as business. An example of the proposition is that Eugene O'Neill, perhaps the most influential American playwright, had his greatest impacts through failures or marginal productions. An example of the latter is *Triumvirate*, which he mounted with Kenneth MacGowan and Edmond Jones in 1916 to try to launch the new Provincetown Players.

Proposition 6.2 can be derived by applying on a larger scale the argument that identity in its fourth sense comes from turbulence. Around disorder and looming disaster there can gather an intense work group that walls off and protects new work and thus provides a sanctuary for the "bad" work that necessarily is precursor to successful work that is genuinely new and thus not in accord with existing convention.

Off-Broadway is the new tryout, the replacement for nearby provincial theatre in this function for Broadway. Off-Off-Broadway, another few scores of even smaller and skimpier theatres scattered around New York City, is on the research end of R&D; it is a concretization of the critical function. These expansions from Broadway depended upon the infusion of new money, of a set of rivulets of NEA money. This infusion was usually in diverse bits around the edges, often for purposes unrelated to innovation, such as special audiences—but all grist for the ingenious mills of professional theatre people.

Off-Off-Broadway is research for Broadway, but also for the American theatre in general, including LORT and other regional and amateur theatre. There are few limits on what can be tried. This is especially true because other professionals are available as audiences. At bottom, that is why the research function is at most occasional elsewhere than New York, even though the better LORT, such as the Guthrie in Minneapolis, and the better university drama setups have separate experimental theatre. Research in the arts is not so different from research in science: It depends on a truly expert and committed (though not necessarily kindly) audience, in short, an audience of other professionals.

What is not developed is some sort of integration of critical analysis in journals (which is partly tied to the literary scene) with the experimental theatre. Critics are most noticed for their remarks least related to research in any sense, namely particular mainline plays and general trends in a season. Too much importance can also be attributed to ad hoc stagings of thin scripts as "research": "The trouble is that related novelties threaten to forfeit their status as novelties, and generalizations that invite us to focus on common ground tend to lose contact with the very diversity they seek to illuminate. ... Criticism needs to move beyond initial concerns about Theatres of Protest, Revolt and the Absurd. ... Today's experimental goal quickly becomes tomorrow's starting-point; today's invention is tomorrow's convention" (Quigley 1985, p. xi). What remains near impossible to judge, here as in other arts, is which productions will survive which test of time. For example, the most famous English playwright of the early part of the century, Arthur Wing Pinero, is, if known, disdained at present, and even Shakespeare's predominance varies.

The NEA-funded study by MATHTECH is the main example so far of social/financial research on the theatre system. Some indication of the sorts of changes that could be engineered is given by the Monday-Thursday proposal appended at the chapter's end. It is perfectly clear that continued subsidy by government is essential, because one very stable finding, from many surveys and studies over the years, is that overall only half the costs of institutional theatre can be obtained from box-office receipts. With maximum effort and under good circumstances, earned revenue may rise above two-thirds of total costs, but the percentage drops quickly for smaller theatres and more experimental repertoire.

Does such research account for Harold Prince's sense of urgency, for the "crisis" of 1976 and the response of the NEA in several forms including the MATHTECH national study? Prince, after all, is a seasoned professional who had had a long apprenticeship to a preceding long-term top producer, George Abbott, who reigned in the 1920s and 1930s. There had been tough times before, not least in the depression.

From 1966 to 1976 there had been indeed an upsurge in gross output: in total number of theatres, in productions, in plays, even in paid attendance. This was an upsurge caused in part by NEA subventions, both organizational and financial. One could see a resulting improvement in the level of income to professionals in theatre. Why then Prince's uneasiness?

Such an upsurge can bring serious problems. The enormous pool of potential participants can yield a flood of new entrants sufficient to dwarf even the increased largesse. Expectations may rise more than do resources. The underlying competition from new forms of drama, from cinema and TV in particular, is not shut down and it may evolve into new forms able to usurp some of the distinctive contributions, and hence the special cachet, of Broadway.

Prince may have added other uneasiness. Directions of NEA funding were influenced by experimental visions of "drama for its own sake" held by academic and repertory centers disdainful of Broadway. Some of the steering by the NEA was toward ethnic and regional and class and other largely social interests and identities because the NEA offers semidemocratic funding. Congressional appropriation tends to insist upon more even distribution of support regionally and other ways. Boards and advisory groups tend over time to include more and more interests beyond professional theatre, however broadly that be construed. As some of these pressures began to have more and more impact, programs directed to other ends were no longer so easy to divert toward experiment in "drama for its own sake." Quests for identities in general society reasserted themselves over artists' high-art ambitions for new sorts of identities and recognitions.

Genre in Theatre

Much in theatre worlds does not change easily, so research and development has a difficult task. Most changes are constrained to stay not only within style but within genre. Return to the definition and discussion of these constructs at the end of Chapter 3.

In theatre a *genre* is a package of plays that come to be especially embraced by theatre worlds, as evidenced by revivals. A genre is almost as definite as a business contract among audience and participants in plays. Revivals are the process in which some plays achieve more than topical success by being resurrected time after time across the country. A very few then continue being resurrected again and again in yet more remote times and locales.

Revivals of an Elizabethan genre on the London stage occurred when that contract—that genre—could be made relevant to the later audiences. The boundaries and contents of a genre are somewhat arbitrary, but less so than for any discrimination that is either entirely social or entirely cultural because some of the cultural distinctions within a genre are being argued and enforced by continuing social organization and conversely. It is the recent separateness of drama as an art world that makes resurrection in revivals feasible. Dramatic traditions can be kept alive as genres within the walls of this specialized theatre world regardless of indifference by the external world. A theatre world sustains genre much as a bureaucracy sustains standard procedures through its stretches of inactivity.

Current avant-garde theatre is a genre, or perhaps a set of genres together called "postmodern." Other arts exhibit the same postmodern thematics: for example, the urge to perform, to not remain on the wall—or on the page. Empty space, standing for alienation, is another postmodern characteristic from the theatre, where a normal stage with its conventional definition of spaces is not wanted: It translates in music into periods of silence and of sound that are ostentatiously "unmusical." Avant-garde thematics, as they are repeated with variations in revivals in one art or another, always concern opposition; they state unremitting hostility to contemporaneous civilization and to one or another of its elite and lower classes, with very little of explicit positive goal: "One look at the average audience gives us an irresistible urge to assault it—to shoot first and ask

questions later. This is the road to Happenings. A Happening is a powerful invention ... behind it is the shout 'Wake up!' ... A Happening was
originally intended to be a painter's creation ... (it) used people to make
certain relationships and forms" (Innes 1981, pp. 54–57).

Within avant-garde genres, performance attempts to come full circle
back to some imagined tribal beginnings in which audience and performer no longer are specialized apart into complex forms of agency. For
example, the Living Theatre developed, in its New York show *Paraders
Now*, a ceremonial cycle designed to incorporate changes from the audience, as in some traditions of oral narrative. You may have yourself seen
performances by the Bread and Puppet Theatre, either a traveling troupe
or its major cycle of performances in Vermont.

Yet according to some, postwar American theatre did not establish itself as central in the avant-garde genre:

> The American stage was a provincial enterprise long after Europe's playbills
> had become international. ... Since the end of World War II, the German
> drama ... is the most variegated, possibly the most chaotic, and probably the
> most daringly experimental of all modern European dramatic writing. Its
> technical innovations, its philosophical themes, its stylistic originality and
> even its unbridled excesses. ... The makers of the American theatre are a dis-
> tinctly lesser breed of bird (eagle). (Bauland 1968)

The longevities of genres differ because of varying difficulties in keeping social organization of art world compatible with cultural form. To explore this, turn from Broadway theatre to genres in the London theatre.
Wendy Griswold (1986) has analyzed with great care revivals of two
genres of that Elizabethan drama widely recognized as central for all
Western theatre. Griswold traces thirteen city comedies and sixteen revenge tragedies:

> City comedy celebrates the adventures of urban and urbane rascals oper-
> ating in the wide-open economic milieu of Renaissance London ... as they
> unblushingly lie, scheme, take risks, ignore propriety, flout conventional mo-
> rality, fleece the gullible, and enjoy themselves hugely all the while. (p. 14)
>
> This study examines the revival careers of thirteen city comedies set in or
> oriented toward London ... which took shape in the so-called private the-
> aters, which catered to a more fashionable audience than did theaters like the
> Globe. (pp. 14, 26)
>
> Revenge tragedy's archetypal interest came from its highly elaborated de-
> piction of horror. And its social significance lay in its display and formal res-
> olution of the tension between centralized authority and individual justice.
> (p. 56)

For each of these clusters of plays that succeeded and came to be seen as similar in their own time, Griswold (1986) pursues why and how the clusters were revived and became enshrined as genres over three centuries:

> Each genre apparently said two rather contradictory things: city comedy promised economic change without economic dislocation, while revenge tragedy suggested that both justice and order were possible under the centralized state despite its manifest tendencies toward corruption or ineffectualness. (p. 198)
> Thus they would appeal to audience segments having some stake in the preservation of the status quo, while paradoxically they would also appeal to those hungry for change ... and both genres were elegant in their ability to represent and resolve problems pressing on different segments of their audiences. (p. 207)

Griswold goes on to explore why both genres were revived little in the nineteenth century, whereas city comedies were revived much in the eighteenth century, a time of sociopolitical reaction, and revenge tragedies much in the twentieth.

On the nineteenth century:

> Why did talented writers avoid drama and hacks dominate it? Why did spectacles flourish in this theatre? What brought the working class into the theatres at the beginning of the century and drove them out at its close? One contributing factor was that high society became enamored of the Italian opera in the late eighteenth century. ... The result was a shift in the overall repertory of the theatres away from legitimate five-act, nonmusical drama and toward a wide variety of other types of entertainment ... of the hastily written and quickly forgotten short works featuring music, spectacle, pathos, and happy endings. ... Of course there were exceptions. A star like Edmund Kean could bring an audience from all classes back into the theatre. (Griswold 1986, pp. 56, 131–40)

Griswold derives eight propositions about theatre-world and audience factors that encourage Renaissance revivals in general and makes seven further findings about revivals of particular plays. She established the importance, in reviving obscure plays, of material factors such as the subsidies from a new postwar British Arts Council, which ballooned regional repertory theaters (which could support large casts for proper dramas) to over a hundred in number, to the near-eclipse of commercial touring companies.

Other arts also intruded in the revival equation of the twentieth century, as did the changing nature of audiences: "Since film and television are better able to produce realistic fourth-wall effects, theatre managers (as well as contemporary playwrights) often rely on stylized productions, actor/audience contact, and distinctly artificial 'theatrical' conventions, for it is in such self-aware theatricality that the stage holds an advantage" (Griswold 1986, p. 191).

The London theatre provided cultural lenses to its audiences for examining social problematics enjoyably. This theatre world is more self-centered than other art worlds and thus better suited to mounting revivals over long stretches. But throughout three centuries this specialized theatre world had to draw, just as does ours, through sprawling networks upon resources across a national society to keep itself afloat and thus able to mount revivals at all. And its cultural lenses could activate a genre only when it could be embedded into contemporaneous social concerns.

Theatre genre can act as the prototype for other art worlds. Just so, in Chapter 2, I analyzed nineteenth-century Pre-Raphaelite genre in terms of individualism expressed in themes of medievalism and spirituality. This resembles the parallel analysis by Griswold in showing similarity between social dynamics in distinct receiving populations at the successive epochs of revival. Similarly, when Bakhtin argues periodic resurgences in the popularity of a writer, Rabelais, he makes points that are similar to Griswold's, but Griswold supplies sorts of quantitative and systematic evidence that would strengthen Bakhtin's work (see Chapter 3).

Theatre revivals depend on having a highly developed art world to reproduce a genre, here of revenge tragedy or city comedy. This case shows that an art can mirror social formations despite and even because of the distortions of its specialized art world. The availability of the same cultural objects, which are being called for differentially over generations as society changes, results exactly from the insularity and rigidity of the theatre world.

In contrast, literature together with cinema provide flexible narrative art to contemporaneously mirror intricate and meandering social formations. Each act of reading can be seen as a revival of its own, in which social configurations from the time of writing can be reflected in whatever the period of reading is, although critics as intermediaries render reading not such an isolated and historically disembedded activity as it might appear.

GUIDE TO FURTHER READING

Raymond Williams (1981) traces evolution of theatre from its sacred roots in ancient Greece. Innes (1981) develops the concept of dramatic theatre performance in today's New York as holy. Csikszentmihalyi (1975) is informative especially on Polish advanced theatre, and Brook (1968) exemplifies American spin-offs.

Connections between drama and identity are well developed from a sociological perspective by Griswold (1986) and from a level of practice by Prince (1974). The paradox of performance is laid out in the writings of Michael Goldman (1975), who develops it in phenomenological terms. Ekman (1972) is interesting on how physiognomy affects communication. Lindenberger (1984), Rosenberg (1972), and Scholes and Kellogg (1966) are lucid on expressive performance concerning, respectively, opera, painting, and oral literature.

Critical assessments of current American theatre abound at all levels of highness and for all degrees of learning, in newspapers and journals of many sorts, beginning with the Sunday *New York Times*. The more academic reviews are *The Drama Review* and the *Performing Arts Journal* (founded only in 1976, after the NEA spigot turned on). *American Theatre*, a monthly magazine put out by the Theatre Research Group, is good on resident nonprofit theatre.

Becker (1982, Chapters 2, 4) has much to say about acting and theatre in general. A distinguished monograph on the American theatre of the postwar era is by Poggi (1986). Wharton (1974) and Little and Canton (1970) assess the state of serious playwriting and production in our base period. See Price (1967) for Off-Broadway as development site. Ten key participants in Off-Broadway offer their views in Greenberger (1971).

Harold Prince (1974) gives the perspective of a major producer, primarily of musical comedies, of which Engel (1967) gives the view from the orchestra pit. For an overview of one Broadway season taken as a whole see Goldman (1969); Novick (1968) performs that service for the hinterlands. Ziegler (1977) gives a realistic assessment of regional theatre from the perspective of a longtime participant.

Simone Whitman (p. 119 in McDonagh 1990) is lucid on Happenings in New York. A marvelous survey of the changing popularity of Shakespeare in nineteenth-century America is Levine (1985).

Quigley (1985) offers astute commentary on Pinero's plays. He also discusses how and why the imagery of art worlds for drama is common and effective. In the first chapter, Quigley argues for the importance of disruption and change for theatre and its proper critique, and he also (1985, p. 26) is a source for the distinction between drama language and theatre language.

Survey tabulations and analyses from the NEA-commissioned study of American professional theatre were issued in a report of February 1978, authored by Anderson and others. The second phase report, on recommendations, was issued in 1981 by the consulting firm Mathematica. But serious study of careers in theatre requires seeing how they embed, especially for actors, in the other performance media of film and TV; a start is Faulkner and Anderson (1987).

FIELDWORK IDEAS

Fieldwork is about obtaining and comparing several points of view at once. It requires interaction with others. This interaction need not necessarily be as conversation or interview, either of which might raise difficult issues of ethics and access. In fieldwork on theatre performances, for example, one might interview market researchers about the audience and its changes rather that trying to directly approach audience members, who may be skittish. Often it is best to try for unobtrusive observation; you can consult Becker (1982) and the chapters in Ragin and Becker (1992) for guidance. Ingenuity and flexibility toward opportunities are the keys.

Expert sources can map the possible sites for you. Current backstage information on professional theatre is most easily available in the weekly *Back Stage* ($1.75 in the New York area and $2.50 elsewhere), which goes out of its way to cover LORT and other outlying theatre. Such information, mixed in with movie data, is also available in the weekly *Variety*, which emphasizes commercial results. NEA subsidies have sparked numerous guides such as *United States Professional Theatre: Geographical Guide* (Los Angeles, Calif.: Logos Enterprises, 1978), with separate indexes for dinner theatres, resident theatres, theatre for young audiences, stock theatres, and industrial show producers. At some point you might think about clothes fashion in art world terms of genre and revival. Schurnberger (1991) surveys the very long history of clothing.

MEASURES AND MODELS

Consider some of the nuts and bolts of how to measure and specify this institutional system of current America theatre. Afterward turn back to Chapter 4 and for one of its six case studies try to sketch out how you would measure and specify an institutional system involved there. (For the first example, the impressionists, one attempt is published in White and White [1965] 1993.)

One can measure book sales and library sign-outs, but it is hard to measure readership or actual attention. Live attendance at a play has greater validity: "Plays offer better data for the study of cultural revival, however, insofar as their production and reception are more centralized, they receive more concentrated critical attention per unit, their commercial success or failure is immediate, and their influence on subsequent revival attempts is often quite direct" (Griswold 1986, p. 12). And instead of examining which of a spectrum of plays or books are hits for a given sort of audiences, logically one can just as well turn the question around and examine what social formations provide the better audience for a given sort of play, as for the revival of Elizabethan drama.

How does one go about making various quantitative estimates for the United States, such as the number of amateur actors? One always starts with the Statistical Abstract of the United States (in any library and available from the Government Printing Office). Common sense applied to some basic Statistical Abstract numbers can carry you to rough estimates. How many high schools are there? Devise at least two different ways to estimate this: say, from the population in a given age range and from the number of school districts. Then estimate what fraction of them put on how many ticketed performances (many have more than one a year).

Then you can search for detailed Census Bureau reports. Each year and even each month, the Census Bureau counts employment in various arts, as in all other occupations, but unfortunately the Census Bureau considers amateur activities in the arts too amorphous to include there. There is pretty good data on amateur participation in a joint NEA/Census Survey of Public Participation in the Arts, which asks people if they've acted on stage or participated backstage in a dramatic performance.

There is now a General Social Survey (GSS), which is funded primarily by government but run, on a shoestring in the university sector, by social scientists (Davis and Smith 1988). It will, from time to time, report on the amorphous and informal sorts of topics that the Census Bureau shuns. But there are problems. GSS estimates extrapolate from a sample to the whole population. That is fine for determining the percentage of Republicans, which is estimated quite accurately even for small samples so long as they are randomly, that is, properly, drawn from the population of interest. But it is no way to estimate the number of professional actors, who are too few to appear except by fluke in a sample. The Census Bureau remains indispensable. However, once you've identified some subpopulation such as actors in unions, you can accurately estimate their attributes from a properly drawn sample without having to interview them all.

Often what you need is not just a number, but ways of assessing and assimilating numbers, and not just numbers but also networks and other social structures. Figure 6.1 is a Venn diagram, which deals with overlaps among sets; the sets here are among memberships in actors unions. Figure 6.2 is a flow chart, a portrayal of a network, where the size of a tie reflects the size of that flow.

There are 17,000 members in Actors Equity, the union of stage actors. There are also 27,000 members in the TV actors' union AFTRA (American Federation of Television and Radio Artists) and 30,000 members in the

Screen Actors Guild (SAG), for a total of 74,000 memberships. But I estimate that because of overlaps there are only 43,000 persons who hold these memberships. The Venn diagram in Figure 6.1 presents the details of overlaps: 5,000 persons, for example, are dues-paying members of all three unions. SAG and AFTRA are the pair that most heavily overlap: The number of persons who hold memberships in both these unions is larger than the remaining number in either union. The number of stage actors employed full time at Equity standard, 2,000, is also the number of actors who are members only of Equity. But this is mere coincidence: The more sought-after actors tend to belong also to other unions.

Numbers and percentages are not enough. Specific social incidents, just like general pattern, gain reality only through actions in networks of relations. Processes of influence must be specified in network terms. In the arts, these social networks operate in especially complex configurations of agency, as we have seen in this chapter. The Census Bureau won't yet count friends and acquaintances, whether artists or others, much less preferences in music or such, so you must turn to special social surveys such as the GSS.

DiMaggio (1982) and Faulkner (1983) show applications of network measures and models to theatre and movies respectively. Network measures use principles of structural equivalence to supplement the concepts of social connectivity pioneered by Milgram (see Chapter 1) and others. Introductory general accounts include Barnes (1972), which is the least technical, and Berkowitz (1982) as well as Wellman and Berkowitz's own chapters in their edited survey (1988) and more recently Knoke (1990).

7

Professionals and Publics

I opened Chapter 1 with professionals on stage in Lincoln Center, but then I turned in Chapter 2 to amateurs, for one does think of the Pre-Raphaelites of Victorian Britain as amateurs. They were gifted amateurs who achieved an amazing resonance with a newly emergent middle class and even helped to create a public of a new kind. The Broadway publics of Chapter 1, by contrast, seem much more specialized, as was confirmed in the previous chapter on American theatre. The following conjecture seems plausible, then:

Conjecture 7.1. Professionalisms and specialized publics go together.

In this chapter I explore implications and trace some correlates across the arts in America today.

An American Mosaic

Struggles in and around production of art in America have become searches for and constructions of publics of recognition. Renewed obsession with identities in this land leads to publics much smaller but more numerous and varied than public ever was before. Such publics of recognition, for genres of artworks, come intertwined with lattices of competing professionalisms under construction by artists. The results are not a tidy system, but instead a mosaic. As we have already seen in Chapter 5, this mosaic reflects, and also distorts, struggles across other social worlds in America, such as ethnicities, hierarchical strata, organizations, locales, and communities of taste.

This mosaic is one of struggles, individual and corporate, for symbolic recognition or predominance, including position in a lineage, and for material support and for recognized agency as artist. Reputation and career develop for artwork as well as for artist, and they can also develop for broker and critic and audience. Careers can tie together an art world and bridge between art worlds. But careers do differ in performance arts from what they are in creative arts, and careers may be confined strictly within a particular art world, such as ballet.

Recognition of careers for artists depends on whether they are seen as professionals. This American mosaic is thus shaped by a basic conflict over boundary between professional and amateur. This boundary often runs right through a particular person, as individuals experience waxing and waning of recognition. This is not just a matter of local incident but also of shift back and forth in criteria for success and serious commitment.

Artists will, in any case, have reputations, and reputation and career can develop quite differently because they are shaped by different publics. For example, a composer of new music, which is intended and seen as serious—as being in the lineage of classical music—will build a career and reputation in purely musical circles, mainly among peers in music. Some of the performers among these peers will, however, have reputations with a much larger musical public for performing some genre of classical music. Their incomes will be enormously greater, or they may have predictable careers in some system of big performing organizations. In any case, they will be professional performers, but they likely will pay deference to the composer rather than the reverse. Professions jostle together into larger clusterings, which typically award highest prestige to those practitioners most removed from a larger public.

In today's view, the amateur-professional boundary is often between the role of teacher and the role of student. This inverts the snobbery of earlier eras in which the split was conceived as one between mere worker drudging for support and refined patron offering guidance. There are complex overlaps and overlays of kinds of reputation and of career even just within artists established as professional. Policymakers can be driven to distraction as they try to spread support aptly across the American mosaic.

Two of the larger tiles in the American mosaic are the cinema of Chapter 3 and the theatre of Chapter 6. The former tile is much less touched by policymakers than is the latter, because support from governments and from philanthropies interacts with commercial earnings. This noncommercial support, often thought of as public or nonprofit support, also is affected by changes in the relative merits assessed to popular arts and to high arts; these changes influence policymakers and brokers and are also shaped by them. But popular arts need not be profitable and high arts can be very profitable as well as prestigious, so there are no simple answers— no answers guaranteed to be right for conscientious patronage.

The greatest potential quandary for noncommercial support, though, concerns the amateur-professional boundary. So far the problem continues to be framed mainly as a problem of entry—the terms of entry. But populist pressures may appear and increase to the point where the importance of distinguishing professional from amateur is disdained in favor of goals of self-expression, for groups as well as individuals.

My argument is that such social pressure cannot be decoupled from sensitivities to artistic content. In particular, pressure toward support of amateurs conflicts with tendencies to favor specialized genres. Amateur creativity can be great in individual artworks, but it cannot sustain specialized genre or, probably, style.

These all are desperate matters. The term is not too strong. To capture this sense of desperate importance I shall rely on case studies; there are no general censuses adequate to provide sampling frames, anyway. I shall put off attempts at general assessment and comments on overall policy until the next, concluding, chapter. I turn first to localities and then move on to individuals, paying particular attention to the professional-amateur divide throughout.

Public Funding for Localities

Very many artists are located neither in regular performances for paying audiences nor in elite realms of high art nor in commercialized art for media, fashion industry, and the like. Who are they? How do they survive? A new answer to the latter question developed during the depression of the 1930s and reappeared with the creation of the National Endowment for the Arts in the 1960s. Considerable experience in public funding for artists and arts has accumulated.

Artworks explicitly tied to ethnicity or gender originally had a hard time getting established in the American mosaic. Ethnicity and gender raised difficulties exactly because they signify the *other* ethnicities and the *other* gender rather than the one assumed as normal and/or preferred. It was hard to associate beauty with them, to justify them by aesthetics, whereas localities were uncontroversial. But there is more material for identity proclamation, more material for artworks, in such tensions and conflicts than in our muted regionalisms, except perhaps for the South, for a few cities, or for enclaves like Mormon Utah or Mennonite South Dakota.

Take just one case study, of a public funding program in Chicago. This program was slipped in, like some of the WPA arts projects of the depression, as auxiliary to some larger program—here the Comprehensive Employment and Training Act (CETA) program—with the ostensible purpose of reducing inner-city unemployment and poverty. It was a program that touched on ethnicities and gender.

I quote a lucid assessment of this case study by a student in my sociology of art course:

Dubin explored the experiences of artists in Chicago (1971 approximately) in working for the state government. These artists were participating in a program called Artists in Residence (AIR) which was part of a federal employment program (CETA [Comprehensive Employment and Training Act]). Dubin presented the wide array of advantages and disadvantages that artists experienced in having their work funded by the government. There was a great deal of tension and conflict between bureaucratic and artistic goals and methods. The contrasting emphases were in part quantity vs. quality, and safety vs. innovation. In working for the city's program, the artist's work had to adhere to the overall goals of the program. Administrators were concerned that the program survive; therefore they focused on and supported work that appealed to a large, unsophisticated and uncritical audience. They (the bureaucrats) wanted artworks that were politically neutral and *not* controversial. They supported work habits and productions that were standardized and resulted in *predictable* responses. ... The artists viewed their duties with AIR as "labor" and not their true artistic work. Furthermore, the standardized format of the AIR program (artists were expected to do residencies, workshops, performances for elderly and handicapped centers, public schools, day-care centers, etc.) left the artists very little time to experiment with other work. Also, the artists were not able to collaborate with other artists (from other mediums) as much.

Working as city employees, the artists gained access to supplies and equipment but they also became involved and concerned with city government issues like budget cuts and policies. On the other hand, working for the state government had some benefits. Most importantly, it offered artists a steady and secure income for a period of time—a situation that artists very rarely enjoy. Also, many artists felt a sense of "professional" accomplishment in being accepted to the program and the program gave them a more certain status as artists. (Rachel Ebling, examination response, May 7, 1992)

Ebling's diverse references to city/state/federal levels suit the confused and complex state of funding!

The very term *funding* would be anachronistic for many contexts where art is built in as a routine that is calibrated to some other purpose—say, graphic art in today's advertising industry or playing instruments for disco. Our high arts are not calibrated so, but neither are they fully supported commercially. Nor are various efforts at community art funded, including the largest examples such as this AIR program just described, which was supported from federal CETA funding. So noncommercial funding patterns are as vital as they are intricate.

In particular, the enormous pool of would-be professionals is enlarged as well as tapped by any offer of additional funding, so that its net effects on terms of agency for artists are difficult to estimate. What is clear is that it is very difficult to build art worlds under these conditions, to achieve stable identity as artists or as agent of artists. Offerings are unpredictable, and they change with bureaucratic and city-political considerations, so that conditions are not conducive to building loyal and committed audiences. Different arts are thrown together somewhat arbitrarily rather than being coordinated according to some artistic rationale. Boundaries among arts are social constructions with a degree of arbitrariness. Dubin's own Chicago account, appraised in the preceding quote, concludes as follows:

> Organizational characteristics imposed limitations on artistic output in various ways after AIR's first program year. There were fewer artists working on individualized projects; reductions were made in the size of those artistic disciplines which challenged their proposed assignments. ... Interrelationships with other organizations were critical so that customers' tastes and preferences took precedence over artists' concepts and proposals.
>
> The artist involved in this situation had previously been active in the "community mural movement," which stressed the representation of social, economic, and political issues relevant to local communities. However, decoration quickly became the preferred mode of muralist expression. ... When agency heads saw the offices of others which had been enlivened with bold graphic designs, they competitively vied for the opportunity to have their own spaces similarly embellished. ... Self-imposed restraint followed directly from AIR's procedural requirements which could delay, frustrate or prevent the execution of projects.
>
> For example, a muralist employed toward the end of AIR's organizational life was commissioned to create a scene capsulizing the history of a local community. The artist worked carefully within AIR procedural guidelines. ... When her proposal was published in a local newspapers, however, some adverse reaction was registered. ... Such themes were too closely associated in the complainants' minds with murals in minority communities which primarily focused on social and political themes. This community, it seems, did not want what some termed a "Puerto Rican mural." (Dubin, pp. 165–168)

Part-Time Paths

Life in each American art world is different, but it is hard to construct a career in any one of these worlds, whether funded publicly or privately. Many artists are, or wish to be, committed as professional artists. Most of those practicing an art are dubious about themselves as having a career within that art, however, because they can't make a living at it. But in this era at least, they do not wish to think of themselves as amateurs. How is one to resolve this quandary? Part-time paths in professionalism.

How do so many artists keep going without commercial support, direct and indirect, and without help beyond occasional public programs such as AIR? One main answer in contemporary America is that they are part-time workers who survive with difficulty, many as loners, with just occasional jobs and teaching stints in art. Many others, perhaps an increasing proportion, turn away from career and livelihood and conceive their production of art in terms of shaping identities for themselves as well as for others, be it as vocation or avocation. The production is part-time because they too usually have to work other jobs.

So far no one has developed adequate ways to survey these "part-time" artists. In the absence of population lists and the ability to sample properly, I shall here just sketch a few I have encountered personally. These I add to examples introduced earlier, such as the co-owners of 17 Wendell Street, and the very many professionals who are full-time only notionally.

Two Poets

Peggy Bowman and George VanDeventer both fit poetry in alongside other concerns and livelihoods. In different ways each is on the outside of a poetry art world that is rickety even on the inside, yet each writes and continues to write poetry:

I wish I could lift up
    your loneliness
hold it in my palm
like a cool flower
    in the morning
enfold it tenderly
feel it warm for a while
in this dawn-fresh garden
    of my wistful dream.

        P.B.

Friends and Neighbors

I want to be more than a neighbor:
Friends. I want to be friends; a
State of loveliness and order
Without the tremble
Of corner stakes and fence lines.
Friends, where the landscape is lush
And the path as wide as the horizon.
Neighbors are good people
That stare strangers away
And speak
Beneath a ribbed hood of community.
Friends. I want someone
To dance with on Main Street;
Sit along the curb
And look at the neighbors.

        G.V.

Peggy Polivka Bowman began work on a B.A. in creative writing after marrying the painter Richard Bowman (see the section "A Scientist Painter"). In her poetry she celebrates nature, especially of the coast south of Half-Moon Bay, where she spends weeks on her own in a cabin of theirs. Cabin for her, studio for him. She has worked at "regular" jobs to keep them (and their medical insurance) going. Jacqueline Onslow-Ford and she were longtime friends, and Peggy has many artworks by other artist friends besides Richard in and around their steep-pitched canyon home.

George VanDeventer has as delicate a touch as Peggy with nature. Neither is much published. George is a survivor from New Jersey city life, blue-collar and unionized, who migrated with wife and daughter to rural Maine. George built his own modern barn to accommodate an Ayrshire herd he built up from 1 to 100 cows. After the 5 A.M. feeding it was poetry time (except in haying season). (Recently, after declines in dairy prices, the VanDeventers converted to the bed-and-breakfast industry.) George, who did not go to college, is also a voracious reader with a considerable library on history and science.

George has, aided by his wife, teacher Arlene VanDeventer, tried everything one could think of to break into more formal recognition, but the outlets are so few and the clamor is so great. George has found some literary resonance, most notably with a British writer and poet, Ronald Blythe, who is famous for his loving study of the village Akenfield. His response to George's letter and poem in response to *Akenfield* illustrates the amazing responsiveness one encounters among artists along with the jealousies and feuds. George has now become central in a Rockland organization, the Live Poets Society, which is active in publicizing and bringing together poets in coastal Maine, just as earlier he helped shape identity for owners of Ayrshires, through their newsletter, and for local groups.

Published, and even "big-name" poets cannot make a living from poetry alone. University posts are not yet fully legitimate in the eyes of poets, who disdain teaching. Thus most serious poets are part-time, with the rest of their livelihood coming from public readings (which are not defined as art because they are not for peers and not defined as teaching because they are not regular), from literary reviews, and from non-art occupations such as dairy farming.

A Concert Pianist

In the I. I. Rabi concert series at Columbia University in early 1991, I heard Katherine play Scriabin, Ravel, and a Beethoven sonata. In tracking her career, I noticed that she used exactly the same biography in the notes for this program as she had for a program three years before in Amherst:

> A native of California, Katherine Teves Mizruchi graduated Phi Beta Kappa from the University of California at Berkeley. She is currently a student of Dorothy Taubman. In the past she studied with pianists Maro Ajemian, William Masselos, and Edna Golandsky.
>
> Ms. Teves has been the recipient of several honors and scholarships, including the Oakland Symphony Orchestra Prize and the Hertz Graduate Fel-

lowship for Performance. Her recent performances include the 92nd Street Y, the Brooklyn Museum, WQXR and WNYC radio, and the Lincoln Center Library. Her recording of an all-Liszt program for the "Discovery" series was aired on National Public Radio.

Ms. Teves has also appeared at the Beethoven Festival in Locust Valley, New York and the Amherst Music Festival in Massachusetts. She is presently on the faculty of the 92nd Street Y School of Music and the Dorothy Taubman School at Amherst College and maintains a private studio in Manhattan.

That studio is of course the site of the teaching that is the principal professional income for her, as for most professionals. This teaching has little connection, however, with the intensive hours of daily practicing that she maintains as a professional.

The form that Katherine gives her biography is as revealing as the form of program notes for theatre actors, which were discussed in Chapters 1 and 6. Clearly, who taught Ms. Mizruchi, perhaps a veritable descent chain of teachers, is a very important issue. As with other arts and sciences professionals, this descent chain and the networks of ties to persons and music sites that result shape the rather few opportunities for performance.

Independently I learned of the particular importance of Dorothy Taubman as an innovator: "Dorothy Taubman has synthesized a way of teaching and playing the piano which ... has a growing number of adherents. ... Application of her principles enables performers not only to play with power, accuracy and musicality, but also to avoid the persistent pain. ... There seems to be a tremendous discrepancy between the practices of piano teaching and those of performing artists" (Alford 1991, p. 1). Alford speaks of strategies to spread the Taubman technique that rely both on her charisma and on professional organization, and he shows videotapes of her approach to posture for the hands of a pianist. Katherine, in teaching at the Y and Amherst, is taking a side in a professional controversy, one that is highly unlikely, however, to end in either clear victory or clear defeat.

A Singer

"Jazmyn" is her professional name, because Debi Gilchrest doesn't count as profession her work as administrative assistant to me in a Columbia University interdisciplinary center. She covers most of her gigs during evenings and weekends: bat and bar mitzvahs galore, plus weddings and parties and singing for churches. After some years she and her longtime accompanying group, or combo, have one regular engagement, in the Thursday evening show at a Manhattan jazz club. Among tours abroad, the important ones so far for her and the combo have been yearly ones to

Japan and the Far East. All have to be fitted into vacations and leaves. Several tapes of her singing have been produced and marketed.

One of the costs of this frenetic form of professionalism is stress, but weighing against that as an advantage is good medical insurance to pay for doctors to help with side effects of the stress. An artistic cost is lack of the blocks of time and the psychological scope needed for practice and experiment sufficient to full development of artistry. The myriad new technologies and blends toward new-wave music of a Philip Glass could suit Jazmyn and her troupe well.

A Writer

Anne Laurin Eccles is a novelist who supported herself at various times working as editor for Boston publishing houses. Her principal adaptation, however, was writing children's books. They, like cookbooks, always have an audience, although for that very reason there also is intense competition for publication and success. Anne kept writing after the arrival of her first child, but now, with three daughters and a son and despite live-in help, her time will be too limited and broken up for the next few years to sustain serious writing.

A Dancer

Ann Dressler earned top grades in non-dance courses as well as in my arts course, belying any stereotypes about dancers not being intellectual.

Ann Dressler, private communication, February 10, 1979:

> Harvard accepted me because I was a dancer. But then when I came here they refused to give credit for dancing ... no matter what she said I would be taking twelve ballet classes a week with or without credit ... I left Harvard-Radcliffe after the fall of '76 for an extended leave of absence ... I loved that first semester of my freshman year and wanted to stay but I did not. I went to New York City, because I am a dancer ... I moved to NYC, studied at a "professional" school, entered a "professional" ballet company and danced professionally. ... Where ever I have gone as a dancer money has always been a problem. I was paid by CETA for a while which was very nice though illegal.
>
> The type of dance training I have had ... a Russian Method, Ragonova technique. It is very scientific. Ballet moves are difficult and somewhat unnatural but all steps can be taught clearly and *intelligently*.

Ann then returned to Harvard and took my course. By Christmas 1980, however, Ann had to go into the hospital to have some tests done on the spine injury she developed while dancing. She had to take the spring semester off for physical therapy, so she went back to New York in 1981. We kept in touch. She wrote me a detailed account of her first New York stay.

Auditions in New York are usually terrifying and inhuman ... I made the audition and stayed on with the company DANCERS, director Dennis Wayne ... a company whose well-being means the dancers' well-being and happiness. ... Dressing rooms are small and intimate, surprisingly comfortable. (New York City ballet has rows of horrible orange lockers that slam and rust.) The ballet mistress was from New York City ballet. She was excellent. Classes were always filled.

DANCERS was not financially sound though. Even with the help of Joanne Woodward the company was losing money. The administrator left. ... We sold T-shirts and handed out pamphlets in Grand Central Station at rush hour. There was such a good feeling of unity and love of the school and company ... I left DANCERS for a company that paid better and was more stable. We had faced the threat of closing down each week at DANCERS but somehow the company has kept together. This past week-end DANCERS performed at the [Harvard] Loeb theatre, looking young and very "New Yorkish." The company's dancers are billed equally in alphabetical order. There is a profile on each one's life in the program. There is also an insert called "The Reason for DANCERS" which explains the company's philosophy. ["Six to seven ballets each and every year newly created on these 14–20 dancers" is stipulated in "The Reason for DANCERS."]

All of the reviews that DANCERS has received, over the last two years have been kind. Most have also been encouraging. Claiming basically that the dancers are good but they need better choreography. (Ann Dressler, private communication, February 18, 1979)

Two Organizers

Many auxiliaries are needed in the arts. Here is one student, Jane Catler, identifying such a calling (to a fellowship application committee in 1985):

I am planning a dual career. I would like to continue my studies in American history and culture as well as help contemporary artists get their work produced, noticed, distributed and collected. ... Coursework has enabled me to explore topics from the literature of nineteenth-century traveling salesmen to Charles Sheeler and Precisionism. My senior honors thesis examines romantic fiction in the *Ladies' Home Journal* from 1889 to 1898. ... This term I am documenting the design and history of a Boston building threatened by development. ... As an intern last summer ... I was charged with updating *Practice and Performance: The Guide to the Arts at Harvard and Radcliffe*. I collected and edited, negotiated and managed distribution of 16,000 pamphlets.

Another student, Rebecca Abrams, focused more specifically on arts administration, taking an advanced degree program in it. She used term papers to write about symphony orchestras, chamber groups, and other aspects of classical music. She developed opportunities of a curatorial kind as well as in subscriptions and tickets for subsidized fine arts, and now she is in the federal arts bureaucracy.

Career as Professional and/or as Genius?

Part-time or not, artists seek to have themselves viewed as professionals. But they have another urge that may be more powerful and which can be used to sidestep some of the conundrums of professionalism. Artists today seek and hope for creativity carried far enough to even be called genius.

Some professions socialize and shape you into looking ahead (medicine or design, say), and some into looking back (perhaps the law), whereas other jobs just keep you in the here and now. The latter are jobs more ordinary than the professional; they are jobs that give up, or have not yet acquired, the social pretensions that are at the core of being professional. The here-and-now jobs also, however, can include working at the highest pitch of intensity and originality, and these are qualities that cannot easily be reconciled with the pomposity, in both demeanor and self-image, that one expects of the traditional professional. Such here-and-now jobs may be less discordant with genius than are professions!

The professional role can interpenetrate with the artist role in various ways. Take painting, to be specific. In our own era and country, painting seems to have the prestige of a minor profession, but does it get packaged in careers like a profession? If there is no career, there also may not be a profession, because career is a principal mechanism of the social pressures and perceptions that can keep a professional system running.

It may be that in painting worlds two opposite forms of career occur together, to much confusion. A backward-looking sort of career comes from the teaching mode of painters. To be sure, much of their teaching is part-time and erratic, but the ideal form of teaching, which alone can justify and shape career imagery, goes with seniority as well as with some order to and sense of cumulation from training. "Proper" training ends with a certificate for the student, which suggests and induces prior credentials for the painter-instructors. Thereby comes movement toward careers and a full-fledged profession.

"Genius" is a social construct, an invention that is parallel to that of secrecy. Genius is a performance measure. Through invoking it one does not need to deny either rule or creativity. Genius provides narrative explanation and justification for transcending the paradox between performance and standard. The seniority of the guild need not thereby be disturbed overmuch. Genuine change is permitted without challenging the legitimacy of the guild's formulation. Genius is a whole new narrative framework for style, in which changes, even sudden and drastic, need not deny validity to what already exists.

The genius construct can be the core of a social institution as potent as guild or profession. The avant-garde is the narrative for such an institution; there is, as for any institution, a paradox within that narrative in that it must simultaneously be narrative of the first mode and narrative of the second mode. These claims concerning genius need not be restricted to the arts. Avant-garde institutions have been attempted also in sciences as well as in scholarly fields. In these other fields, however, alternatives to genius are better developed than in arts today.

In all the arts today, narratives are central to wrestling with issues of originality. Just as one can note that literature has long-standing homologies from its own narrative artworks to painting, as well as social ties with painting, one can note that literature uses about the same narratives of avant-garde and genius as were early developed around the impressionists in French painting. These narratives are "performance measures." What is striking from my own and other interview studies of painters is the extent to which they resemble writers—and dealers and critics—in how they keep constructing such narratives around, but not confined to, their own artworks. They also, of course, devise career narratives of the first mode.

Painters are also geniuses and members of an avant-garde. That is, all—scores of thousands of them—conceive themselves, in their best moments, as pressing forward the frontiers of vision and concept, in opposition to some shadowy in-group called the "establishment." This is the second, opposite form of career. All painters (including those in the others' establishments!) have their own establishment to fight and thus their own personally centered sense of genius. Instead of training students, the goal here is to advance the avant-garde and down the establishment.

Professionalism obtrudes also, in this second mode of career, at least as an orientation or goal that impels painters to cluster in groups, designated variously as schools or trends. Such groupings induce an auxiliary corps of interpreter-critics, including some curators for museums. These groupings remain but temporary camps, however, in the march of the avant-garde.

Although creative originality is the principal claim about the "genius," another main thrust of professonalism in the avant-garde is commercialization of career. That was the great invention, the enormous social achievement to emerge from the impressionist movement in Paris from the 1850s to 1880s. The energy and creativity of one person, the dealer Durand-Ruel, was central in this first of the six art revolutions that were surveyed in Chapter 4. A new system of career emerged out of his efforts to replace an older academic system.

The difficulty is to judge impacts, if any, upon theme and tone and technique of work from the mix of career forms and social disciplines of the art worlds involved. And one may wonder if the argument about painting carries over into careers in other arts. All these issues can be brought together by looking at arts within universities.

CalArts is a revealing extreme case. CalArts was to be, in the vision of its founder, Walt Disney, an elite institution for the arts. It was to parallel Cal Tech (the California Institute of Technology, known as a home for Nobel prizes in sciences). Like Cal Tech, CalArts had to function within the commercial and guild environment of greater Los Angeles. Disney died before the actual construction was completed and before most of the practical decisions were made.

CalArts was conceived by its organizing artists as a utopia. In a utopia each human is assigned an embracing super-role. This therefore entailed a paradox, because CalArts was also conceived as a breakthrough institution, which is to say it was to be generating a narrative of the second mode, but its charter pronouncements were in utopian terms of narrative of the first mode.

In studying CalArts, one must treat mundane concerns of professonalism and academe and audience and specialization and control and status cheek by jowl with aesthetic concerns of content and theme and technologies. Thereby one can hope to enlighten the debate on whether arts can survive in the American university. All these aspects can be traced in the narrative of Walt Disney's CalArts (which is an ex post narrative in the first of the two modes defined in Chapter 3):

> By the end of the Institute's second year of operation a rift had developed between the school's principal backers and its chief academic administrators. As the Institute's laity firmly disciplined its artists, cutting their budgets (which means firing personnel) and forcing them to defer to noncollegial opinion and desire, amateurism was ritually condemned, and "professional craftsmanship" became the new watchword. ... The trustees' announcement ... shattered the fantasy of unlimited financial resources which had underpinned so many other utopian projections. ... The imagination of "open sharing" in a "community of artists" which transcended disciplinary boundaries ... their project to combine aesthetic and social radicalism in an avant-garde institution. (Adler 1979, pp. 126, 107)

A Scientist Painter

In the street mural movement, artists strove to derive their own and other identities communally. Other American visual artists struggle for identity almost entirely as individuals under the doctrine of *l'art pour l'art*, which was seen in Chapter 4 to drive the impressionists. Thirty-five years ago I bought a wonderful, large oil painting from Richard Bowman when he was my wife Cynthia's teacher, evenings, in the Palo Alto art league. Bowman has spent forty-odd years painting the implications of a vision. This vision of his came only after years of academy training in the Art Institute of Chicago. At graduation in 1942, he was awarded the Ryerson Travelling Fellowship for a year. Europe being at war, Richard went to a village in southern Mexico, where blazing sun and rugged mountains combined to trigger his vision of seeing as energy.

Bowman grew into his vision during the same years as the abstract expressionists, described in Chapter 4, but he was drawn more to the imagery and depths of natural sciences than to what he saw as shallow ripples of fashion in New York art.

The painting we bought was *Summer Hill*. It captured the sheer exuberance with which Bowman *saw* California upon returning from four years in Manitoba as associate professor of studio art. This was a dutiful stint that he had obtained through a friend from his first job at the University of Iowa who had been selected to start an art department at the University of Winnipeg. Stunning as they were, many others of Bowman's canvases in 1957 were hard to conceive living with in one's home. Such canvases could best play their avant-garde role through exhibits, but this requires ownership by museums or major collectors, which in turn presupposes considerable critical attention combined with exposure in one or more established galleries. How had Bowman fared?

This was my question on May 3, 1992, as I wound up the steep road of the Bowmans' canyon home south of San Francisco. I was on the trail of a new acquisition for myself. Also, a new edition of my and Cynthia's book on the impressionists, *Canvases and Careers,* was to come out, and I wanted to look in our own era and country for images and transpositions of experiences from the impressionist era. So I wished to learn more of Bowman's career, because I suspected that Bowman could be portrayed as a lineal descendant of the impressionists with their spotty, difficult careers. I was sure also that he was an inheritor of the avant-gardism that their revolution created. I had in mind Howard Becker's treatment of the American composer Charles Ives and his specification of maverick roles more generally. Later, I will contrast Bowman with a nonmaverick painter of my acquaintance, a young man I will call George Mitchell.

Richard maintained a network of contacts from his Art Institute days. And his lifetime good friend was British artist Gordon Onslow Ford, whom he had met in that village of Erongaricuaro in Michoacan, Mexico, in 1943. From the two together came Bowman's only exposure to the New York art scene, which was in 1944. Armed with introductions from both

Onslow Ford and the Art Institute director, Richard visited, with his roll of paintings, two famous European painters who were living in New York, Fernand Leger and Max Ernst, as well as an inane museum curator. Richard also showed his roll to Sidney Janis, who was then a private collector but later founded a gallery that became world famous. A visit to the Pinacotheca Gallery led the next year to a well-reviewed one-man show. There were important reverberations in Chicago: inclusion in Art Institute shows and purchases by local collectors.

Onslow Ford pulled Richard along with him to California, where Bowman got a temporary job in the Stanford art department before his stint in Manitoba. All this came after Richard's marriage in Chicago to Peggy Polivka (who subsequently became a poet—see earlier) and his first job, two years at the University of Iowa, which was followed by Richard's burst of glory in Chicago. Onslow Ford had, back in Mexico, spotted the moment of Richard's maturing an original vision. Onslow Ford's own paintings were more monochromatic, but he continued to resonate with Bowman's growth and early on introduced him to Clyfford Still, Mark Rothko, and other major artists and writers who were then in the San Francisco area.

Bowman was formed as person and painter in the Midwest, could not abide the East, and fled to the Far West. He, and his poet wife, Peggy, build their social life as much with literary and musical artists as with visual artists.

Thus far Bowman's life is sounding like a cross between college teacher and free-lance artist. The subsequent years in the Bay area, after Stanford and Manitoba, have been lean in career terms. The income to be expected from museum and government acquisitions is tiny because their streams of acquisitions are dwarfed by the annual flow of works from gifted professional painters. This also had been true of France's art worlds, both in royalist and in republican eras. And in the United States most museum acquisitions, in any case, come as gifts from private collectors.

Richard has had other patrons, such as the San Francisco lawyer Harold Allen Parker, who also published in 1986 a retrospective book on Bowman's work. Also there was a European couple, the de Schulthesses, who supported him with stipend in the way that Durand-Ruel had combined with his picture dealing. But they took in return, during those few years, only a portion of Bowman's output. I guessed that many, if not most, of his canvases remained stacked around the edges of his studio. So, had the teacher vocation become the only career left to so original a painter as Bowman?

Bowman has offered self-narratives in occasional prefaces and notes in catalogs for shows including his works. But Bowman and his sponsors have not been as effective in public relations as others. Bowman's primary narrative is in and of his works.

Creativity Bowman did have. It welled forth in series after series, with as many as a hundred per series, mostly of oils, large canvases as often as small. These go from the early *Rock and Sun* series on through *Kinetograph* and *Micromacrocosmos* to *Kinetogenics*. Then followed *Synthesis* and *Dynamorph* series (which Bowman notes in retrospect returned to the *Rock and Sun* and the *Kinetogenics* idioms). A catalog reads: "Interwoven among the last three of these series is the *Environs* series, begun in 1960, of paintings based upon fluorescent phenomena occurring in the vicinity of my home and studio in the country hills."

Onslow Ford's help has continued, as when in 1979 Gordon pulled Richard into what became one of Richard's most prestigious group shows. This was at the Galerie Schreiner in Basel, Switzerland, alongside luminaries: W. Baziotes, Morris Graves, Henry Moore, Joan Miro, R. Matta, Mark Tobey, Yves Tanguy. These artists are luminaries in part because they, or their dealers, understood better than Richard, or even Gordon, the commercial ethos of that dealer-critic system that was still flourishing in postwar Europe and New York but was flourishing now around offshoots of abstract expressionism instead of impressionism.

A basic mistake for any American was never to be in New York. Yes, Bowman usually had a gallery, one with permanent exhibition space, but never a gallery in Manhattan, where the bulk of the buying and of the inveigling of publics occur. Manhattan now has some 600 galleries as well as much of the print and electronic media.

Only in one period did Bowman have a gallery that really pushed, in hand-tailored fashion, his oeuvre to particular clientele, who were perhaps local, as well as sought out shows for his work. This was from 1959 to 1977, with the gallery of Rose Rabow of San Francisco. Rabow believed in Bowman's work, but unlike Durand-Ruel she was not in the predominant city, and art collecting had yet to reach a middle/upper class broad enough to sustain markets in separate cities.

Bowman has had three retrospective solo exhibitions: in 1956 at Stanford University Art Gallery, in 1970 at the San Francisco Museum of Modern Art, and in the 1986 at Harcourts Contemporary Gallery in San Francisco. His most recent major show that I know of was in 1987 at UCLA's Wright Gallery, along with such luminaries as Sam Frances, plus Mark Tobey and Morris Graves again, as well as Onslow Ford. Several other times, Bowman has been recognized by museum directors and has been included in beautiful exhibition catalogs containing critical appreciations. He has pictures in five museums, all in the West and two paintings of his from a private collection were reproduced in the December 1992 issue of *Architectural Digest.*

Despite such recognition, Bowman's income from painting continues to be erratic and minimal. Major paintings continue to be bought only by the same collectors: The twenty-two private collectors who are listed in the 1986 book are the same set of collectors as those who were in the back of the catalog for his major one-man show of 1961 at the San Francisco Museum of Modern Art. To make time for his powerful development of a vision, akin to a scientist's basic research program, Bowman has confined his teaching posts to casual, part-time, local ones without medical or retirement benefits.

A Business Painter

A younger American painter, call him George Mitchell, has aimed to make painting his business as well as his career. I learned much from watching George, a student early on in my sociology of art courses at Harvard. Mitchell, unlike Bowman, has a livelihood as well as a career; of that he made sure. To these ends George, who was very intelligent, meticulously planned, was disciplined in production, and was attentive to the gods of foundations as well as of commerce. His choice of this liberal arts college, even though it offered only makeshift provision for studio instruction, was unusual. It was an early career calculation.

Business first, professionalism second, pure art third—but superb quality throughout: Such was the Mitchell Creed as I perceived it. Let me expand upon each of these goals: If you cannot develop a product with regular sales, you will not live well. If you do not maintain establishment credentials, your market value goes down. But, finally, if you cannot get to some unbridled painting at least some of the time, there is little point to the career. Mitchell, after all, knew he had, besides artistic talent, the energy to succeed in another profession or business, with looks and charm to spare.

Mitchell's particular key, which Bowman never turned, was multiple-impressions art, that is, engravings and prints and all their varied progeny. Mitchell often crossed such work with collage and such. Often there would be clever ways to quickly add a touch of handwork to each in a series of prints, increasing their value.

Mitchell's approach can remind us of how, a century earlier, Monet deliberately probed the market by bringing out his canvases as staged series, as an art historian argues: "He possessed a superb sense of the art market in which he was operating ... subscribed to two clipping services ... had a 600 book library" (Tucker 1989, p. 9). Monet maneuvered the average prices of his series up from 3,000 francs for each in the original series, *Grainstacks*, to 5,000 for the *Poplars* and on to 15,000 francs for the *Cathedrals*, with the aid of a variety of expedients.

Even in his senior year, George was exquisitely crafting sets for selling, perhaps to dentists' offices: Those were boom times for professional atriums, which made use of inoffensive and yet if possible also striking and high-quality artworks in their suites and corridors. George also had his eye on the more lucrative market for art in lobbies of banks and major businesses.

Agents, more than dealers, were conduits for Mitchell's work. These often were people with some art know-how and taste who worked for or hired those to whom the furnishing of hotels and motels was subcontracted, for example. Networks of contacts were as key to Mitchell as to some young lawyer or accountant building a practice. It was not career in a bureaucratic sense.

Yet the prototype for high art from Durand-Ruel's day, the dealer-critic system, still carried on, in Boston and across other cities. Mitchell, a prudent soul, could keep his same key turning there too in high art for collectors. Probe most galleries and you'll find higher gross sales, I suspect, from prints than in the more glamorous single oils à la Bowman. Just think through the economics. A large oil painting might take a month and sell for say $7,000, if it sold at all, but with the gallery, itself struggling to pay its rent and clerks, taking half. And prints go at prices that an enormously greater number can and will pay, even after, once your reputation becomes established, you ask $1,000 or more. Those magnificent oils you see in a gallery may be the same kind of come-on luxury item that Saks Fifth Avenue uses for bait. You no more have wall space (or decor) for such an oil than you have pocketbook for that Armani suit.

Still and all, the more reliable path for a visual artist to good livelihood within this huge economy is fastening on as a component in the production process for finished space. Such catered space is by far more for business than for home. Mitchell thus took on a business environment. Later interludes on foundation and government support—at artists' colonies, in elite resort areas, and so on—were mainly for prestige. But Mitchell could also learn that quite a bit of finished space is for government in any of its myriad local forms of county, city, borough, region, authority, state agency, and so on. And George was alert enough to early spot and spend time in Europe to share in its return to preeminence in art.

Two Careers Compared

Richard Bowman did not seize any of these practical keys that Mitchell wielded toward business and professional survival. Yet Bowman did have the technical skills: For example, he had taught printmaking back in Iowa. Bowman, unlike Mitchell, has never traveled to Europe, but he felt immediate kinship with the impressionists after a 1940s Chicago Art Institute exhibit of its last master—or alternatively an early postimpressionist—Pierre Bonnard.

Bowman is akin to the artists of these French movements not only in devotion to his local (San Francisco–area) landscape but also in how he was taken with new materials: "The discovery and use of fluorescent lacquer in 1950, fluorescent oil in 1956 and fluorescent acrylic in 1965 was for me a natural medium to integrate and express more fully my concept of the great forces, unseen but known, in the universe" (from a November 1975 flyer).

Mitchell resembles Bowman in exploring new materials, but differences in their cultural and social embeddings make for important differences between Bowman and young Mitchell in their art. Mitchell is a performer, a formalist able to offer what fits. Bowman, himself an awkward bear of a man, is gripped by a master narrative, his vision of the master narrative of our time, science.

Mitchell may be closer than Bowman to the multiple subjectivities of Rousseau, but studying the life of either American can lead toward more general insights about careers. We examine their canvases and look for their careers. In both these lives of twentieth-century American painters, we can see continuing influences from, as well as echos of those problems that generated and bedeviled, the impressionist revolution.

Bowman, unlike most artists (including Mitchell) but like many of the postimpressionists, has always had passionate interest (and total lack of training) in new science and engineering topics. These include cloud chambers and black holes, radioactivity and the insides of cells as well as solar-flare close-ups. Bowman feels that his vision of natural phenomena predates and then is verified by scientific accounts. This becomes an aspect of Bowman's single-minded commitment to developing an artistic vision in its own right.

Bowman needs a kind of social setting that is just not there. He has friends, good friends, and admirers and so on, but those do not add up to a social setting. The closest approximation to a social setting in which he would no longer be hurting is exactly the settings of the research scientists who generate the findings that enthrall Bowman. And such settings are just as appropriate a prototype for other artists pursuing new visions, visions that have no reference to natural sciences.

Bowman behaved as if the same academic institutional support that makes basic science viable was available to him, too, for new directions in art. It wasn't and it isn't. One obstacle is that unlike sciences, art worlds, and in particular their critical auxiliaries, have not managed to integrate their versions of how identity and relations are formed—to integrate them into coherent rhetorics. Science has become known as rhetorics that are both general in applicability, once specified, and reliable if rules are followed; so they are worth material support directly and also are valuable to higher education. All this was accomplished despite—or was it because of?—the sciences not having a separate apparatus of critics. Perhaps support for arts can be evolved commensurate with those for sciences, but perhaps, instead, such support is winding down even for American science.

Bowman may be clearer on his own identity than his own livelihood; the reverse may be true for the Mitchell I knew. We should of course be on guard against the avant-garde tendency toward caricaturing any artist, Mitchell or Bowman, as being either wholly pure or wholly crass, wholly maverick or wholly conforming. Such a tendency was strong during the impressionist era, as an art historian points out:

> An oscillation between shrewd businessman and creative genius punctuates the unpublished correspondence of Théodore Rousseau. ... They provide an illuminating glimpse into a successful landscapist's economic strategy at this period. ... The letters reveal an artist permanently late with delivery, ever eager to put a final and more perfect touch on the canvas, and a man who cleverly manipulated such delays to extract advances or extra payments. ... Contrast all this with the dominant image of the artist laid down in Sensier's posthumous biography. ... Published in 1872 and itself part of the panoply of contemporary dealer publicity, this empirically detailed life history portrayed Rousseau as an unworldly man, a genius insufficiently recognized by the state, misunderstood by the critics, and exploited by venal speculators. This is precisely the kind of mythical portrait that revisionism has worked so hard to deconstruct. But hold on a minute. Do not dismiss the faithful Sensier too lightly. In fact there is plenty of material in the letters to suggest that such a persona was not merely biographical fiction. ... He was always full of bile against superficial painters such as Cabanel, whose "trite" nudes and commercial success obscured his and Millet's "true" glory. ... Now, the point is not that one or another of these personas revealed the "real" artist. ... For in some sense all these things were true. (Green 1989, pp. 32–33)

Many of the Pre-Raphaelites were extremely attentive to their income: They perfected a sort of triple-dipping in which a painting was toured to be shown for an admission fee to large numbers. Thousands of copies were struck off and sold from etchings or other print masters derived from the painting, and the painting itself was then sold. The PRB paintings, with their bold outlines and literary subjects, were especially suitable for prints, and unlike modern painters, the Pre-Raphaelites often sold

Notes to Plates

Adelaide Alsop Robineau, Editor's statement and designs from *Keramic Studio*
1907.

Robineau is a significant figure in American art. She was an innovative ceramicist, working in carved porcelain and experimenting with European glaze techniques. She was a teacher, most notably in bringing together expertise from major artist-craftspersons and transmitting it through the journal *Keramic Studio*, founded in 1899, with her husband, Samuel Robineau, a collector of ceramics. *Keramic Studio* was the interface between the professionals and the host of amateur and semiprofessional china decorators, most of them women. This statement introduces an extensive portfolio of designs and models for transforming a sketch from nature into stylistic conventions of the British Arts and Crafts movement, originally the stock of Morris and Company. The emphasis was on using natural forms native to America, with direct observation as source. As can be seen, the tone is serious and is calculated to confer artistic validity upon both beginning and "more advanced" workers.

Courtesy of the Fine Arts Library, Harvard University.

Frederick A. Rhead, Design for a plate, from *Keramic Studio*
1911.

Not only design aesthetics but also detailed technical procedures were taught in the pages of *Keramic Studio*. This illustration is from an article giving instruction on etching a design with acid to obtain a relief effect. It was one of a series of "pottery classes" describing various processes. The design wakes faint echoes of Arthurian Pre-Raphaelite themes. Indeed, F. A. Rhead was British, head of a Staffordshire "pottery family" and director of art pottery for Wileman and Co. His son, Frederick Hurton Rhead, having been trained under his father, emigrated to the United States in 1902, where he was to have far more scope and influence than if he had stayed within the pottery establishment of England. He frequently contributed to *Keramic Studio*, sometimes collaborating with his father, as in this example. He was associated with burgeoning commercial art pottery in the Middle West. He was one of a group of what might be called the "pottery all-stars" who became artists-in-residence of the Peoples University in University City, suburban St. Louis. This was a venture of the American Woman's League and included a correspondence school for the cultural and educational improvement of rural and small-town women. Later, Rhead established his own studio, Rhead Pottery, in Santa Barbara, California. Rhead had a major impact through training students, again mostly women, to shape and throw pottery for themselves (this work had been considered "too taxing," mucky, and unsuitable for women). The craft of pottery—that is, the whole process—became much more accessible to women in the United States than in Britain. An American art world of pottery and ceramics developed where amateur-professional boundaries were constantly being redefined.

Courtesy of the Fine Arts Library, Harvard University.

Richard Bowman, *Micromacrodyne*
Charcoal and fluorescent lacquer on canvas. 51" x 65". 1952.

Shimmering Personage
Acrylic and fluorescent acrylic on canvas. 31" x 35". 1992.

Both these paintings, forty years apart, exhibit Bowman's intensely observant and reflective approach to organic and physical structures. As other artists have done, especially in the twentieth century, he uses new technology to explore and release new energies. In *Micromacrodyne*, the combination of dark charcoal's sweeping, rhythmic definition of the organic shapes with the fluorescent lacquer's points of emphasis makes an image of dynamic extension and expansion. In *Shimmering Personage*, the quality of the paint lines, their echoes and reflections, suggests a continuous energy system. Getting at and playing with core structures and dynamics of the natural world has been a preoccupation of both nineteenth- and twentieth-century artists; often the stimulus came from watching science at work and incorporating its procedures and theories. The nineteenth-century interest in color experiment and theory comes to mind. Another strand has been the meticulous recording of externals, phenomena and objects, much as a Victorian artist-naturalist might do. In identifying what he understands as the intuitive mode of the scientist, Bowman forms a stronger linkage: He says, in effect, "You the scientist are like me, the painter."

Photographs by C. J. Vroman.

Anita Jung, *Not Then, Now*
Etching, lithography, and collage on paper. 31" x 48". 1992.

This work is an evocation of the way memory's fragile artifacts endure. It is created with the faint, etched words, the floating screens of tissue paper, and a suggestion of dust and darkness through the lithographic tones. Jung's referent here is surely archaeology: "Memory is the ruin of experience." She is presenting a structure of memorylike fragments to be explored. Indeed, the viewer is intended to participate by gently lifting the tissue paper to read what is etched beneath. Number 25 in Daniel Schacter and Susan McGlynn's Memory Collection, this work was tracked down through a friend who found an interesting gallery in Madison, Wisconsin, and brought a Polaroid print of *Not Then, Now* to Schacter on a visit to Boston. On the strength of the photo and some phone conversations with the gallery owner, Schacter bought the work on trial. He notes "... the piece exceeding expectations ... it was an easy and quick decision to keep it." Anita Jung was teaching in the Art Department at the University of Southern Illinois when this work was purchased.

Courtesy of Daniel Schacter and Susan McGlynn.

Deborah Putnoi, *The Patchwork of Our Lives*
Oil and drypoint plate on masonite. 24" x 25". 1992.

This work has, in its line drawings and brilliant colors, a quality of naive/subtle symbolism reminiscent of Chagall (who might be considered as a memory artist par excellence). When Putnoi produced this work, she was a graduate student in Education at Harvard, working with Howard Gardner, whose first major studies in psychology and education were concered with the development of children's image making (for example, *Artful Scribbles*, 1982). *Patchwork* has the bright colors of a quilt; the small ladders are to represent "mental time travel" among events, people, experiences. Intrigued by its references to childhood, memory, and psychology and stimulated by the popularity of Putnoi's works in a local prestigious gallery show, Schachter and McGlynn made this Number 37 in their Memory Collection.

Courtesy of Daniel Schacter and Susan McGlynn.

Cheryl Warrick, *S Series #3*
Charcoal. 11" x 21". 1991.

"I would do a drawing, and erase the entire drawing, and find ghosts of what was left later on." "We live our lives as layers. We have to peel away all the layers to get to who we really are." These statements by Cheryl Warrick were quoted in an interview for a local neighborhood arts journal. They indicate a way of working that exactly corresponds to the very thought process being represented. Warrick is not just representing the probings of memory and association; she is acting them out. Charcoal, a particularly malleable medium, was very satisfactory to Warrick because "... it's the smudging and pushing and pulling. You can see the human hand in it." Schachter and McGlynn acquired this triptych and *Visible Past*, a small painting by Warrick, as a package, from Gallery NAGA, Boston.

Courtesy of Daniel Schacter and Susan McGlynn.

Deed of Gift to The Museum of Fine Arts, Boston, 1993

Warrick, a young black artist, was originally an intensive care nurse who painted on the side. She went back to school to earn a B.F.A. from Massachusetts College of Art. Nursing became a weekend activity. Now she was becoming more well known, selected to exhibit in national-level shows. Daniel Schacter was interested in a new work by Warrick, also memory related. He first proposed a "trade-up," in which he would acquire *Imbrue* in place of *S Series #3*. The dealer suggested another transaction: Schacter was to offer *S Series #3* to The Museum of Fine Arts, and if it were accepted, Schacter could acquire *Imbrue* at an attractive price. There was reason to think that the curator of prints and drawings would be interested in Warrick's drawing, since he had curated the drawing show where *S Series* first appeared. Such proved to be the case. After approval, in stages, by the curator, the museum's director, and the Acquisitions Committee, the work was officially accepted, and Schacter made out this Deed of Gift and acquired his new Warrick piece.

Notes prepared by Cynthia A. White

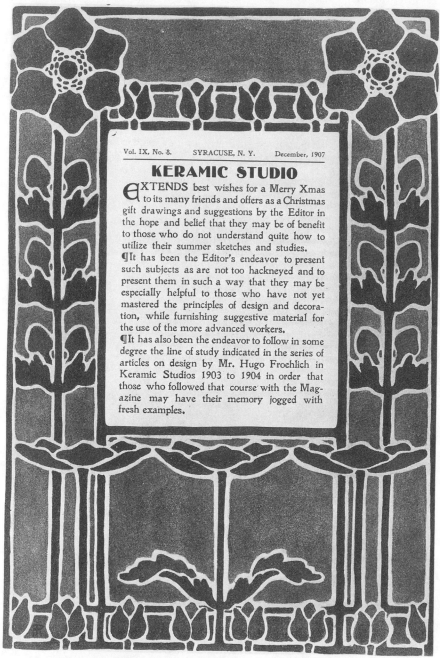

Vol. IX, No. 8.   SYRACUSE, N. Y.   December, 1907

KERAMIC STUDIO

EXTENDS best wishes for a Merry Xmas to its many friends and offers as a Christmas gift drawings and suggestions by the Editor in the hope and belief that they may be of benefit to those who do not understand quite how to utilize their summer sketches and studies.

¶It has been the Editor's endeavor to present such subjects as are not too hackneyed and to present them in such a way that they may be especially helpful to those who have not yet mastered the principles of design and decoration, while furnishing suggestive material for the use of the more advanced workers.

¶It has also been the endeavor to follow in some degree the line of study indicated in the series of articles on design by Mr. Hugo Froehlich in Keramic Studios 1903 to 1904 in order that those who followed that course with the Magazine may have their memory jogged with fresh examples.

Adelaide Alsop Robineau, Editor's statement and designs from *Keramic Studio*

Frederick A. Rhead, Design for a plate, from *Keramic Studio*

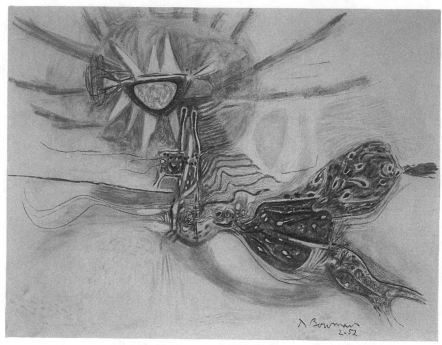

Richard Bowman, *Micromacrodyne*

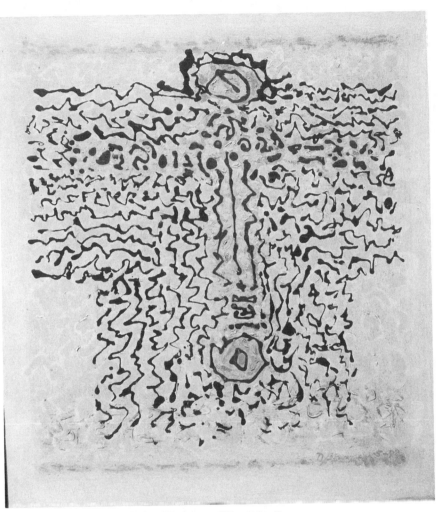

Richard Bowman, *Shimmering Personage*

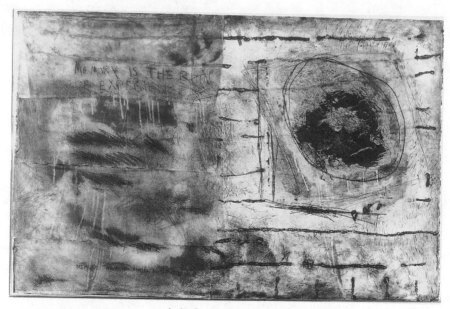

Anita Jung, *Not Then, Now*

Deborah Putnoi, *The Patchwork of Our Lives*

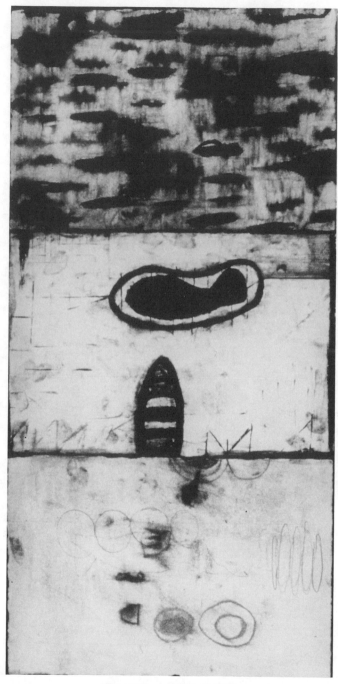

Cheryl Warrick, *S Series #3*

Museum of Fine Arts   465 Huntington Avenue   Boston, Massachusetts 02115

DEED OF GIFT

I hereby give and deliver to the Museum of Fine Arts, Boston, Massachusetts, the property described below as an unrestricted gift. I understand that it is the purpose of the Museum to promote by all appropriate means a wide public knowledge and appreciation for fine arts, and I further understand that the management, use, display or disposition of my donation shall be in accordance with the professional judgment of the Trustees and Director of the Museum.

I further warrant that I am the sole owner of the property having acquired it by PURCHASE/INHERITANCE from:

Gallery NAGA   October 31, 1991
Source (dealer/donor)   Date acquired

Signed and sealed this 10th day of February 1993   Daniel L. Schacter
                                                    Name(s) and Address

Daniel L. Schacter   138 Woodchester Dr., Newton, MA
Signature(s)

I/We wish that the gift be identified to the public and in the records of the Museum as:

"Gift of Daniel L. Schacter and Susan M. McGlynn   "

DESCRIPTION and CONDITION of the work(s) donated:
attach additional pages if necessary — please date and initial

    One drawing by Cheryl Warrick, U.S., born 1956
                S Series #3, 1991
                Charcoal on paper
                overall (three sheets): 22 1/2 x 11 in.
                            side by side

COPYRIGHT: Was the work created after January 1, 1978? ☑ yes ☐ no. If yes, do you own the exclusive, or non-exclusive rights relating to the copyright of this work? ☑ yes ☐ no ☐ unsure. If no, or unsure, please provide the name and address of the current copyright owner or previous owner of the work.

State/Commonwealth of _Massachusetts_ , County _Middlesex_

Personally appeared before me _Daniel L. Schacter_ on _Feb. 10,_ 19 93

and acknowledged the foregoing instrument to be _his_ free act and deed.

MARI M. TAVITIAN
NOTARY PUBLIC
My Commission Expires September 23, 1999

mari m. Tavitian
                                                    my commission expires
Notary Public

MUSEUM OF FINE ARTS hereby accepts the foregoing gift and delivery.

Director   date

Deed of Gift to the Museum of Fine Arts, Boston, 1993

the reproduction rights to printers rather than using galleries to sell prints.

The problems of any one painter differ from those of another, and their problems seen personally need not map into problems of their art world, or conversely. The problems of painters differ from the problems of other sorts of American artists now or the problems in an earlier era, but there is commonality on two sad central truths: There does not begin to be enough support. What support there is does not conduce artists and their collaborators toward either the best work possible or the most original work.

A Collector with a Theme

It may be that changes in roles today that are thought of as auxiliary will prove crucial to the reshaping of art worlds under tensions between professionalism and genius and under limited material support. Almost by chance, patterns of interactions can get started around art worlds that grow into new mini-publics of recognition. I found one such growing around a new collector, Daniel Schacter.

Schacter is an experimental neuropsychologist with whom I overlapped at the University of Arizona, where he and his spouse, Sue McGlynn, also a psychologist, built a small collection dominated by southwestern themes. Dan is now through art celebrating the professional identity as scientist of memory built up over more than a decade of research. Dan remembers deciding soon after he moved to Harvard that he was building a "memory collection."

Recently I accompanied Daniel in Manhattan down below Houston Street for a tour of art galleries in SoHo (and neighboring TriBeCa and other areas). Dan covered about thirty-five galleries that afternoon and found nothing, which is just normal for a serious collector. But of course he found out lots about trends, he tuned up his eye, and he left his visiting card around while picking up other cards and announcements in return. Acquisitions will follow. Appended at chapter's end are sample entries from the detailed notes that he has kept on the acquisitions he does make. I lay out their gist in seven points:

1. Schacter probes for specific memory interpretations from the artist, in writing and by phone if not in person. He also gives some reliance to interpretive comments by critics in reviews, of which he keeps many clippings. Several of the artists are very responsive to his probing for conceptual bases in memory function. I quote from a seven-page memo that Temple Lee Parker wrote, in connection with his purchase #30, *Memory*. (I italicize her use of themes from Chapter 3; note that she, like Bowman, commits to science.)

I put the "limitation," the shape, into relation with itself thus using that shape and whatever symbolical meaning it may have as a means to break itself apart. What happens simultaneously is that this very shape can be seen as reemerging from itself. ... I hope to show a fusion between the static and dynamic aspects of time. Linear time itself or even linear cycles of time can be interpreted as "limitations," here represented by the circle, that can be used to explode themselves. Insofar as the viewer perceives destruction and re-creation of the circle shape to be simultaneous, coinciding, and integral occurrences, he or she can perceive the time element involved as being non-linear; the aim is to catalyze in the viewer a non-linear, rhythmic sense of time culminating in a sense of time-out-of-time. The result is another paradox: a cause and effect situation catapulting one beyond cause and effect.

The idea for "Memory" emerged from a series of paintings I originally entitled my "line" paintings before I really had any notion of how such line paintings would relate to the ideas concerning "time" represented in my earlier work. ... I didn't start deciphering all of what I had done until later. ...

This exploration of *linear, temporal change ... allowed me to create a sense of narrative, however abstract, and thus a bridge between my more figurative and my more abstract work.* ... The line paintings, on the other hand, give the possibility of depicting a linear narrative through time in a more dynamic, and yes, since the lines are not straight, less linear fashion. ...

"Memory" came forth quite spontaneously after a period of almost neurotic immersion in the examination of the peculiarities of my own memory. ... When people share their memories and find discrepancies among themselves, the creative act of remembering becomes all the more volatile, and, as depicted in my shape paintings, *a single event can give rise to multiple perspectives and interpretations.* ...

If we were not able to access memories randomly and could only arrive upon a particular memory by looking at past events in a reverse sequential manner, if we were unable to take a memory out of its linear context, then, depending on the rapidity of our thought processes, we would be perhaps incapable of expression or creativity, or even *a sense of identity.*

One final point that may be of interest is that as a teenager I harbored the romantic notion that I would one day make great scientific discoveries. I was especially interested in the brain and was naive enough to think that it would be possible to find the exact network of synaptic impulses that triggers aesthetic experience.

This all suggests:

Conjecture 7.2. We may be witnessing, as higher education diffuses through much of a new cohort of artists, a new sort of more interactive—and cognitive—relation between artist proper, as now conceived, and new roles such as the collector-of-a-theme exemplified by Schacter.

2. Dan often develops and maintains a tie with the artist. At least six artists have visited this growing Memory Collection, which Dan and Sue hang in their large home. And Dan uses such ties as when, after seeing some of his subsequent pieces, he got Robert Goss to modify an intricate piece that Dan had acquired in November 1991, Transaction #13.

But many of the total of thirty-seven artists represented are scattered elsewhere—Louisiana, Wisconsin, Georgia, California—with their works being scanned initially via color slides or videotapes. Recently Schacter corresponded with Richard Shaffer, who had painted Dan's first memory acquisition from four years ago in Arizona. Dan wrote about publication of this first work, *Color of Memory,* on the cover of the *Journal of Cognitive Neuroscience,* for the Spring 1991 issue. Dan also acquired two new pastels on memory from Shaffer, Transactions #24 and #26.

3. Social network tracing (discussed in Chapter 1) is prominent throughout Schacter's notes. Dan is attracted by and considers works, often repeatedly, in numbers much greater than his purchases. Reviews of gallery shows provide leads, but he locates many through indirect referrals.

A recent acquisition, Transaction #31, from Loretta Harms, who was graduating from the Museum of Fine Arts School in Boston, depended on Dan's remembering being introduced to her months before at a reception at the NAGA gallery (see the "Fieldwork Ideas" section at the end of this chapter). The introducer was NAGA's director, Arthur Dion, who indeed was now, most unusually, taking this neophyte on and giving her a solo show.

Earlier, Dan followed up his memory from a West Coast neurobiology conference of a conversation about an Alabama artist doing a major "installation" piece about memory. The artist drew heavily on the "monohierarchical" scheme of memory systems proposed by Endel Tulving, a distinguished psychologist who was married to an artist. This led to Transaction #21 with Pat Potter.

The artist of Transaction #19 (discussed further later on) also is collected by a professor at the Harvard Education School. This professor thereby becomes a new non-artist contact in Dan's networks. Dan's most recent transaction, #37 (see *The Patchwork of Our Lives* on p. 171), was by a young artist who was doing an M.A. thesis in education under the professor of Transaction #19, Howard Gardner, author of a delightful book on children's art.

4. Agency (compare Chapters 1 and 5) recurs in all sorts of ways in Dan's building of the Memory Collection. Quite often the Schacters go looking with friends whose judgments can be significant. Transaction #30 shows that Temple Parker, whose essay was excerpted earlier, had been sent by director Kelly Barette of the Beck Gallery, who, on the strength of

discussion with Schacter a year earlier concerning Transactions #7 and #8, probed for memory connections when Temple Parker sent in unsolicited work (see the "Fieldwork Ideas" section at the end of this chapter). Similarly, art consultant Judith Green Cheloff, after being brought in as agent for Transaction #15, kept alert to Dan's criteria and eventually brought about Transaction #35: This is one of the two most expensive pieces to date; #36 is the other (see the "Fieldwork Ideas" section at the end of this chapter).

Artists also scouted for him among other artists: For example, Pamela Sienna, who had driven up from Hartford to bring the Schacters her painting in Transaction #19, and thereupon discussed the Memory Collection, later sent them an *Art News* review on the memory-related work of Mildred Howard in San Francisco, two of whose works they subsequently acquired. And gallery director Christina Lanzl, after handling a sale, Transaction #23, by a young German woman painter of wartime memories, later told Dan of her own memory-related work; he then commissioned a new piece along those lines, Transaction #32.

5. Dan has several times commissioned new works from painters of previous acquisitions, such as in Transaction #32, just discussed. Sometimes this is triggered by his repeated negotiation over price and other matters on each painting. Sometimes it has to do with constraints from hanging the Memory Collection in their Newton home (there are also a few reproductions in his office).

6. The collection has been funded largely by money from a major prize in psychology, which Dan won for his research discoveries on implicit memory. The fund is nearly depleted after his last two "blockbuster" purchases, so the Memory Collection will now grow more slowly. It may focus tighter than ever on the work's conception in memory terms. Dan and others think that this tight focus accounts for the notably high artistic quality of his collection.

Perhaps Dan will, instead or also, build around more specific subthemes. He already has two works set off by Alzheimer's disease in relatives of the artists: the work *Alzheimer's I,* by Stoepel Peckham (Transaction #29 in the "Fieldwork Ideas" section at the end of this chapter), and *Tangled Memories III,* by Kim Zabbia (Transaction #34). Perhaps Dan will acquire only works with expositions as scientifically articulate as Parker's. Or he could combine these two criteria, as in the Pat Potter piece mentioned earlier. He bought two later works from Schaffer that had specific reference to retrograde amnesia and its relative preservation of older, remote memories, which is known in psychology as Ribot's law.

What seems unlikely is that Dan will shift to criteria that would be scientifically arbitrary, such as size of the piece or its medium of execution.

7. Dan's obsessive pursuit of memory had led him to African American

artists by quite a different path from mine (described in Chapter 5). Mildred Howard's pieces—see item 4 above and #28 in the "Fieldwork Ideas" section at the end of this chapter—are about memory in a social and political way. Her major pieces in the spring 1991 show at the San Francisco Art Institute were memories about black children killed in Soweto in 1976. And Schacter had acquired two other pieces by a black artist, Cheryl Warrick, Transactions #10 and #11, that attracted him by psychological memory overtones; #11 (see *S Series #3* on p. 172) has since been donated to the Boston Museum of Fine Arts (see p. 173).

All seven themes suggest bases on which additional publics of recognition may be developing—for example, a collaborator in Dan's research has acquired two pieces by Cheryl Warrick.

GUIDE TO FURTHER READING

Mukerji and Schudson (1991) survey recent social science assessments of popular versus high art; see also the sustained argument by Gans (1974).

The basic source on CalArts is Adler (1979). Abbott (1988) discusses the social metabolism of professions.

Sociologist Howard Becker, in his comprehensive analysis of art worlds, clarifies maverick roles in general (1982, Chapter 8). His treatment of American composer Charles Ives, for example, can be a model for maverick painter Richard Bowman. There is one book on Bowman (1986). There is also one article by him (1973) that explains the development of his uses first of fluorescent lacquers and subsequently of fluorescent oil paints and acrylic paints. In a magnificently illustrated volume, Waddington (1970) argues and demonstrates the close relations between science and painting in this century to which Bowman's vision points.

Since *Akenfeld: Portrait of an English Village,* Ronald Blythe has published (1979) a study on aging, also researched by in-depth interviews. Instructive interviews with poets are found in Packard (1974), and observation of newer breeds of modern dancers are found in Novack (1990).

Simpson (1981) gives artists' perspectives on the SoHo neighborhood, whose business ecology Zukin (1989) traces and explains.

FIELDWORK IDEAS

1. The next time you spend some time in a large suburban shopping mall (preferably an enclosed one), explore the answers to the following questions: In what ways are the arts (what arts, exactly) represented, and in what sense are the various identities making up the mall proclaimed and celebrated in arts? What ties, literal or figurative, are being accounted—both ties within the mall and ties to the larger world? By what artistic forms? Could some new arts be emerging here in suburbia?

2. I used the historical present in writing of the part-timers. Have they remained part-time? In finding and then tracing one or more of them to the present, you will learn a good deal about how art worlds do and do not keep track of themselves. (Only one pseudonym is used—George Mitchell.)

3. The notes kept by Daniel Schacter on his art collecting are a model of precision and clarity for you to emulate. See this excerpt:

Memory Collection

Works are listed in chronological order of acquisition; order is defined by take-home date, which signifies entry into the Memory Collection (MC). The abbreviation "IV" represents the initial viewing.

28. *Cedar Bayou*   Mildred Howard   Gallery Paule Anglim, San Francisco

    24x24", mixed media on window frame

    IV: April 29, 1992   MC: April 29, 1992 $1800

Memory link: Uses reworked photograph (circa 1920s) of relatives from artist's family album printed on an old wooden window frame to address role of memory at personal, familial, and socio-cultural levels; buttons from artist's childhood clothes, attached to window frame, are used as symbols of memory.

Comments: Received a letter from Pamela Sienna on 4/6/92 with an attached review of a Mildred Howard exhibit in November 1991 *Art News*. The review made clear that Howard's work focused on memory, and Sienna suggested that I might want to look into it. Wrote to the gallery the same day, and received a reply on 4/20 together with slides and a catalogue devoted to Howard on the occasion of her receiving a major award in 1991. The essays in the catalogue indicated that memory, in both the personal and socio-cultural senses, was the core motivation for most of Howard's work. Sue and I both loved one of the slide pieces in particular, and I called the gallery the next day and worked out a deal for it with gallery rep Jon Sorenson, including a 10% discount. He indicated that he had to call Howard to check on the availability of the work, because she had it with her. He called back a little later with "bad news and good news": bad news was that the Seattle Arts Commission had the day before decided to purchase the piece that we wanted; good news was that the gallery had another piece that used a similar photographic image. Sorenson claimed that this other work was at least as strong and perhaps stronger than the first, but it did not show up well on slide so he hadn't sent it. He was so sure that if we liked the first one that we would love this that he agreed to send it on the condition that I could return it if not pleased and he would cover the shipping. Work arrived in wooden crate a day earlier than expected via FedEx. Colors are indeed subtle and require ideal lighting, but the piece is extremely evocative, and I called Sorenson with decision to keep it the same day that it arrived.

He mentioned that Howard was excited about the idea of one of her pieces going into a memory collection and wanted to hear more about it. Wrote her a letter on 5/4.

29. *Alzheimer's I*   E. Stoepel Peckham   Pindar Gallery, New York

21x16", mixed media collage

IV: May 7, 1992   MC: May 7, 1992 $650

Memory link: Meditation on loss of memory and intellect by artist's father as a consequence of Alzheimer's disease.

Comments: After attending Gerry Edelman's conference on selectionism and the brain at the Neurosciences Institute on May 5 and 6, allowed a couple of hours to walk through SoHo on Thursday morning the 7th before taking the shuttle back to Boston. Went to Pindar in part because it was on the route, and in part because the title of Peckham's show, "Fine Lines and Asymptotes," sounded interesting. Potential concern with memory was indicated by a couple of large sculpture/installation-type pieces entitled "Picnic with Memories." Then saw the Alzheimer I and II collages, together with artist's statement in accompanying materials that the pieces are meditations on her father's loss of memory/intellect during AD. Alz II wasn't particularly appealing, but Alz I was visually strong and symbolically rich in its treatment of amnesia and dementia. Had some brief discussion with the gallery people, who told me that if I wanted the piece I could take it with me, since the show would be closing in a couple of days. Relatively easy decision to go for it. Took the wrapped piece back to the hotel via subway and then got a cab out to LaGuardia. Received a letter from the artist on 5/18 containing a few thoughts about the piece and an expressed interest in seeing the memory collection next time she came to Boston. Wrote back on 5/21 and received another note on 6/15 indicating that she and her husband would likely make their visit in the fall.

30. *Memory*   Temple Lee Parker   Randall Beck Gallery, Boston

20x30", acrylic on canvas

IV: May 9, 1992   MC: May 20, 1992 $900

Memory link: Uses contrasting bright/dark colors and overlapping shapes to depict ideas about relation between clearly recollected memories and contextual background of dimly recollected or nonconscious memories; memory as means of escaping constraints of linear time by allowing "random" retrieval from temporally noncontiguous parts of the past; and the overlap among temporally noncontiguous memories.

Comments: Received package from Kelly Barrett on Saturday May 9, delivered by mailman as we were saying goodbye to neighbors Peter and Karen Wood, who had just dropped by with their daughter Nina. Contained a letter from Kelly saying that she had received some (unsolicited) slides from an artist named Temple Parker including a piece entitled "Memory," that she contacted the artist and told her about my interests, and that it was important for me to know about the conceptual bases of the piece and why it is called "Memory." Parker then sent Kelly a seven page typed essay, with illustrations, concerning the background of the painting, its relation to earlier work of hers, and the kinds of ideas about memory that it explores. Kelly sent along the essay with a slide and photos. The piece was strong visually and the ideas and verbal expression of the artist were remarkably lucid and intriguing. Called Kelly Saturday afternoon and indicated my strong interest. She said that she would call Parker and arrange for her to send the piece down to the gallery (from Hampden, Maine, where she lives). Called on 5/19 indicating that the piece had arrived. I went down to view it on the morning of 5/20 and had no hesitation about going for it on the spot. Wrote Parker on 5/26, sending along a few articles and extending open invitation to come and see collection. Received 6 page reply from her on Monday 6/8, indicating among other things that she would be visiting Boston in a few days and wanted to come by for a visit. Called her on Tuesday afternoon 6/9 and set it up for Monday morning 6/15. She came out to the house via T and spent a couple of very interested hours touring the collection. Brought along some info on her current activities, a picture of a new piece on a memory theme (quite similar to "Memory"), and mentioned that she was in the process of doing a couple of pieces on amnesia. Told her to send me slides as they become available and that it was likely that I'd want another piece at some point in the future. Drove her to Harvard Square on the way to work.

Addendum: When giving a colloquium at BU (Steve Grossberg's center) on 12/8/92, was approached by vaguely familiar face during question period—turned out to be Temple Parker, who had just moved to Cambridge. Said that she had completed some new memory pieces and would soon send along photos and text. Received packet on Monday 12/14. Most of the works were like *Memory*, but was intrigued by a small piece, *Static*, that combined collage with the abstract material. Given that I had been having doubts about the viability of *Memory* in the collection because of its degree of abstraction and "distance" from the memory theme, I wrote and proposed a trade of *Memory* for *Static*. Received reply from Parker on 12/21 indicating that she didn't feel right about the trade because *Static* was a much smaller and in some sense lesser piece than *Memory*. Wrote back indicating that was OK, and then followed up with a call on 12/23 asking whether I could actually see the new works in person. Went by her Cambridge studio, just a few blocks from WJH, on the afternoon of 12/23. Agreed that *Static* was indeed too small of a piece to trade for *Memory*, and had long discussion about relevant issues. She offered to do a new piece using the basic approach laid out in *Static*, comparable in scope to *Memory*, and swap it for *Memory*. In the meanwhile, she also agreed to lend *Static* after cleaning up the frame a bit. She brought *Static* by the office on the afternoon of 12/24. Received favorable comments on during 1/93 visits to the collection from Anne Turyn and Nina Neilsen, and passed these on to Temple in the form of brief notes; she responded indicating appreciation. Indicated that she would likely complete the new to-be-traded-for piece sometime during March or April 1993.

31. *It Shines by Its Absence*   Loretta Harms   Museum of Fine Arts School, Boston

   13x25", mirror, silkscreen, coverseal

   IV: April 26, 1992   MC: May 21, 1992 $600

Memory link: On one side, shows silhouette face looking in partially colored-over mirror, where coloring represents traces of memory, to express idea that memory is often illusory and that past exists only as a reflection that is reconstructed in the image of the rememberer; on the other side, figural allusion to ambiguous event that could be remembered in different ways.

Comments: Went to fifth-year competition exhibit by graduating MFA students at Museum of Fine Arts School on drizzly Sunday afternoon. While looking through catalogue that contained statements by each of the artists, came across paragraph-length statement by Harms indicating that the purpose of her work was to use mirrors and other reflecting materials to illustrate how the mind attempts to "bring back and reorder" the past. Checked out her work, which was highly distinctive and mature, and was able to have a long chat with her about it, since this was the opening reception for the exhibit. Thought I recognized her from an encounter at Gallery NAGA a few months earlier, when Arthur Dion introduced me to her as a young artist who he was signing up with the gallery. This was confirmed when I asked her what she would be doing next year and she indicated that she had just signed on with NAGA and would be in a group show and solo show there; at that point, we both remembered the earlier encounter. She had been a philosophy major at Tufts and was conversant with a fair amount of philosophical and psychological writing on memory, which provided the conceptual motivation for her work. After talking to her and looking over all of her pieces fairly carefully, I chose "It shines ..." because it had the clearest memory link and was strong visually. When I went to talk to the person who handles sales from the exhibit, was informed that 3 of her 8 pieces had already sold that afternoon, and that an hour earlier someone had been torn between "It shines ..." and another piece, finally choosing the other. Had to wait until show ended for delivery of piece, but paid for it and had correspondence with Harms in the interim, including sending her a couple of my articles, which she apparently read with interest and thought would give her some new ideas to explore. She came out to the house via the T to deliver the piece in the early evening on Wednesday 5/20, and was eager to see the rest of the collection, which she liked a lot. Also was eager to read more about amnesia with a view toward doing some pieces on an amnesia theme, so I sent her a packet of articles the next day. She also invited us to her Gallery NAGA opening in June and for a visit to her studio sometime during the summer.

* * *

36. *Children of the Wood*   Catherine McCarthy   Nielsen Gallery, Boston

   60x44", diptych, oil and varnish on canvas

   IV: June 6, 1992   MC: June 20, 1992 $4800

Memory link: Contrasts blurred memories of artist's childhood with persistence of emotional bonds developed during childhood, symbolized by bright red ribbon that ties ghost-like figure of artist as child to fragmentary figure representing her brother; "Children of the wood" is name of a fairy tale that is partially written on canvas in block letters, mostly obscured by layers of paint.

Comments: Bought Art New England from Reading International on Thursday, 6/4, and saw review of McCarthy's show at Nielsen Gallery in March (which I had missed). Included statement that for McCarthy, "paint is memory," and went on to discuss various ways in which memory is focal point of the works in the show. Went by Nielsen on Saturday 6/6 to see if they had anything around. They were in the midst of redoing the gallery, but I managed to get a bunch of slides, printed materials, and a videotape of the show. Both Sue and I were particularly taken by "Children of the wood," but the quality of the videotape was poor and I hadn't gotten a slide of it. Went back on Thursday 6/11 on the way into work, and it turned out that all the slides were gone but the piece itself was there. Nina Nielsen and colleagues had to work hard to pull it out from behind a bunch of other pieces in the midst of their reconstruction. Was very impressed by it, but even with Nielsen's upfront offer of a 20% discount, the $4800 tab was steep. Asked them whether they could bring in a couple of other pieces for comparison. Showed videotape Saturday night 6/16 during family visit. Returned again to gallery on Wednesday 6/17 to view it with Sue and Janie before having 40th birthday lunch at Cactus Club. Nina N. said that she had told McCarthy about the memory collection, and that she was thrilled by the idea of one of her pieces going into it, because "that's what I'm doing." A couple of the pieces from the videotape couldn't be brought in because they were being exhibited at a show of hers in San Francisco, but they had a couple of new ones that were about to be hung for a group show, one of which, Taproot, took an interesting, more intellectual approach to memory than did "Children... ." Nina N. praised "Children ..." to the limit, noting that while the others were nice paintings, "Children ... " was a major work, one that had a chance to be shown in the Whitney Biennial because of Whitney director and former ICA director David Ross's interest in McCarthy. Sue loved "Children ... ," Janie liked it a lot but had some misgivings, I was strongly attracted to "Children ... " and to "Taproot" for different reasons. Couldn't get a true fix on the piece because it wasn't hung and the gallery was in disarray during the hanging of their new show. Was told that McCarthy would be present at opening of group show on 6/19, so went back late that Friday afternoon, just before the beginning of the opening, to meet her. Saw the piece hung properly with good lighting for the first time and was blown away. Had long talk with McCarthy about it, which confirmed my earlier impression of what the piece was about. Although not actually part of the show, "Children ... " attracted the biggest crowd of onlookers, including the admiration of an artist from NYC who had driven up to Boston specifically to meet McCarthy. McCarthy indicated that she thought Nina N. would loan the piece out on a trial basis, and she was indeed delighted to do so. Arranged to pick it up the next day on the way back from picking up Mom at South Station; got there around noon but had to sit in the car for several minutes as a thundershower passed. Agreed with Nina that decision would be made within the week. Took some time to get it hung properly but finally succeeded. Sue was already sold, and I came to a decision within a couple of hours. Janie came out to the house and was super enthusiastic. Called back Nina on 6/26 indicating positive decision, and she indicated that she and Catherine M. would love to come out and see the collection and also read some of my articles. Agreed to set up a visit for end of July, and sent them both a packet of papers. Received reply from Catherine M. on 7/9, saying that she enjoyed the articles and that she would look forward to seeing the collection after going out to SF for an opening of a group show there. She came out to view the collection Friday afternoon, 8/7, and had a very positive response to it.

MEASURES AND MODELS

I was one of three non-theatre members of the advisory group to the theatre survey commissioned by the National Endowment of the Arts, the results of which occupied the previous chapter. I outlined an intervention for building new and larger publics. (It never made it into the final recommendations from this NEA study.) In the proposal I suggested a design for field studies of how social networks shape publics: the "Monday–Thursday Proposal."

Rationale. Audiences are the central concern and challenge of the American professional theatre. Professional theatre in America has established its appeal to mature men and women with shows—dramatic, comedic, and musical—that each draw 100,000 and more in a year to combination theatre and nearly as many over several years in subscription audiences for repertory. Special-audience theatre organizations have found how to reach with special troupes many other audiences, such as children and teenagers.

Our professional theatre proposes with government aid to break through the financial barrier, and barriers of habit, which at present tend to limit audiences to upper middle class professional and business couples. This proposal is at the same time another means to enhance the vitality of all sorts of community, voluntary, and working groups of Americans. Attendance at a performance by members of an affinity group not only will stimulate their corporate life but also will bring fresh life and new independence to the professional theatre. Word-of-mouth assessment and publicity will come to predominate over published accounts of shows by the few media critics.

This proposal addresses chronic problems: Performances throughout the week are necessary to cover the fixed overhead costs of theatres, yet attendance on weekday nights often is less than half the weekend attendance. The estimated maximum cost per year to the Endowment would be $37,000,000.

Proposal. The National Endowment for the Arts will administer a matching program to help more groups attend American professional theatre. This aid is eligible to any size and type of professional theatre. Prototypes have run successfully in New York among upper-income groups, and such a program seems to lead to a permanent increase in theatre-going habits, partly through the social reinforcement of joint attendance.

1. The NEA will match payments for blocks of contiguous seats for joint attendance by affinity groups at any evening or matinee performance on Monday through Thursday under the following conditions:

a. All performers must be paid at the appropriate Actors Equity scale for that theatre size.

b. Eligible groups are those defined as affinity groups by regulations of the Civil Aeronautics Board or by the International Air Transport Association.

c. Payment from the group is a lump sum from its representative on or before the performance date, in amount equal to one-half the minimum posted seat price times the number of seats in the block. Payment is made to the producer's agent, with matching payment from the NEA to the same agent within thirty days.

d. The group payment may be in advance, at half the reduced rate for subscription series, for any number of performances so long as attendance is restricted to group members and immediate family and dependents; the NEA matches this payment within thirty days.

e. The group must pay for a minimum of thirty seats at a performance.

f. At the end of each theatre season, a producing organization that has participated shall obtain from the NEA, upon presentation of a schedule of as many performances and productions as the preceding year, an interest-free advance payment equal to one-half of the total matching payments in the preceding year.

2. Each participating production organization must hold available for affinity group purchase at least one-quarter of all seats, excluding season

tickets, until one week before a performance, for performances on Monday through Thursday. This applies to all productions. At least half the seats held must be those with the highest posted prices.

3. Each participating producer must, within thirty days, pay to the treasury of the attending affinity group, through its ticket purchaser, a fee of 7.5 percent of total receipts for the block of seats, including any government matching funds, pro rata.

8

Conclusion

Our current arts are vastly and magnificently inventive technically, and they proliferate in volume and avenue despite their niggardly share of our national income. Your fieldwork should give you some sense for the intense concentration and also for the shared elations of these artworks, constructions and performances alike. Within our art worlds there is enough richness of relation, together with sufficient intricacy of conceptual development, to equal earlier culminations in renaissances. Yet their alignments with their own and others' troubles with identity are as yet awry, in America as elsewhere.

Creativity is inescapably social by its main criterion, that others not have uttered such an artwork before. And in case after case, we have seen how it was interplay among many successive efforts across an art world network that cumulated into creativity of greatest scope, yielding artworks that help set a new genre or style. The growing ubiquity of agency, the professionalization of art, thus can be more stimulus than inhibition to creativity, depending on how social networks and boundaries are shaped.

What is not so clear, however, is how much such delegated creativity, such art through agency, contributes to a full spectrum of identities and especially to strivings for expression and assertion of identities other than for artists and elites. Artworks, along with arts themselves with their styles and genres, can be seen as narratives available for use by identities and in constructing other identities. Artists' goals in their careers, however, in either commercial or academic variants, need not lead to artworks that aptly or adequately generate representations of other identities, personal and group.

Strivings for richer identities are the social source of all art. Argument about the spectrum of identities today usually comes in the idiom of popular versus high culture. One impulse is to argue for popular culture as descended from tribal art, which represents a people—but is that today an ethnicity (which particular one?) or a nation or a city or ... ? The second impulse is to support artworks evolving in lines able to sustain critical appreciation; one then suppresses the knowledge that such coherence is unlikely to be sustained without framing and support by elites that will show up, however indirectly, in the art.

The arts are as varied and messy and fascinating as the social worlds that they help us to experience and reconstruct. Ripples of fashion inundate the artworks produced in our time; so this book looked behind fashion. This book looked at the juncture between tangible social arrangements and artworks to see how and when shifts in style occurred. Of course there occurs, in most periods and contexts, just reproduction or refurbishing instead of whole shifts of style, but that requires explanation too. And which spectra of arts are seen as distinct deserves explanation too.

In conclusion, I develop three themes that have been left largely implicit thus far—differences among arts; art and reality; and, finally, prognostication about arts from our identity needs.

Spectrum of Arts

Separate arts are constructs, not exogenous facts. There is no particular number of arts, whatever Aristotle or later cultural arbiters have said. Instead, all the boundary lines are constructed and hence negotiable. Nor are the arts fixed by physical nature. Some arts do relate more to one and some more to another of the human sensory capacities. Music cannot be much mimetic, for example, whereas painting originally must be mimetic, with literature intermediate; this combination of truths can be shown to explain much about opera. But what does mimesis have to say, for example, about dance or about the possibility of an olfactory art?

We have seen that style in art production balances among competing tensions between social and cultural faces and that distinct arts are but styles writ large. One need not expect logic or reason to decide what is and isn't in or out of a particular art. We can probe why today's particular arts are distinguished from one another, but it is not up to us to define particular arts. Each art in its time and place is a social fact more massive than, but otherwise like, the styles being reconstructed around us in our arts today.

Approaches to beauty are argued and constructed within particular social contexts of arts, although the separate approaches may, like ideas of truth in sciences, come to share features. Each separate art world, like each science, comes to reflect a larger institutional system that enfolds a whole gamut of art worlds and reaches out into and across still other worlds, perhaps out as far as a civilization. And views of truth and beauty in such larger context get reflected back—only sometimes through conscious agency by elites—and shape views and voices, outside the parties' own knowledge. Thus an aesthetics comes to any critic or critics largely as a given, despite a core of it being from their own deeply sited concerns about identity.

Fuzziness characterizes the separations between one art and another, just as aesthetic discriminations of quality are fuzzy. Mixed media, such as in video arts, are not just a modern peculiarity. And the internal differentiations and complementarities that characterize each art world shape also the mode, as well as the content, of art production. Just as social formations themselves are in fact heterogeneous matters of networks rather than the crisp societies or organizations supposed in our rhetorics, so also artistic formations are heterogeneous. One attempts to impose order through terms like *genre* and *artwork* and *performance* and so on, yet these terms in fact shade into one another.

Should, for example, art-rock be considered a new genre? It draws on dance and performance art as well as rock music. It derives to some extent from conceptual art and from minimalism in visual arts. It shares with other new music formations like jazz-rock fusion the use of high-tech electronics and found sounds (be it water-tap dripping or traffic noise) together with a preoccupation with social change.

The distinctive problem, though, is that the artists are themselves highly aware of—and determined to manipulate, to draw impact out of—the perceived relation of art to society. And they also combine elements from a number of aesthetic canons while at the same time rejecting each. What art-rock is becomes a moving target, and whether it is a genre must be assessed exactly with an eye to the shifting intentions of its authors to keep it a shifting process. By contrast, in jazz-rock fusion "each work draws on very similar sets of elements, within a strong canon, making genre membership relatively unambiguous" (Bodinger-deUriarte 1989, p. 40).

This author goes on to draw out similar ambiguities as to genre status for the well-known earlier art complexes of Dada (urinals and nonsense writings as art) and Bauhaus (the first distinctly modern-looking design and architecture, from 1920s Germany): "The definitional core for each of the three genres is an interactive oppositional ethic combining anti-canon orientation, interdisciplinary approach, and multi-media expression" (Bodinger-deUriarte 1989, p. 40).

Here is an art historian on shifting boundaries among other modern arts:

> Artists since Impressionism have often proclaimed a separation of art from literature, the breaking of a relationship that was certainly close to the heart of classicism. A looser affiliation with music has often been offered in exchange. Music, it was said, reached deeper levels of response than could be

reached by an art dependent on learned interpretation. The abstract elements of art—colour, form, scale, their deployment in hard, soft, rhythmically assertive or quiet ways—would strike through man's veneer of house-trained understanding to the instinctive, natural man beneath. ... Art abandoned, or seemed to abandon, its duty of instructing, but that did not mean it was willing to yield its high status to books, newspapers, and films. Like music it aimed at an even more exalted plane: that of religion—and in seeking that role it sought also its primordial place at the center of human experience. (Lynton 1980, p. 160)

Lynton here is dealing with abstract expressionism, which was the last of the six cases of style change in Chapter 4.

On mechanisms of intermixing, one can for example point to New York City, and within it to Happenings. These served to tie visual arts into the idea of theatrical time—of one time common between audience and performers, who now included painters as well as actors. Dance also shared in this sense of time, and visual artists like sculptor Charles Ross and painters Robert Rauschenberg and Robert Morris contributed to dance performances in New York, especially with Merce Cunningham.

All these sorts of linkages among and with the arts have limitations. Here is the assessment of a student (already quoted in Chapter 7) who had catholic tastes for other arts yet always remained a dancer:

I usually see "ART" as a clump. The clump is a certain type of person, a frame of mind and Emotions. There are base lines, art themes if you will, that flow through all different types of artistic work. Yet if taken individually, as we get closer we see how individual and different each art is.

Recently a close friend of mine asked me to read a screenplay that he had spent the entire semester working on. I have had a lot of trouble deciding what I think of the play. The biggest problem is the camera. I can't seem to visualize his descriptions of "soft focus," or "close-in," "pan-out quickly." But I am forced to consider my reactions because this person is a friend. I am forced to relate. ... An added shock was when I found that a ballet scene had been written into a dream sequence. Now there was my art—enclosed within—though clearly in its own right. Often I feel the same thing with Degas' paintings/sketches of dancers. I am drawn to the subject and what he is trying to represent. I appreciate his desire to portray dancers and thank him yet he cannot truly reach them [the dancers]. (Ann Dressler, private communication, April 14, 1979)

This student is uneasy with non-ballet dance as well:

The remainder of my week was spent reading Marge Theeman's Ph.D. thesis [Harvard sociology department—a participation-observation study of national networks of new movements in dance in America]. I studied it over a period of two weeks, which really turned out (no pun intended) to be a wise idea since my initial reaction was fear. This brings up a block of feelings that I have yet to sort out. I do not like most articles, books etc., that I read on dance. The cause could be my conservative upbringing or part of the ballet snob syndrome; a major part seems to be frustration that people are not writing with the good of the art in mind. These feelings are the same for most dance performances that I see. What are these people doing? I'm wary of the yoga and creative movement stuff because it makes dancers sound all freaky and bizarre. We don't need that, haven't we got enough problems spreading the art as it is? (Ann Dressler, private communication, February 23, 1979)

Perception and Extremes

No ordinary book like this one can adequately convey to you the magic of art's levels of reality. Exploring contexts, social and cultural, that are pushed to the extreme provides one way to probe how art can induce distinct levels through its portrayal of reality. Return to the theatre.

What happens when the audience becomes part of the cast? In a sense that was the case before drama and before ritual even earlier. But the interesting question is different: It concerns what happens after drama, both in its everyday role sense and in its ceremonial theatre sense, is well established. *Now* what appearance is taken by a social formation in which the audience is coterminous with the cast?

One such appearance is the state of liminality. Liminality is an occasion, a Mardi Gras, for the suspension of all normal rules. This is a suspension conceded as legitimate by all. Liminality is signaled by ceremonial boundaries; that is, there is a self-conscious embedding within a temporary culture, which is made explicit usually as rejection of some other cultural set of rules. The period of liminality serves to interrupt causal chains of agency and gaming. Usually this suspension holds only for some short, very specific period.

Other such appearances are in social states of extreme order, states that are the antipodes on degree of order to states of liminality. A prime example of such extreme order is the dominance hierarchy resulting from a tournament, such as in tennis. The tournament is a conscious enactment of the pecking order found in chicken flocks. A tournament consists in a set of pairings among a population in which within each pair one dominates the other. A perfect, or near-perfect, dominance ordering is one in which if one actor dominates a second who dominates some third, then the first also dominates the third in direct paired encounter. The outcomes of pairings are to be arrayed to permit inference of a transitive ordering from the outcomes, divorced from positions in other social networks and thus from institutional position.

Tournament and Mardi Gras are mutual extremes. These two extremes, of tournament and liminality, are perfect converses. In the tournament the social standing of each actor is totally clear and there is, as a result, complete ambiguity as to the cultural basis of the social standings. In liminal formations, however, there is zero ambiguity because there is an agreement on an extremely simple "new" culture of rules. Usually this is just an erasure of previous rules. At the same time, there is complete indefiniteness in social patterns of relation.

Liminal occasions mush together disparate and remote swirls of action; so they are the antipodes to the specialization that becomes characteristic with art worlds. Liminality breaks up agency even while it embeds in overall context. One can see this duality in Mexican fiesta, in student strikes, in pilgrimages, in masses, in reunions, around a dramatic stage, at imperial apotheoses (royal inaugurations). Liminality does cope with phenomenological confusion, but liminality deals with identity by dissolving it.

Tournaments break apart larger contexts. This is at the cost of erasing verifiable cultural content as criterion of dominance. By-products, such as hierarchies, may emerge in the larger context around the tournaments. Various tournaments, each with relatively arbitrary cultural bases, can be fitted together in projects for control. Chickens build their flock's pecking order sincerely, but unlike humans they have no capacity to concatenate tournaments into ladders of mobility and hierarchies of control.

Liminality and tournaments both emphasize discontinuity. Time in social life has a picaresque quality overall, but moment by moment it is remorselessly locked into the previous step, derived from the preceding configuration. Memory, whether as vengeance or forethought, interrupts the lock-in only occasionally. Most of the picaresque is generated for each actor from interruptions through gamings by others. Liminality produces the illusion of an enlarged present in which lock-ins are broken. Liminality is essential to art. Tournaments impose an enlarged present by fiat. Tournaments make mock of preceding continuities of interdependent action. Tournaments are essential to art.

Proposition 8.1. Liminality and tournaments are essential to art, in both its production and its reception.

Liminality is signaled by ceremonial boundary; that is, by there being a self-conscious embedding within an explicit culture, an embedding often as rejection. At the same time, the period of liminality serves to interrupt causal chains of agency and gaming. Usually this suspension holds only for some short, very specific period.

Hear Agnew again on market and theatre:

> So closely identified were the institutions of market and theater during the later Middle Ages that few contemporaries even thought to compare them. It was as if they shared a common anatomy or frame that occasion might dress out differently according to the needs of the ecclesiastical and commercial calendars. ... Market crosses and city gates were converted to platforms for spectacular civic pageantry quite as easily as hucksters' stalls were adapted to the more modest demands of booth theater. *Both forms of exchange evoked the experience of a threshold; both occupied extraterritorial, extratemporal spaces that served imagination as well as interest, cosmology as well as commerce;* and both operated as containers or crucibles of social antagonism. Events repeatedly showed the capacity of ritual drama to reconcile social conflict. (Agnew 1988, p. 40, emphasis supplied)

Liminality includes and directs attention back to the audience. Perception is as requisite as performance to achieving artwork; audience, like performer, require both. Perception depends upon reinforcement and support in social networks and collectivities. One can see this not only among visitors to art museums but also in discussions at home over what music to hear. Perceptions become joined and trained into accustomed perspectives.

Contrast two examples. Italian painting of the Renaissance period was "history" painting, painting of elevated topics. It basically concerned action, of heroic sort, leading to dogma, and *so it takes a unique perspective as through a transparent window.* Dutch descriptive painting is very different. In it boundaries are blurred even as objects presented well; this was an art of persistence that was concerned above all with practice and what is popular, as produced by guilds and crafts throughout northern European cities: *So it takes a static scene, as in a mirror.* The Dutch were a whole people in search of identity:

> Once freed from imperial authority, [the Dutch Republic] was left to make itself up without any of the self-evident markers of territory, tribe, language or dynasty that were customarily held to be criteria for national self-consciousness. ... Unlike the Venetians, whose historical mythology supplied a pedigree of immemorial antiquity and continuity, the Dutch had committed themselves irrevocably to a "cut" with their actual past, and were now obliged to reinvent it so as to close the wound. (Schama 1987, p. 67)

Social constraints on and from perception are not limited to the visual. Perception is to performance as hearer is to talker: In any art, cultural en-

actment is a continuing conversation. Return again to Agnew's colloca-
tion of theater with market, from Chapter 4:

> In their earliest versions, the mystery and miracle plays brought the time-
> less, placeless, and essentially emblematic characteristics of ritual enactment
> into a milieu (the marketplace) whose ancient ambiguities had already
> drawn to it a complex, confining, and controlling body of ceremonial and le-
> gal practices. ... The medieval market square became the site where actors
> and spectators—the roles were interchangeable—could mime, mum, and
> mock the hierarchical principles of the surrounding society.
>
> Festive celebration of this kind sought to revive ... a collective affirmation
> of group identity and of the social rank by which that identity was struc-
> tured. ... The legitimacy of the marketplace as a social institution was insepa-
> rable from its theatricality, for the medieval criteria of authority and authen-
> ticity required that both attributes be bodied forth: *deliberately displayed,*
> *performed and witnessed.* (Agnew 1988, pp. 33, 40, emphasis supplied)

Such perception is a communal achievement, not a matter of vision. No
artwork is an artwork except as it is received as such, received within a
code.

The code of perception can become the stuff of controversy in the
hands of critics. Consider the case of Cézanne's artworks. One critic
writes: "I am concerned with the meaning of the layers of interpretation
superimposed on Cézanne's art as much as with any 'original' meaning
that might be ascribed to his work. ... The changing state of interpretation
thus seems to transform a work of art in advance of its being seen, even as
it preserves the work by keeping it before the public's attention" (Shiff
1984, p. xiii). This is not just the problematic of art, it is the problematic of
ordinary life.

In Chapter 3, I argued that social organization can be seen as the interlocking of stereotyped stories that actors proffer and through which they
perceive and perform and maneuver. Cultural and social organization
thus wind around each other. These stereotyped stories that make up the
cultural side of social organization settle into packages. These packages
are standard; they are held in common within some social formation and
indeed serve to map the formation's boundaries. Such packages also provide the flexibility needed for useful accounting of ordinary social life, erratic as it in fact is, so that there is call for stories of liminality and tournament.

All arts contribute to stories of identity and relation, so the arts are con-
stitutive rather than superfluous for social organization. Sets of stories are
the stuff of daily socializing: They are used in its endless reconstructions
by interpretation of selves and of social organization. And such sets also
embrace extremes in stories such that a set can bracket all the possibilities

that may need mapping. Perception is enhanced through provision for liminality and tournament.

Identity Urgencies and Public Support

Art was crucial to social life long before there were artists, or particular arts, because identities and ties always are being celebrated and announced with the help of artworks. Each of us looks forward to fresh action but also looks backward in rendering accounts of how ordinary social action came about, and such unending tension is demanding and difficult to live through. Art provides help, and thus artworks and their artists reflect these tensions between innovation and control in social networks among human identities.

Artworks contribute to ceremonial, domination, and ostentation as well as to entertainment (cf. Schudson 1989). This remains true whether or not arts are perceived as also contributing, like a science or theology, to shaping some sort of higher reality, some beauty. From the beginning, works of art are involved in and also reflect and identify social formations, be they tribe or class, generation or market, sect or gender, or that complex social formation that we describe as person.

In earlier eras, when artists were workmen or artisans, the focus was the work of art, which was thought of as conceived, as it was controlled, by the principal or patron, individual or corporate. The artwork represented the patron's identity and ties rather than the artist's. There can come displacements to ever new foci of control. The displacement process can thus spiral further into identities of new levels, during which artists' reputations come to appear central.

The Pre-Raphaelites of Victorian London were an intermediate example. Particular identity, such as Dante Rossetti's, and particular relations, as of Rossetti to his shop-girl fiancée, became represented, accounted, and celebrated in particular artworks. Other themes emerged, including medievalism, that coupled the young men's identities with Victorian England's emerging class dynamics. Across the Atlantic, much the same themes and fervors as in the PRB circles of Ruskin and Morris were activated a generation later in the United States, where they were especially associated with increasing roles of women in the arts.

Others besides artists can enter the identity sweepstakes of artworlds in new ways as artists' preeminence becomes established. Back in the Pre-Raphaelite era, one T. Butts became the devoted patron of William Blake despite his own humble station in life and limited income, and much the same was found among the impressionist crowd. Another prototype in our own time and place is the collector described at the end of the previous chapter. In this emerging reconstitution of aesthetics there is not a sharp line between critic and artist nor between artist and appreciator. The individualist bias from the Pre-Raphaelite era also is eroding along with distinctions and separation between artists. There is nothing easy and nice about these processes. Births are painful.

Identity troubles both come from and help to trigger the reversion of artists toward other artists as their audience. The public, such as it is, must either twist itself into a self-view as artistic professional or in some sense it may be left out—and left bereft of help with identity. This of course just recaps what has happened in regard to science since the last century, when—as is now inconceivable—great scientists were laboring and glorying to include the public (which was not yet a laity) in their audience.

As with science, there is a good side to the growing involution. There is elation and comradeship among what becomes a self-segregated elite and perhaps sharply enhanced progress as well. But there is not, as yet, the cultural safety net provided by a mandate such as science's to teach the laity (albeit grudgingly) as part of a deal giving them secure livelihood in universities. But science does not begin to have the web of part-time, offline instructional contexts for amateurs, which is one of the ways artists eke out livings.

Ours is an era of identity troubles intensified, so it seems. This need not be a personal sign. Identities go much broader and narrower, much deeper and shallower, than our conventional notions of adolescent uncertainty about self. The ancient Hellenes captured an essence of identity in their construct of the polis—the city-state seen as a soul for a society of equally striving members. Their arts, which should include their athletics as well as their amphorae and temples and music, were as much about polis as about person. And just so in the Middle Ages, of Europe and elsewhere, did confraternities, churches, quarters, lineages, and classes all urgently concern themselves with asserting and explaining and celebrating their identities, and sometimes with some larger overarching identity.

Identities and their relations, while being celebrated in performance, are also being folded into some larger groupings, as are the performances. There is nothing new or odd, for example, in teenagers identifying passionately with some rock group and in so doing helping to carve out, say, a punk-rock genre. At a more sophisticated level, Wagnerian enthusiasts by their support and disdain established a new genre within opera.

A more advanced and specialized economy brings more specialized arts and thus increases art worlds' problems of identity formation and reproduction. These arts of more specialized agency also provide more varied story sets for representing ties of identities. These newly specialized arts often are counted as low or popular art, even though elites may have as much need for them as anyone else, because there hasn't yet been time for the rhetorical work of conforming them and canons to one another.

There are worthy books by American policy analysts and economists that lay out various budget and balance-sheet problems of revenue and costs, public and private, state and local, mostly for high arts but also for some popular arts. Yet they miss the central point, which is that our arts primarily concern our identities, both as these identities are and more especially as various "we"s in the making would have them be.

These identities are newly urgent. There is no limit to our arts and no counting of our artists because agency is being left behind by many, despite any economic loss, as artists grapple with and figure out new ways to express searches for identity that include themselves or even center on themselves. Ours is an era of identity troubles.

One network's image is another network's mockery or blasphemy, which breeds tensions within persons, spread as they are across disparate social networks. It breeds as well bitter conflicts among networks and various formal organizations that figure in their identities. Surely at least a Solon is needed to solve the resulting riddles of public subsidy. The intensity of the struggles for such subsidy belies the following claim by an otherwise astute analyst of the transformation of art that began around 1800 in France: "The more complex and fluid the society, the less attached to, or expressive of, specific groups are styles in art or in life" (Pelles 1963, p. 149).

The pitifully small sums of National Endowment for the Arts support, which are at the focus of arguments, are but tickets for the attention sought by groups. Gender identities are perhaps the most urgently expressed concerns among us at the present time. On one side the stakes are emergence and survival of fragile new identities, but at the cost on other sides of fragmentation and disappearance of longtime identities. These are all variously expressed in changing visual signs, in narratives, in music and motion. Abroad, what we call ethnic identities may be the most urgent in expression, but we need not expect the resulting flows of art to be manifest to us, to be exportable as aesthetics.

Conjecture 8.1. Despite recessions and apparent conservatism, the 1990s should be a time of importance for the arts because the economy is specializing and in particular is engaging, and disengaging, new groups and existing strata—especially of women—in new ways.

Nor do the old identities fade away. The figure of the avant-garde artist, such as Richard Bowman of the previous chapter, may be with us for generations to come, producing modernist works whose concern is with our identities as living creatures vis-à-vis the physical world. Collectors will be finding new ways to tie aesthetic sensibilities in with other social worlds. And so the American art mosaic becomes more colorful as new publics of recognition are woven in.

Nor should more traditional concerns about identity formation be discounted, particularly the endlessly vexing problems of whether and how to teach arts in grade school. These teaching problems are now compounded by the crisscrossing of newly explicit concerns with inculcating other kinds of corporate identities in children. And not to be overlooked is the traditional concern with helping children develop and express identities as separate persons, in the modern sense of the educator and philosopher of pragmatism John Dewey. And finally, to what extent can and should the role of art teacher in schools be structured so as to encourage some art professionalism in them, parallel to that for art teachers of adults and in college?

GUIDE TO FURTHER READING

Gans (1974) is trenchant on the divide between popular and high culture. Sennett (1977) argues the demise of that product of the Victorian era, public man, whose disappearance permits creation of many publics—in lattices that may exhibit a good deal more of elite control, however.

Andersen (1970), Hammacher (1969), and Wallock (1988) relate sculpture to Happenings, which crossbreed theatre and literature with visual arts.

The view of liminality taken earlier has been developed in, for instance, the essays of drama theorist Schechner (1977) and anthropologist Victor Turner (1969). A chapter on liminality experiments in Polish theatre by Grotowski is included in Schechner and Schuman (1976). For interesting illustrations one can turn to Christian (1981) on Spanish religious procession and Cannadine and Price (1988) on royal coronations.

The social aspects of tournaments are developed by biosociologist Chase (1980). Their mathematical properties are surveyed by Moon (1968).

The contrast between Italian and Dutch painting is from Alpers (1983).

Jakobson (1990, Chapter 5) lays out the linguistic basis for sets of stories as recognized and used by critics. I develop the theme of story sets at length elsewhere (White 1992a).

Insightful analyses of patterns of support for the arts in America have been provided by Netzer (1978) and by Banfield (1984) and for theatre by Moore (1968). Dubin (1987) reports with insight as well as fact a troubled passage in social support for the arts in Chicago.

Dubin (1992) also provides a massive survey of recent controversies about new visual art in America; he is especially vivid on those concerned with gender identities. Freedom of expression and, paradoxically, the right of artists as corporate bodies to exclude others from choice of works are the idioms in which proponents argue for funding. See also Broude and Garrard (1982).

Colley (1991, 1992) surveys and analyzes the problems of teaching arts in the schools.

FIELDWORK IDEAS

This book and the readings it surveys will show you a lot about careers and creativity and the associated themes, but spending time around producers of art is essential, as is spending time, and more time, with art-works. In this conclusion I again quoted a good deal from students' papers, and I hope that your own fieldwork can contribute what this text cannot. A book cannot give you a good sense of the actual labor of art.

Here are fieldwork ideas corresponding to the three sections in turn:

1. You can draw on others to help you with fieldwork, and you can make your fieldwork more analytic. Here is a task that combines the two possibilities in taking up the spectrum of arts:

Get a group of friends to help you develop an inventory of all the arts of which you can find evidence (what is evidence?): for example, chants, statuary, cinema, painting, pottery, tales, mime, liturgical ceremonial, costumery, watercolor, drum and bugle corps, street organs, Ice Capades.
...

You will need to develop some agreed rules of the naming game, much as you do with other parlor games. More specialized forms of this game might appeal to you more: for example,

- How many kinds of songs and singing are there? (Barber shop quartets, a capella, Gregorian chants, blues, soul, country, arias, modern atonal ...)
- How many sorts of dance are there? (Contact improvisation, modern, tap, ballet, ballroom ...)

2. From the discussions of liminality, it seems clear that strategic moments and situations for gaining insight on acting and drama include

- how actors unwind after performance, how they adjust to non-acting roles
- how audiences adapt to differences in intermission, both in interruptions by time and by various alternatives in boundary—and breaking boundary—in space

And how does a magician specialize and focus the same skills as the actor? Does the mime require a more accomplished actor than the magician? than the theatre actor?

3. Scan local art collections for examples of visual art by women who announce feminist commitments. Look for signs of the kinds of dual mappings between perceptions and social ideology that are explored in Dubin (1992), which is a survey of the contested terrain of how gender identities are portrayed in current American artworks. Or ask yourself, What will be artistic reflections of the coming of the second millennium? You can search for religious sects with enormously heightened expectations that could show up in artworks.

MEASURES AND MODELS

Again I comment separately for the preceding three sections, in turn:

1. Multidimensional scaling programs can be used to picture degrees and bases of overlap among arts: Consult your computer center or methods course for specifics.

2. Complete linear orders of precedence are antithetical to experiences of time and sequence and interdependence in social processes. So they signal enacted social structure and typically invoke ceremony and artwork. Mathematical analysis is possible.

A tournament (Moon 1968) is a complete set of pairings among a population in which within each pair one dominates the other. The pairings are to be strictly divorced from positions in other social networks and thus from institutional position. A perfect, or near-perfect, dominance ordering is one in which if one actor dominates a second who dominates some third, then the first also dominates the third in direct paired encounter. Call this a perfect tournament: It defines a transitive order, a complete linear order. The outcomes of pairings are to be arrayed so as to permit inference of a transitive ordering from the outcomes.

Dynamics of social encounters are more complex to model. The mathematical term for locked-in social sequence is Markov process; for a nontechnical introduction to this see Bradley and Meek (1986).

3. As a sociologist, Bodinger-deUriarte (1989) backed up her assessment of art-rock with a systematic content analysis of 100 songs of the corpus presented between 1971 and 1987. This analysis was reinforced by fifty-five interviews with leading figures about, for example, the purposes behind their techniques of directly challenging the audience during these presentations.

References

Abbott, Andrew. 1988. *The System of Professions*. Chicago: University of Chicago Press.

Abell, Peter. 1987. *Social Syntax*. Oxford: Clarendon Press.

Adler, Judith. 1979. *Artists in Offices*. New Brunswick, NJ: Transaction Press.

Agnew, Jean-Christophe. 1988. *Worlds Apart: The Market and the Theater in Ango-American Thought, 1550–1750*. New York: Cambridge University Press.

Alford, Robert. 1991. "Cultural Innovation and Practical Knowledge: The Case of Piano Technique." Memorandum, Department of Sociology, Graduate Center, City University of New York, January.

Alpers, Svetlana. 1983. *The Art of Describing: Dutch Art in the Seventeenth Century*. Chicago: University of Chicago Press.

Andersen, Wayne. 1970. *American Sculpture in Process: 1930–1970*. Boston: New York Graphic Society.

Anderson, Perry. 1974. *Lineages of the Absolutist State*. London: New Left Books.

Anderson, Robert J., Hilda Baumol, Sonia Maltezou, and Robert Wuthnow. 1978. "The Condition and Needs of the Live Professional Theater in America. Phase I Report: Data Collection and Analysis." Princeton: MATHTECH, Inc., under contract to the National Endowment for the Arts, February 17.

Antal, F. 1962. *Hogarth*. London: Routledge and Kegan Paul.

_____. 1965. *Florentine Painting and Its Social Background: The Bourgeois Republic Before Cosimo de Medici's Advent to Power: XIV and Early XV Centuries*. London: Routledge and Kegan Paul.

Ascher, Marcia, and Robert Ascher. 1981. *Code of the Quipu: A Study in Media, Mathematics and Culture*. Ann Arbor: University of Michigan Press.

Auerbach, Erich. 1953. *Mimesis: The Representation of Reality in Western Literature*. Princeton: Princeton University Press.

Baker, Wayne E., and Robert R. Faulkner. 1991. "Role as Resource in the Hollywood Film Industry." *American Journal of Sociology* 97:279–309.

Bakhtin, M. 1968. *Rabelais and His World*. Cambridge: MIT Press.

Balfe, Judith H., and Margaret J. Wyszomirski, eds. 1985. *Art, Ideology, and Politics*. New York: Praeger.

Banfield, Edward C. 1984. *The Democratic Muse: Visual Arts and the Public Interest*. New York: Basic Books.

Barnes, J. A. 1972. *Social Networks*. Reading, MA: Addison-Wesley.

Bauland, Peter. 1968. *The Hooded Eagle: Modern German Drama on the New York Stage, 1894–1965*. Syracuse, NY: Syracuse University Press.

Baxandall, M. 1975. *Painting and Experience in Fifteenth Century Italy*. New York: Oxford University Press.

_____. 1979. "The Language of Art History." *New Literary History* 10:453–465.

_____. 1980. *The Limewood Sculptors of Renaissance Germany*. New Haven: Yale University Press.

Becker, Howard. 1982. *Art Worlds*. Berkeley: University of California Press.

Bell, Daniel. 1982. *The Cultural Contradictions of Capitalism*. New York: Harcourt Brace Jovanich.

Belz, Carl. 1973. *The Story of Rock*. 2d ed. New York: Harper-Colophon.

Berezin, Mabel. 1991. "The Organization of Political Ideology: Culture, State, and the Theater in Fascist Italy." *American Sociological Review* 56:639–651.

Berger, Peter, and Thomas Luckmann. 1967. *The Social Construction of Reality*. Harmondsworth: Penguin Books.

Berkowitz, S. D. 1982. *An Introduction to Structural Analysis: The Network Approach*. Toronto: Butterworths.

Bloch, R. Howard. 1977. *Medieval French Literature and Law*. Berkeley: University of California Press.

Blythe, Ronald. 1979. *The View in Winter: Reflections on Old Age*. New York: Harcourt Brace Jovanovich.

Bodinger-deUriarte, Cristina. 1985. "Alternative Status Judgments Among Freelance Musicians." In *Art, Ideology, and Politics*, edited by Judith H. Balfe and Margaret J. Wyszomirski. 1985. New York: Praeger.

_____. 1989. "The Impact of Artists' Perceptions on the Form, Content and Presentation of a Genre." Ph.D. thesis, Department of Sociology, Harvard University, May.

Boime, Albert. 1987. *Art in an Age of Revolution: 1750–1800*. Chicago: University of Chicago Press.

Boris, Eileen. 1986. *Art and Labor: Ruskin, Morris and the Craftsman Ideal in America*. Philadelphia: Temple University Press.

Boster, James S. 1986. "Exchange of Varieties and Information Between Aguaruna Manioc Cultivators." *American Anthropologist* 88:428–435.

Bourdieu, Pierre. 1984. *Distinction: A Social Critique of the Judgment of Taste*, translated by Richard Nice. Cambridge: Harvard University Press.

_____. 1985. "Social Space and the Genesis of Groups." *Theory and Society* 14:723–744.

Bové, Paul A. 1986. *Intellectuals in Power: A Genealogy of Critical Humanism*. New York: Columbia University Press.

Bowman, Richard. 1973. "Paintings with Fluorescent Pigments of the Microcosm and Macrocosm." *Leonardo* 6:289–292.

_____. 1986. *Richard Bowman: Forty Years of Abstract Painting*, edited by K. R. Eagles-Smith. San Francisco: Harold Parker/Harcourts Gallery.

Boyle, Wickham. N.d. *On the Streets: A Guide to New York City's Buskers*. New York City Department of Cultural Affairs, Koch administration.

Bradley, Ian, and Ronald L. Meek. 1986. *Matrices and Society.* Princeton University Press.

Brain, David. 1989. "Discipline and Style: The Ecole des Beaux-Arts and the Social Production of an American Architecture." *Theory and Society* 18:807–868.

Brook, Peter. 1968. *The Empty Space.* New York: Athenum.

Broude, Norma, and Mary D. Garrard, eds. 1982. *Feminism and Art History.* New York: Harper and Row.

Bryer, J. R. 1982. *The Theatre We Worked For: The Letters of Eugene O'Neill to Kenneth MacGowan.* New Haven: Yale University Press.

Bryson, Norman. 1981. *World and Image: French Painting of the Ancien Regime.* New York: Cambridge University Press.

Burns, Elizabeth, and Tom Burns, eds. 1973. *Sociology of Literature and Drama.* Harmondsworth: Penguin Books.

Burns, Tom. 1977. *The BBC: Public Institution and Private World.* London: Macmillan.

Burrows, J. F. 1987. *Computation into Criticism: A Study of Jane Austen's Novels and an Experiment in Method.* Oxford: Clarendon Press.

Campbell, Colin. 1987. *The Romantic Ethic and the Spirit of Modern Consumerism.* Oxford: Blackwell.

Cannadine, David, and Simon Price, eds. 1988. *Rituals of Royalty.* Cambridge and New York: Cambridge University Press.

Chambers, Frank P. 1928. *Cycles of Taste.* Cambridge: Harvard University Press. Reprint. New York: Russell and Russell, 1967.

Chase, Ivan D. 1980. "Social Process and Hierarchy Formation in Small Groups: A Comparative Perspective." *American Sociological Review* 45:905–924.

Christian, William A. 1981. *Local Religion in 16th Century Spain.* Princeton: Princeton University Press.

Clark [Ferguson], Priscilla P. 1987. *Literary France: The Making of a Culture.* Berkeley: University of California Press.

Cockcroft, Eva, J. Weber, and J. Cockcroft. 1977. *Toward a People's Art.* New York: Dutton.

Colley, Bernadette. 1991. "Finding Common Ground: Art Schools and Ed Schools." *Arts in Education* (November/December): 35–47.

_____. 1992. "The Artist in Residence Program: An Evaluative Report." New Hampshire State Council on the Arts, August.

Cornell, Stephen. 1988. *The Return of the Native: American Indian Political Resurgence.* New York: Oxford University Press.

Corrigan, Robert W. 1977. *The Theater in Search of a Fix.* New York: Dell.

Coser, Lewis A., Charles Kadushin, and Walter W. Powell. 1982. *Books: The Culture and Commerce of Publishing.* New York: Basic Books.

Crane, Diana. 1987. *The Transformation of the Avante Garde: The New York Art World, 1940–1985.* Chicago: University of Chicago Press.

Csikszentmihalyi, M. 1975. *Beyond Boredom and Anxiety.* San Francisco: Jossey-Bass.

Culler, Jonathan. 1975. *Structuralist Poetics: Structuralism, Linguistics and the Study of Literature*. Ithaca, NY: Cornell University Press.

———. 1983. *On Deconstruction: Theory and Criticism After Structuralism*. Ithaca, NY: Cornell University Press.

———. 1990. *Framing the Sign*. Norman: University of Oklahoma Press.

Damrosch, David. 1987. *The Narrative Covenant*. Ithaca, NY: Cornell University Press.

Danto, Arthur. 1981. *The Transfiguration of the Commonplace*. Cambridge: Harvard University Press.

Dauber, Kenneth. 1990. "Pueblo Pottery and the Politics of Regional Identity." *Journal of the Southwest* 32:576–596.

———. 1992. "Object, Genre, and Buddhist Sculpture." *Theory and Society* 21.

Davidoff, Leonore, and Catherine Hall. 1987. *Family Fortunes: Men and Women of the English Middle Class, 1780–1850*. Chicago: University of Chicago Press.

Davis, James A., and Tom W. Smith. 1988. *General Social Surveys, 1972–1988: Cumulative Codebook*. Chicago: National Opinion Research Center.

DiMaggio, Paul. 1982. "Cultural Entrepreneurship in Nineteenth-Century Boston: The Creation of an Organizational Base for High Culture in America." *Media, Culture and Society* 4:33–50.

———. 1987. "Classification in Art." *American Sociological Review* 52:440–455.

Doezma, Marianne. 1980. *American Realism and the Industrial Age*. Cleveland: Cleveland Museum of Art.

Dubin, Steven C. 1987. *Bureaucratizing the Muse: Public Funds and the Cultural Worker*. Chicago: University of Chicago Press.

———. 1992. *Arresting Images*. London: Routledge.

Eccles, Robert G. 1991. "The Performance Measurement Manifesto." *Harvard Business Review* 69:131–137.

Ekman, P., ed. 1972. *Emotion in the Human Face*. London: Pergamon Press.

Engel, Lehmann. 1967. *The American Musical Theater*. New York: Macmillan.

Ennis, Philip. 1993. *The Seventh Stream: The Emergence of Rocknroll in American Popular Music*. Hanover, NH: Wesleyan University Press of New England.

Fantasia, Rick. 1992. "From McDonald's to Kitchburger: The Place of Fast Food in France." Manuscript, Smith College, Department of Sociology, January.

Faulkner, Robert R. 1971. *Studio Musicians*. Chicago: Aldine.

———. 1983. *Music on Demand: Composers and Careers in the Hollywood Film Industry*. New Brunswick, NJ: Transaction Books.

Faulkner, Robert R., and Andy B. Anderson. 1987. "Short-Term Projects and Emergent Careers: Evidence from Hollywood." *American Journal of Sociology* 92:879–909.

Feller, William. 1968. *An Introduction to Probability Theory and Its Application*. 3d ed. New York: Wiley.

Ferguson, Robert A. 1984. *Law and Letters in American Culture*. Cambridge: Harvard University Press.

Findley, Carter V. 1980. *Bureaucratic Reform in the Ottoman Empire: The Sublime Porte, 1789–1922*. Princeton: Princeton University Press.

Finn, David, and Dena Merriam. 1988. *A Grace of Sense: The Sculpture of Joan Sovern*. Redding Ridge, CT: Black Swan Books.

Fortes, Meyer. 1945. *The Dynamics of Clanship Among the Tallensi*. London: Oxford University Press.

———. 1949. *The Web of Kinship Among the Tallensi*. Oxford: Oxford University Press.

Fredeman, W. E., ed. 1975. *The PRB Journal: W. M. Rossetti's Diary of the PRB, 1849–53*. Oxford: Clarendon Press.

Frye, Northrop. 1947. *Fearful Symmetry: A Study of William Blake*. Princeton: Princeton University Press.

———. 1957. *Anatomy of Criticism*. Princeton: Princeton University Press.

Gans, Herbert. 1974. *Popular Culture and High Culture: An Analysis and Evaluation of Taste*. New York: Basic Books.

Gardner, Howard. 1982. *Artful Scribbles*. New York: Basic Books.

Gartman, David. 1991. "Culture as Class Symbolization or Mass Reification? A Critique of Bourdieu's *Distinction*." *American Journal of Sociology* 97:421–447.

Gayle, Addison, Jr., ed. 1972. *The Black Aesthetic*. New York: Anchor Doubleday.

Gayle, Margot, and Michele Cohen. 1988. *Guide to Manhattan's Outdoor Sculpture*. New York: Prentice-Hall.

Gibson, J. J. 1950. *The Perception of the Visual World*. Boston: Houghton-Mifflin.

———. 1979. *The Ecological Approach to Visual Perception*. Boston: Houghton Mifflin.

Gilmore, Samuel. 1987. "Coordination and Convention: The Organization of the Concert World." *Symbolic Interaction* 10:209–227.

———. 1988. "Schools of Activity and Innovation," *Sociological Quarterly* 29:203–219.

Goldman, Michael. 1975. *The Actor's Freedom*. New York: Viking.

Goldman, Peter B. 1977. "Galdos and the Nineteenth Century Novel: The Need for an Interdisciplinary Approach." *Anales Galdosianos* 10:5–18.

Goldman, William. 1969. *The Season*. New York: Harcourt Brace World.

Gombrich, E. H. 1963. *Meditations on a Hobby Horse*. London: Phaidon.

———. 1973. *Ideals and Idols: Essays on Values in History and in Art*. London: Phaidon.

Gossett, Philip. 1992. "Scholars and Performers." *Bulletin of the American Academy of Arts and Sciences* 45:32–51.

Granovetter, Mark. 1974. *Getting a Job: A Study of Contacts and Careers*. Cambridge: Harvard University Press.

Green, Nicholas. 1989. "Circuits of Production, Circuits of Consumption: The Case of Mid-Nineteenth-Century French Art Dealing." *Art Journal* (Spring): 29–33.

Greenberg, Clement. 1986. *The Collected Essays and Criticism: Arrogant Purpose, 1945–49*. Vol 2. Edited by John O'Brian. Chicago: University of Chicago Press.

Greenberger, Howard, ed. 1971. *The Off-Broadway Experience*. New York: Prentice-Hall.

Greenhalg, Michael, and Vincent Megaw, eds. 1978. *Art in Society: Studies in Style, Culture and Aesthetics.* London: St. Martin's Press.

Griswold, Wendy. 1981. "American Character and the American Novel: An Expansion of Reflection Theory." *American Journal of Sociology* 86:740–765.

_____. 1986. *Renaissance Revivals: City Comedy and Revenge Tragedy in the London Theatre, 1576–1980.* Chicago: University of Chicago Press.

Grout, Donald J. 1965. *A Short History of Opera.* 2d ed. New York: Columbia University Press.

Haley, John W., and John von Hoelle. 1990. *Sound and Glory: The Incredible Story of Bill Haley, the Father of Rock 'n' Roll and the Music That Shook the World.* Wilmington, DE: Dyne-American Publications.

Hammacher, A. F. 1969. *The Revolution of Modern Sculpture.* New York: Harry N. Abrams.

Hampton, Christopher. 1990. *The Ideology of the Text.* Bristol, PA: Open University Press.

Hebdige, Dick. 1979. *Subculture: The Meaning of Style.* New York: Methuen.

Hilton, Timothy. 1970. *The Pre-Raphaelites.* New York: Oxford University Press.

Hirsch, Paul M. 1972. "Processing Fads and Fashions: An Organization-Set Analysis of Cultural Industry Systems." *American Journal of Sociology* 77:639–659.

Horwitz, Morton J. 1977. *The Transformation of American Law, 1780–1860.* Cambridge: Harvard University Press.

Huaco, George. 1965. *Sociology of Film Art.* New York: Basic Books.

Huggins, Nathan I. 1972. *Harlem Renaissance.* Oxford: Oxford University Press.

Hunt, John Dixon. 1982. *The Wider Sea: A Life of John Ruskin.* London: J. M. Dent.

Hutchinson, Sidney, 1986. *The History of the Royal Academy: 1768–1980.* London: Robert Royce.

Huxtable, Ada Louise. 1986. *Goodbye History, Hello Hamburger.* Washington, DC: Preservation Press.

Innes, Christopher. 1981. *Holy Theatre: Ritual and the Avante Garde.* New York: Cambridge University Press.

Isaacs, Jennifer, ed. and comp. 1980. *Australian Dreaming: 40,000 Years of Aboriginal History.* Sydney: Lansdowne Press.

Jakobson, Roman. 1990. *On Language.* Edited by Linda R. Waugh and M. Monville-Burston. Cambridge: Harvard University Press.

Jordy, William H. 1972. *American Buildings and Their Architects.* New York: Doubleday Anchor.

Kaye, Phyllis J. 1977. *National Playwrights Directory.* New York: Gale Research.

Kendall, Elizabeth. 1984. *Where She Danced: The Birth of American Art-Dance.* Berkeley: University of California Press.

Knoke, David. 1990. *Political Networks: The Structural Perspective.* New York: Cambridge University Press.

Kochen, Manfred, ed. 1989. *The Small World.* Norwood, NJ: Ablex.

Korte, Charles, and Stanley Milgram. 1970. "Acquaintance Networks Between Racial Groups: Application of the Small World Method." *Journal of Personality and Social Psychology* 15:101–108.

Krumhansl, Carol L. 1991. "Music Psychology: Tonal Structures in Perception and Memory." *Annual Reviews of Psychology* 42:277–303.

Kuspit, Donald B. 1979. *Clement Greenberg: Art Critic.* Madison: University of Wisconsin Press.

Lachmann, Richard. 1988. "Graffiti as Career and Ideology." *American Journal of Sociology* 94:229–250.

Lamont, Michelle, and Marcel Fournier. 1992. *Cultivating Differences: Symbolic Boundaries and the Making of Inequality.* Chicago: University of Chicago Press.

Lane, Michael. 1980. *Books and Publishers: Commerce Against Culture in Postwar Britain.* Lexington, MA: Heath-Lexington Books.

Larson, Magali S. 1983. "Emblem and Exception: The Historical Definition of the Architect's Professional Role." Pp. 49–86 in *Professionals and Urban Form,* edited by Judith R. Blau, Mark E. La Gory, and John S. Pipkin. Albany: State University of New York Press.

Le Goff, Jacques. 1984. *The Birth of Purgatory.* Translated by Arthur Goldhammer. Chicago: University of Chicago Press.

Lentricchia, Frank, and Thomas McLaughlin, eds. 1990. *Critical Terms for Literary Study.* Chicago: University of Chicago Press.

Lepenies, Wolf. 1988. *Between Literature and Science: The Rise of Sociology.* Translated by G. J. Hollingdale. New York: Cambridge University Press.

Levine, Lawrence W. 1985. "William Shakespeare and the American People: A Study in Cultural Transformation." *American Historical Review* 89:35–66.

Lévi-Strauss, Claude. 1983. *Totemism.* Translated by Rodney Needham. Boston: Beacon Press.

Lindenberger, Herbert. 1984. *Opera: The Extravagant Art.* Ithaca, NY: Cornell University Press.

———. 1990. *The History in Literature: On Value, Genre, Institutions.* New York: Columbia University Press.

Ling, Roger. 1991. *Roman Painting.* New York: Cambridge University Press.

Little, Stuart W., and Arthur Canton. 1970. *The Playmakers.* New York: Norton.

Lucie-Smith, Edward. 1985. *American Art Now.* New York: Morrow.

Luhmann, Niklas. 1990. "The Work of Art and the Self-Reproduction of Art." Chapter 11 in *Essays on Self-Reference.* New York: Columbia University Press.

Lynes, Russell. 1955. *The Tastemakers.* New York: Harper's.

Lynton, Norbert. 1980. *The Story of Modern Art.* Ithaca, NY: Cornell University Press.

McDonagh, Don. 1981. *Complete Guide to Modern Dance.* New York: Popular Library Edition.

———. 1990. *The Rise and Fall and Rise of Modern Dance.* Chicago Review Press: A Capella Books.

McKinzie, R. D. 1975. *The New Deal for Artists*. Princeton: Princeton University Press.

Macleod, Dianne S. 1987. "Art Collecting and Victorian Middle-Class Taste." *Art History* 10:328–350.

Mainardi, Patricia. 1989. "Editor's Statement: Nineteenth-Century French Art Institutions." *Art Journal* (Spring).

Marling, Karal Ann. 1982. *Wall-to-Wall America: A Cultural History of Post-Office Murals in the Great Depression*. Minneapolis: University of Minnesota Press.

Marsh, Jan. 1988. *Pre-Raphaelite Women: Images of Femininity*. New York: Crown-Harmony.

Mathematica, Inc. 1981. *Conditions and Needs of the Professional American Theatre*. Report no. 11 (May). Princeton: National Endowment for the Arts, Research Division.

Mayer, Adrian C. 1960. *Caste and Kinship in Central India*. Berkeley: University of California Press.

Meiss, Millard. 1978. *Painting in Florence and Siena After the Black Death*. Princeton: Princeton University Press.

Metropolitan Museum of Art. 1968. *The Great Age of Fresco: Giotto to Pontormo: An Exhibition of Mural Paintings and Monumental Drawings*. Florence: Art Editions "Il Fiorino."

Meyer, Marshall W. 1992. "Organizational Design and the Performance Paradox." Chapter 11 in *Explorations in Economic Sociology*, edited by Richard Swedberg. New York: Russell Sage.

Milgram, Stanley. 1967. "The Small-World Problem." *Psychology Today* 1:62–67.

Moon, J. W. 1968. *Topics in Tournaments*. New York: Holt, Rinehart and Winston.

Moore, Thomas Gale. 1968. *The Economics of the American Theater*. Durham, NC: Duke University Press.

Moulin, Raymonde. 1987. *The French Art Market: A Sociological Perpsective*. Translated by Arthur Goldhammer. New Brunswick, NJ: Rutgers University Press.

Mukerji, Chandra, and Michael Schudson, eds. 1991. *Rethinking Popular Culture: Contemporary Perspectives in Cultural Studies*. Berkeley: University of California Press.

Netzer, Dick. 1978. *The Subsidized Muse*. New York: Cambridge University Press.

Nicoll, John. 1970. *The Pre-Raphaelites*. New York: Dutton.

Nissen, Hans J. 1988. *The Early History of the Ancient Near East, 9000–2,000 B.C.* Translated by Elizabeth Lutzeier. Chicago: University of Chicago Press.

Novack, Cynthia. 1990. *Sharing the Dance: Contact Improvisation and American Culture*. Madison: University of Wisconsin Press.

Novick, Jules. 1968. *Beyond Broadway*. New York: Hill and Wang.

Packard, William, ed. 1974. *The Craft of Poetry: Interviews from the New York Quarterly*. Garden City, NY: Doubleday.

Pelles, Geraldine. 1963. *Art, Artists and Society*. Englewood Cliffs, NJ: Prentice-Hall.

Peterson, Richard A., ed. 1976. *The Production of Culture*. Beverly Hills, CA: Sage.

Poggi, Jack. 1968. *Theater in America*. Ithaca, NY: Cornell University Press.

Potter, Rosanne G., ed. 1989. *Literary Computing and Literary Criticism: Theoretical and Practical Essays on Theme and Rhetoric*. Philadelphia: University of Pennsylvania Press.

Praz, Mario. 1964. *An Illustrated History of Furnishing*. New York: Braziller.

Price, Julia S. 1967. *The Off-Broadway Theater Since 1905*. New York: Scarecrow.

Prince, Harold. 1974. *Contradictions*. New York: Dodd Mead.

Quigley, Austin E. 1985. *The Modern Stage and Other Worlds*. New York: Methuen.

Ragin, Charles, and Howard Becker, eds. 1992. *What Is a Case: Issues in the Logic of Social Inquiry*. New York: Cambridge University Press.

Raine, Kathleen. 1970. *William Blake*. London: Thames and Hudson.

Rewald, John. [1946] 1973. *The History of Impressionism*. Rev. ed. New York: Museum of Modern Art.

Ricoeur, Paul. 1988. *Time and Narrative*. Vol. 3. Translated by K. Blamey and D. Pellauer. Chicago: University of Chicago Press.

Robinson, Charles. 1979. *Reviewer Response to Novels About Race Relations Published During the 1950s*. Honors B.A. thesis, Department of Sociology, Harvard University.

Rose, Barbara. 1975. *American Painting Since 1900*. New York: Praeger.

Rosenberg, Harold. 1969. *Artworks and Packages*. New York: Horizon Press.

———. 1972. *The Dedefinition of Art*. New York: Collier Macmillan.

———. 1982. *The Anxious Object*. Chicago: University of Chicago-Phoenix.

Rosengren, Karl E. 1968. *Sociological Aspects of the Literary System*. Stockholm: Natur och Kultur.

Rostovtzeff, M. 1930. *A History of the Ancient World*. Vol. 1: *The Orient and Greece*. Translated by J. D. Duff. Oxford: Clarendon Press.

Roth, Leland M. 1979. *A Concise History of American Architecture*. New York: Harper and Row.

Rothenstein, Sir John. 1962. *British Art Since 1900*. London: Phaidon.

Rueschemeyer, Marilyn, I. Golomshtok, and J. Kennedy. 1985. *Soviet Emigré Artists: Life and Work in the USSR and the United States*. Armonk, NY: M. E. Sharpe.

Runciman, Steven. 1971. *Byzantine Style and Civilization*. London: Penguin.

Ruskin, John. 1987. *Modern Painters*. Edited and abridged by David Barrie. New York: Knopf.

Salmon, Jaely, ed. 1987. *Philanthropy and American Society: Selected Papers*. New York: Center for American Culture Studies, Columbia University.

Sambrook, James, ed. 1974. *Pre-Raphaelitism: A Collection of Critical Essays*. Chicago: University of Chicago Press.

Schama, Simon. 1987. *The Embarassment of Riches: An Interpretation of Dutch Culture in the Golden Age*. New York: Knopf.

Schechner, Richard. 1977. *Essays on Performance Theory, 1970–1976*. New York: Drama Book Specialists.

Schechner, Richard, and Mady Schuman. 1976. *Ritual, Play and Performance: Readings in the Social Sciences/Theatre*. New York: Seabury Press.

Schmidgall, Gary. 1990. *Shakespeare and Opera*. New York: Oxford University Press.

Scholes, Robert, and Robert Kellogg. 1966. *The Nature of Narrative*. New York: Oxford University Press.

Schudson, Michael. 1989. "How Culture Works: Perspectives from Media Studies." *Theory and Society* 18:153–180.

Schurnberger, Lynn. 1991. *Let There Be Clothes: 40,000 Years of Fashion*. New York: Workman Publisher.

Sennett, Richard. 1977. *The Fall of Public Man*. New York: Random House–Vintage.

Shapiro, David, and Cecile Shapiro. 1990. *Abstract Expressionism: A Critical Record*. New York: Cambridge University Press.

Shiff, Richard. 1984. *Cézanne and the End of Impressionism*. Chicago: University of Chicago Press.

Simpson, Charles. 1981. *Soho: The Artist in the City*. Chicago: University of Chicago Press.

Spencer, Baldwin, and F. J. Gillen. [1903] 1927. *The Arunta*. Rev. ed.

Stillinger, Jack. 1991. *Multiple Authorship and the Myth of Solitary Genius*. New York: Oxford University Press.

Thomson, Virgil. 1962. *The State of Music*. 2d ed. New York: Random House.

Tomars, A. S. 1960. "Introduction to the Sociology of Art." Ph.D. thesis, Columbia University.

Travers, Jeffrey, and Stanley Milgram. 1969. "An Experimental Study of the Small World Problem." *Sociometry* 32:425–443.

Tucker, Paul Hayes. 1989. *Monet in the "Nineties": The Series Paintings*. New Haven: Yale University Press.

Turner, Victor. 1969. *The Ritual Process*. Chicago: Aldine.

Udy, Stanley. 1970. *Work in Traditional and Modern Society*. Englewood Cliffs, NJ: Prentice-Hall.

Verdaasdonk, D. 1991. "Feature Films Based on Literary Works." *Poetics: Journals of Empirical Research on Literature, the Media and the Arts* 20:405–420.

Vinson, James. 1977. *Contemporary Dramatists*. London: St. Martin's.

Waddington, C. H. 1970. *Behind Appearance*. Cambridge: MIT Press.

Wallock, Leonard, ed. 1988. *New York: Culture Capital of the World, 1940–1965*. New York: Rizzoli.

Wanderer, J. J. 1970. "In Defense of Popular Taste: Film Rating Among Professional and Lay Audiences." *American Journal of Sociology* 78:262–273.

Watt, Ian. 1957. *The Rise of the Novel*. Berkeley: University of California Press.

Weill, Stephen. 1983. *Beauty and the Beasts*. Washington, DC: Smithsonian Institution.

Wellman, Barry, and S. D. Berkowitz, eds. 1988. *Social Structures: A Network Approach*. New York: Cambridge University Press.

Wharton, John F. 1974. *Life Among the Playwrights*. New York: Quadrangle/New York Times.

White, Elizabeth A. 1992. "Sentimental Entrepreneurs: Profit and the Cultural Rhetoric of the Middle Class, 1840–1890." Manuscript thesis, Department of American Studies, Yale University.

White, Harrison C. 1970a. *Chains of Opportunity: System Models of Mobility in Organizations.* Cambridge: Harvard University Press.

_____. 1970b. "Search Parameters for the Small World Problem." *Social Forces* 49:259–264.

_____. 1985. "Agency as Control." Chap. 8 in *Principals and Agents: The Structure of Business,* edited by J. Pratt and R. Zeckhauser. Boston: Harvard Graduate School of Business Administration Press.

_____. 1992a. *Identity and Control: A Structural Theory of Social Action.* Princeton: Princeton University Press.

_____. 1992b. "Agency as Control in Formal Networks." Chap. 3 in *Network Organization: Its Emergence and Implications for Management Theory and Practice,* edited by Nitin Nohria and Robert G. Eccles. Cambridge: Harvard Business School Press.

White, Harrison C., and Cynthia A. White. [1965] 1993. *Canvases and Careers.* New York: Wiley. Reissue with new Foreword and Afterword. Chicago: University of Chicago Press.

Whiteside, Thomas. 1981. *The Blockbuster Complex.* Middletown, CT: Wesleyan University Press.

Williams, Raymond. 1977. *Marxism and Literature.* New York: Oxford University Press.

_____. 1981. *Culture.* Glasgow: Fontana.

Wittkower, Rudolph. 1978. *Sculpture: Processes and Principles.* New York: Harper and Row.

Wolff, Janet. 1983. *Aesthetics and the Sociology of Art.* London: Allen and Unwin.

Wright, Gwendolyn. 1980. *Moralism and the Model Home: Domestic Architecture and Cultural Conflict.* Chicago: University of Chicago Press.

Ziegler, Joseph W. 1977. *Regional Theater.* New York: Plenum–Da Capo.

Zolberg, Vera L. 1990. *Constructing a Sociology of the Arts.* New York: Cambridge University Press.

Zukin, Sharon. 1989. *Loft Living: Culture and Capital in Urban Change.* New Brunswick, NJ: Rutgers University Press.

About the Book
and Author

How much does art provide escape from everyday life, and how much does it aid in controlling life? How are art worlds built and maintained? Are new styles the creations of whim or genius? Or are stylistic changes the product of the social and political world in which the artist lives? How does art itself shape these worlds? How are art worlds built and maintained?

In a book that ranges across cultures, artistic forms, and the centuries, Harrison White offers his unique vision of expression and artistic production embedded in a world of complex social networks. Participating in this process, artists, audiences, entrepreneurs, collectors, and critics form identities for themselves and others. Cultural and social forces both near and distant interplay here, often in ways not immediately apparent to observers or even to the participants.

With chapter-by-chapter annotated guides to further reading and ideas for field work, this is also a book to be used as an investigative tool for students and general readers.

Careers and Creativity will change the way we think about artistic careers, creativity, and the production of meaning in art.

Harrison C. White is director of the Center for Social Sciences and professor of sociology at Columbia University.

Index